San Antonio's Monte Vista

Architecture and Society
in a Gilded Age
1890–1930

For Christina

SAN ANTONIO'S
Monte Vista

Architecture and Society

in a Gilded Age

1890–1930

Donald E. Everett

Foreword by W. Eugene George

MAVERICK PUBLISHING COMPANY

MAVERICK PUBLISHING COMPANY
P.O. Box 6355, San Antonio, Texas 78209

Library of Congress Cataloging-in-Publication Data

Everett, Donald E.
    San Antonio's Monte Vista : architecture and society in a
    gilded age, 1890–1930 / Donald E. Everett.
      p. cm.
  Includes bibliographical references and index.
  ISBN 0-9651507-8-X, ISBN 0-9651507-9-8 (pbk.)
  1. Mansions–Texas–San Antonio. 2. Eclecticism in
  architecture–Texas–San Antonio. 3. Monte Vista National
  Historic District (San Antonio, Tex.) 4. San Antonio (Tex.)–
  Buildings, structures, etc. 5. San Antonio (Tex.)–History. I. Title.
      NA7511.4.S36 E94 1999
      728' .09764'351–dc21
                                      99-32160
                                        CIP

08 07   10 9 8 7 6 5 4 3

Printed in China

First page: One of two gilded griffins guards the entrance to the Adams house on Belknap Place (1890, McAdoo & Worley, architects).

Frontispiece: The bright San Antonio sun highlights Spanish Colonial Revival detail work at the entry of the Stowers house on West Lynwood Avenue (1925, Adams & Adams, architects). Photo by W. Eugene George.

Contents

Foreword

Good houses require good architects. But good houses also require good clients, good contractors and good artisanry. In addition, good architecture requires an adequate construction budget. San Antonio's Monte Vista had all these ingredients.

More than fifty architects produced work in Monte Vista during a forty-year period. Through their accomplishments one can see that this area was blessed with design talent far beyond the ordinary. Architects of the period were highly competent in design, structure and construction. Working in collaboration with their clients, they developed projects at significant creative levels.

Some architects were shared with other cities. San Antonio's Atlee Ayres also built in Kansas City and Oklahoma City, and Hal Thompson of Dallas built in Monte Vista as well as in Houston. But, perhaps because of the dynamics in the fast-growing San Antonio of the time, the net result in Monte Vista excels.

When Monte Vista was established during the late nineteenth century, a period of eclecticism in architecture had begun. Designers borrowed freely the architectural elements of the past, sometimes commingling parts from various eras into a single statement. But examples found in the reference journals of the day usually responded to climatic conditions found in Europe or in the American northeast. They required adjustments to serve the sunnier environment of San Antonio.

Monte Vista responded to sylistic trends and regional modifications in a magnificent way. Many modifications were made throughout the South. Homes had more and larger windows, often going to the floor line when they were next to outdoor galleries, a feature more extensive in the South than the Northeast. Ceilings were higher so warm air could rise.

A particular adaptation in San Antonio was made to catch the summer evening's southeast breeze from the Gulf of Mexico. Whether houses faced north or south, bedrooms in these pre-air conditioned times were ideally positioned on the southeast. An example is the Marshall Terrell

Marshall W. Terrell's newly finished Craftsman-style home at 223 West Agarita Avenue (1914, Atlee B. Ayres, architect) incorporated a common local architectural feature—galleries at the southeast, to catch the summer evening's Gulf breeze.

house, built facing south on Agarita Avenue. It has a southeast porch sheltering two stories and living areas tucked back in the shade where they can be ventilated with privacy. This is a southern house. Imagine snow piling up on that upstairs (and downstairs) porch were it in the North.

When Mediterranean and Spanish Colonial Revival houses entered the scene, their light appearance was very well suited to the magnificent daylight in San Antonio. That also happens in Spain and in Southern California, but it works especially well in San Antonio.

As Monte Vista developed, changing technology was also affecting the design of homes. Hygenic bathrooms with heated water became standard. Kitchen equipment went through major advancements. Room for ice-making refrigerators was needed. Milk and ice no longer had to be delivered daily from horse-drawn wagons. Space to house domestic servants remained a necessity for larger homes, though development of such time-saving innovations as the portable vacuum cleaner was reducing dependency on live-in help.

Vital to Monte Vista were the high standards of quality that remain in the work of such contractors as G. W. Mitchell, H. H. Moeller and John Westerhoff & Sons. Similar levels are reflected in the interior work of Prassel Sash and Door Company and Steves Lumber and Millwork. Carpenters, masons and plasterers showed expertise exceeding much of the work done today.

Of particular importance is the usually unidentified work of Hannibal Pianta, who as a young Italian immigrant came to work on ornamental plaster for the Columbian Exposition, the great 1893 World's Fair in Chicago. In San Antonio he later designed, fabricated and installed much of the ornamental cast stone work for perhaps most of the remarkable Italian and Spanish-style doorways that were a major focus of Monte Vista architects. Pianta, who was really a sculptor, did these doorways full size in clay, made plaster molds from the clay and then cast them in a special concrete. Unfortunately, he did not sign his work and there seem to be no records of his designs extant.

Another common architectural embellishment in Monte Vista is the extensive use of decorative tiles, some by Batchelder and Rookwood.

Monte Vista is a sort of time capsule. By the time the Depression arrived, the neighborhood

One example of Monte Vista's ornamental cast stone work attributed to Italian immigrant Hannibal Pianta is the lunette over the entry of 100 East Gramercy Place (1927, Richard Vander Stratten, architect).

was virtually complete, though a few examples of Art Moderne architecture did go up in the late 1930s and there was some residential and apartment construction in the 1940s and later. Remarkably, Monte Vista did not suffer the decline and destruction that decimated other residential neighborhoods of the era in Houston, Dallas, Fort Worth and Austin.

Thus Monte Vista uniquely invites a stroll on a pleasant day to enjoy its sense of place, formed by those able to carry out the highest goal of residential architecture—creating a pleasing neighborhood where one can live, grow, relate with family and neighbors and assemble all the memories of home.

W. Eugene George, AIA

Mary Ann Castleberry Endowed Professor
Division of Architecture and Interior Design
The University of Texas at San Antonio

Introduction

The Monte Vista National Historic District is located one and a half miles north of downtown San Antonio and is home to approximately 3,000 people. Its distinguished residential architecture, primarily from San Antonio's "Gilded Age," defined as extending from 1890 to 1930, forms the most extensive and intact neighborhood of this era in Texas.

Monte Vista's approximately one hundred blocks comprise fourteen platted subdivisions. The district takes its name from the largest of these developments, platted in 1920.

Mark Twain is credited with coining the term *Gilded Age*, the title of a novel that he and Charles Dudley Warner wrote in 1873. A satire on business and political corruption of the day, *Gilded Age* became an expression applied to the ostentatious display of the generation following the Civil War, in which an economic revolution reshaped the lives of the American people and urban life and thought became secularized.

The phrase eventually acquired one dictionary definition as something "displaying [a] fine but deceptive outward appearance." Although many residences in Monte Vista date from this period, strictly speaking the term can hardly be applied here. Monte Vista indeed has many fine homes, but these structures are not of "deceptive outward appearance."

In terms of solid foundations and interior appointments, many of these houses are among the most substantial ever built in San Antonio. But fine as they are, the wealth that built them could not compare with that of the northern tier of the nation, which benefited from a second industrial revolution with a concomitant rapid urbanization.

San Antonio, which in 1877 became the last major city in the nation to obtain a railroad, could neither identify nor compete with the lifestyle and luxurious edifices that embellished the landscapes of the metropolitan East.

Unmitigated optimism, however, prevailed in the city following the arrival of the "Iron Horse." San Antonio's railroad enabled the city to become a wool market for the growing sheep industry in the Uvalde area and to develop a livestock center in the ensuing decade. The numbers of health seekers increased as they no longer had to depend on the bone-crushing stagecoach journeys of yesteryear. Land speculators joined in the hegira to San Antonio, whose citizens could boast a commercial ice factory, electric streetcars and telephones by the 1880s, a decade in which the population increased by 83.3 percent.[1]

Travelers from throughout the country began to praise the "most prosperous" city in Texas. An 1891 visitor wrote his hometown newspaper in Youngstown that residential lots in San Antonio were selling in excess of those for similar property in the Ohio city. Less prophetically, the correspondent wrote, "The people here claim they have oil and natural gas. I visited what they call a gas well and I would not give a dollar for all the oil and gas in southwest Texas."[2]

Full knowledge of such riches, however, did not come until the 1920s, when oil-rich entrepreneurs began building mansions even more impressive than cattle barons' homes—which had begun to appear in Laurel Heights by the turn of the century—and those of the earliest residents, whose fortunes had been made in banking, mercantile trade and the sale of inherited lands.

Exhibiting the opulence typically associated with the Gilded Age is the detail on brewer Otto Koehler's home (1901, Carl von Seutter, architect), adjoining the Monte Vista district's southern boundary along West Ashby Place.

Such imposing residences as these wealthy citizens constructed, though, seldom displayed the excesses evident in some homes of the northern nouveau riche. One explanation is found in the fortunate presence of a number of exceptional architects, whose designs still merit praise from their latter-day colleagues.

Despite disclaiming its appropriateness for Monte Vista, the Gilded Age designation in America has a particular connotation in San Antonio, though it must be dated at a later period (1890–1930) than elsewhere in the nation. The era produced several opulent suburbs in San Antonio—Government Hill, West End, Alamo Heights, Tobin Hill, Laurel Heights and Monte Vista.

Unsympathetic encroachments have overwhelmed three of these areas; Alamo Heights became a separately incorporated municipality in 1922. Only Laurel Heights and Monte Vista (with its extension to the east) have retained their essential integrity. To protect it, in 1975 residents successfully acquired the municipal designation of Historic District for the era's last surviving neighborhood near downtown San Antonio.[3]

The entire Monte Vista neighborhood achieved national landmark status on December 10, 1998, when it was listed on the National Register of Historic Places. This marked the conclusion of a long-term effort supported by the Monte Vista Historical Association, organized in 1973 as enthusiasm, mingled with a sense of repsonsibility, reflected the spirit of neighborliness hundreds of Monte Vista residents have demonstrated during the last quarter of the twentieth century.

One reason for the district's ability to survive the urban decay that destroyed such neighborhoods elsewhere is suggested in the exhaustive National Register nomination form, prepared by Maria Watson Pfeiffer:

The neighborhood's resilience was at least partially attributable to the wide variety of housing stock—eclectic in its range of sizes, materials and designs (and therefore prices)—found in the area's numerous subdivisions, each built for a different segment of the homebuying public. Wealthy ranchers lived in close proximity to modest schoolteachers, each in houses designed and constructed by noted architects and builders.

The resulting array of architectural styles summarizes a booming period in San Antonio's history when popular national design trends influenced local tastes.[4]

This text first appeared as a supplement to *The North San Antonio Times* on January 28, 1988. I am grateful that it has been of use to readers and researchers and, with some corrections and updating, can now reach a wider audience. Treated herein are approximately one-third of the 1,500 homes in Monte Vista. While these include most significant ones, plus many of lesser importance, further research remains to be done.

Those who actively participated in preparing the manuscript include Lois Boyd, Dorothy Williams, Linda Clark, Grant Morrison, Mary Everett Potter and Mary Lou Everett. My gratitude is likewise extended to Trinity University, which provided much of the funding for the initial project; to Maria Watson Pfeiffer, Tom Shelton and Jon Thompson; and to publisher Lewis Fisher, who has supported the Monte Vista movement from its inception and who has taken charge of the illustrations for this volume. I am also grateful to architectural historian Eugene George for use of his color photographs and for the foreword.

W. EUGENE GEORGE

From his artistic family's vantage point in a still sparsely settled neighborhood, Julian Onderdonk in Afternoon Back of Laurel Heights *(1913) captured the feel of a brushcountry landscape hospitable mainly to goats.*

"Laurel Heights Speaks for Itself"

1. Mrs. Kampmann's Goat Pasture

Mrs. Kampmann's goat pasture seemed an unlikely setting in 1889 for a real estate development that would attract some of San Antonio's most affluent citizens. Where goats grazed, jackrabbits and cotton tails abounded, and an occasional wolf, coyote, or jaguar could still be shot, the rocky hills with unexplored caves for adventurous boys extended northeastward from San Pedro Springs.

This dry and barren wilderness, which sustained only mesquite brush, cat claws, chaparral, and wild mountain laurel, had long since been declared "fit for nothing" by most citizens of San Antonio.[1]

These hills lay within the eight leagues of land granted to the City of San Antonio by the Spanish government in the 1730s; most of it had been sold following a Texas Supreme Court decision that permitted the sale of public property (Lewis v. City of San Antonio, 1851).[2] Thus, Major J. H. Kampmann and D. C. Alexander, among others, acquired such acreages before the Civil War. Subsequent generations would be critical of these sales, and as the years passed the accounts of these transactions became exaggerated in the retelling, as in this aged gentleman's recollection in 1922:

One business incident . . . . that made a deep impression on me then and still, was when James R. Sweet, mayor, [and] the city sold all of what has come to be celebrated as Laurel Heights at fifty cents an acre, on fifty years time, with interest at six percent . . . It is still more interesting that during the Civil War and when money was depreciated into practically nothing the men who had bought Laurel Heights paid their debt in this almost worthless currency. The City of San Antonio disposed of this big property now worth millions . . . . for even less than a good song is worth nowadays.[3]

Perusal of the D. C. Alexander abstract reveals that J. M. Carolan, not Sweet, was mayor at the time of the 1854 purchase of 128.59 acres for $541—one-third paid in cash and the balance to be paid at 8 (not 6) percent interest over fifty years. Some five hundred additional acres of city-owned land were purchased by Alexander and paid for in the spring of 1862, but only $1,420 was paid in Confederate States notes. In 1870, moreover, Thomas H. Stribling, son-in-law and executor of the Alexander estate, paid $665.54, "the difference in value between said Confederate Notes when received (1862) and specie," and thus cleared the Alexander estate of all indebtedness to the city.[4]

No one really concerned himself about the Alexander and Kampmann purchases, however, until Jay Adams allegedly profited by $100,000 through real estate dealings in what had come to be known as Laurel Heights. It began after Denver real estate man Jay E. Adams, with an eye to land development, visited San Antonio en route to Corpus Christi in December 1887. By the following year older brother Lee Adams, in broken health that had not improved in either Denver or San Diego, joined hundreds of others who sought the favorable climate in San Antonio. Lee Adams later wrote:

[Jay] came to San Antonio on a visit and prospecting tour in February 1889. I had previously selected that rough, rocky hill country north and east of San Pedro Springs for the best probable development in a residential way in San Antonio.

I often drove with my father out into the brush on this hill and said to him, "We are some of us liable to see this the best residential part of San Antonio."[5]

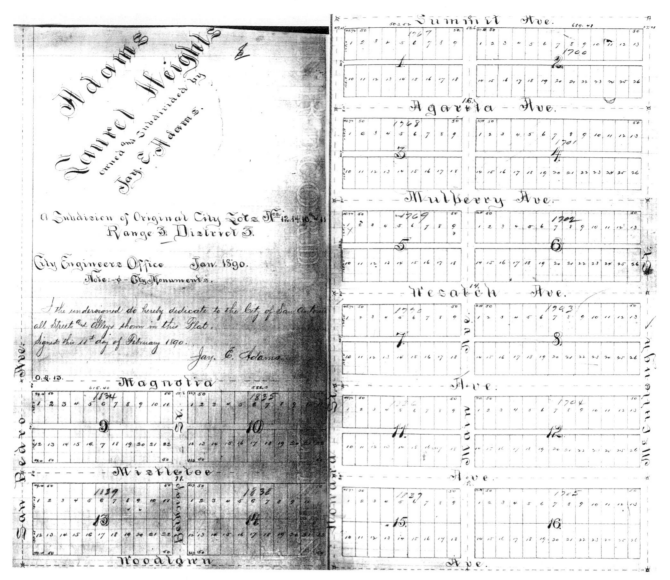

Major development in today's Monte Vista district began with the platting of the sixteen-block Adams Laurel Heights subdivision between San Pedro and McCullough avenues north of Woodlawn Avenue in 1890 by Jay Adams. The Coloradoan's misspelling in one street name of the South Texas huisache tree as "wesatch" was soon corrected.

Denver's real estate boom began to dissipate with inflation of land prices by the end of the 1880s. Young Jay Adams saw in fast-growing San Antonio to the southeast an investment outlet for his profits. In the autumn of 1889, Jay and Lee Adams purchased an eighteen-acre tract south of Summit Avenue from the Kampmann estate at the seemingly exorbitant price of $350 per acre. Before moving to San Antonio the following spring, Jay Adams acquired fifty-five more contiguous acres south to Woodlawn. Seventy-three acres bounded by Summit and McCullough, south to Woodlawn, west to San Pedro, and back to Howard at Magnolia were plotted as Jay Adams's Laurel Heights.[6]

This property was the first real estate development in the present Monte Vista National Historic District, even though several very distinguished San Antonio families had already built stately homes along French Place adjacent to the then-northern terminus of Main Avenue. Morrison and Fourmy's city map, dated April 19, 1883, indicates that lots had been plotted as far north as San Pedro Place (now Ashby Place) and French Place, between San Pedro and Howard avenues.

Nathan Gould, father-in-law of artist Robert J. Onderdonk, built what is the oldest structure in the Monte Vista Historic District. Emily Gould Onderdonk's diary entry of April 18, 1882, read, "Mother, Father, Robert and I moved into our new house Wednesday the 12th of April."[7] Joining the Gould-Onderdonk family on French Place that decade, Judge Leroy G. Denman, banker Josiah Townsend Woodhull, Colonel Augustus Belknap, financier E. B. Chandler and the two Talcott families (on Ashby) constructed some of the outstanding homes in the city. Proximity to the homes of these well-known citizens encouraged Jay Adams to be optimistic in his plans to develop an exclusive neighborhood.[8]

Promotional advertising in local newspapers exceeded any that prospective home buyers had ever witnessed. Entrepreneur Adams called on St. Matthew in his initial announcement of January 1890. "Therefore, whosoever heareth these sayings of mine, and doeth them, I will like him unto a wise man, which built his house upon a rock. And the rain descended, and the floods came, and the winds blew, and beat upon that house, and it fell not; for it was founded upon a rock."[9]

Limestone formations in the Laurel Heights hills, the secret of the permanence of homes today in the Monte Vista Historic District, did not escape Adams's attention. "Dr. [Frank] Paschal paid $2,800 for the foundation put in for his new house on Maverick Street, Tobin Hill [just to the South], while W. B. Clarkson paid $300.00 for his new foundation on the same street in Laurel Heights and Paschal's house will crack, while that of Clarkson's will not."[10]

An early advertisement extolled other advantages:

"LAUREL HEIGHTS"

Is the only hill that is reached without crossing railroads and passing poor houses. The improvements are all good and the streets are graded almost to this beautiful hill. It is 100 feet about the city and is adjoined by the best houses in the city.

Has the finest view.

The purest air, best shade.

Widest streets and avenues. The best ocean breezes and the healthiest location about the city.

Every lot contains a few nice natural trees and shrubs, such as live oak, wesatch, agarita, laurel and persimmon, with shade trees set out around every block. In this country shade and sea breeze are essential. The water-mains and gas-pipes run to the addition now and will be extended through it.

San Pedro, Belknap, Howard, Main and McCullough avenues all run directly through this property.[11]

Adams claimed that his fifty-foot lots were worth $1,000 each, but early buyers could acquire them in the $200–$400 range. The plat was laid out with eighty-foot avenues and twenty-foot alleys. If homes were to be commenced at once no cash was required; otherwise, one-fourth cash and the balance at 8 percent were required.[12]

When buyers did not immediately ascend the Heights in numbers, Adams announced in March 1890 that he would give a $400 lot to the first individual who would build an acceptable house in the area. The second builder would receive a "fine $150 parlor mantel," and the third a "fine $50 gold watch." Minimum construction cost on each house would be $1,500.[13] The free lot went to a Mr. Hatfield, who built the first house in Adams's Laurel Heights at 117 Woodlawn.[14] A later (December 1891) gimmick offered a $25 discount for those who would give a lot for a Christmas present.[15]

Meanwhile, verbal enticements proliferated during the spring of 1890 as the developer promised that no lots would be sold to speculators. Adams declared that "Laurel Heights speaks for itself to those who see it." Brush rapidly disappeared as the hills were grubbed and native shrubs and such trees as existed were retained. Additional trees were set out along the streets, and they would flourish as San Antonians in the 1890s became increasingly aware of their subterranean water resources.[16] Otherwise, the land in

G. Bedell Moore named his since-razed 1880s home at 202 West French Place Laurelia in homage to the profusion of hardy mountain laurels in the new neighborhood.

Gardens like those behind E. B. Chandler's French Place home—the carriage house is in the left background—helped prove developers' point that the seemingly poor Laurel Heights soil could be coaxed into lushness, sometimes with the help of an above-ground irrigation system such as that using the pipes at right.

the area would have remained submarginal. A 1904 soil survey in the San Antonio area, later published by the United States Department of Agriculture, indicated that the soil of Laurel Heights, and that of its Alamo Heights contemporary, was Colton Stone Clay.

The Colton stony clay consists of from three to six inches of loose, dark-colored clay, underlain by a rotten white limestone. . . The shallow covering of soil on the surface is residual, having been derived from the underlying limestone . . . The Colton stony clay is characterized by its stubby, stunted growth of liveoak and mesquite and cactus . . . under present conditions this type of soil is of no agricultural value, except for the scanty pasturage it affords. It would make an excellent soil for goat ranches or vineyards.[17]

Happily for Jay Adams, he could point to the lovely nearby gardens of Judge Denman and E. B. Chandler to prove that flowers, shrubbery and even fruit trees could flourish on the Heights. Moreover, Adams could boast of fine views from an elevation of at least a hundred feet above the

downtown business section and the cool sea breezes from the southeast. Here one would come upon neither mud nor mosquitoes. Plans followed quickly for extension of water mains, lights, gas, and the streetcar line into the addition.[18]

By March 15, 1892, Adams listed some twenty readily identifiable purchasers of Laurel Heights lots.[19] Newspapers in late spring reported rapid resale of local real estate, which sometimes doubled or tripled in price in two months' time. Within two years a reporter noted that "there is a growing disposition on the part of newcomers and even among older residents of the city to seek the purer air and freedom of the outskirts."[20]

Not surprisingly, other real estate developers sought to participate in this rising market. Financier E. B. Chandler had in 1888 purchased eighteen acres south of Woodlawn between Howard and San Pedro for $6,000. Several investors from Denver belonged to the Christian Church, so-called "Campbellites."

Two years later, Adams's fellow Denverite and Campbellite, the Rev. Dr. William Bayard Craig, in association with two of his prominent Denver church members, Frank and Logan Russell, purchased some Chandler property that would subsequently be known as Craig's Laurel Heights. Immediately to the south, a Mr. French of Pittsburgh owned a block of ground. Thus, French

---

Previous pages: Perhaps San Antonio's finest example of Victorian residential shingle style architecture is the Monte Vista home built by attorney Thomas H. Franklin (1891, James Riely Gordon, architect) on French Place at Main Avenue. Sold in 1944 to become part of the Saint Mary's Hall campus—since 1968 the campus of San Antonio Academy—its restoration was completed in 1988.

W. EUGENE GEORGE

Place, Russell and Craig acquired their names. Adams, on the other hand, selected native Texas trees as his choice for such street names as Huisache, Magnolia, Mistletoe, Agarita, and Mulberry.

Other Denver Christian Church members later joined with Adams in developing Beacon Hill to the west of San Pedro and Laurel Heights Terrace to the east of McCullough. Unrelated Denver groups also purchased large acreages in Alamo Heights to the north of town, and in Denver Heights to the south.[21]

A certain ambivalence characterized local reaction to the arrival of Denver investors. Exultant articles in the newspaper prophesied a great future for San Antonio, but "knowledgeable" local landmen ridiculed the newcomers for paying exorbitant prices for worthless land. Jay Adams, in his later years, related an episode that occurred in Tax Collector Gustav Frasch's office which reflected local opinion. Adams, unknown personally by Frasch, stood by as the tax assessor explained his policy to a New York investor. A property the New Yorker proposed to buy at an excessive price would not suffer a tax increase, Frasch declared.

"Oh, no," the Assessor replied. "I always assess a man's possessions at just what they are worth. Now, there is a man from Denver [Adams] one hears about. He has bought Laurel Heights and paid $350 an acre for it. But I assess him exactly what the land is worth, and all it will ever be worth. That is $100 an acre. The man from Denver was a fool."[22]

Sales in Laurel Heights continued at a profitable pace through the spring of 1893. Four lots sold "at a figure [in March] in advance of the price paid for the same property during the zenith of the activity of 1890, thus conclusively showing that well-located lots are in good demand."[23] Building likewise continued at an increasing tempo in April and May 1893, as City Assessor Frasch reported for that two-month period:

Laurel Heights Addition—Nineteen 2-story frame dwellings; three 1-1/2 story frame dwellings; twenty 1-story frame dwellings; four 2-story brick dwellings; one 1-1/2 story brick dwelling; one 1-story brick dwelling; one 2-story hard rock dwelling; one 1-1/2 story hard rock dwelling; one 1-story soft rock dwelling; one 2-story private boarding school; one frame pavilion; one 1-1/2 story rock and brick outhouse; fifty-one lumber outhouses.[24]

The man who headed the Denver rush to San Antonio earned a modest fortune on Laurel Heights within three years, but the disastrous depression that befell Colorado in the late 1880s became widespread as the Panic of 1893 extended across the nation and reached the Alamo City. Adams's extensive real estate investments were in jeopardy by year's end. As his brother Lee wrote, "Jay E. Adams was a great spender as well as a great money maker and in those hard years when there was no sale of property he came very near having to make an assignment, but he was the best squirmer I ever saw and he wormed himself out and retained his fortune."[25]

As elsewhere in the nation, the depression continued until the defeat of William Jennings Bryan and his free silver platform in the presidential campaign of 1896. Historians often suggest that election of William McKinley that year restored the confidence of the American people, but it was the turn of the century before the local real estate market again became very profitable.

Part of its resurgence also resulted from population growth. Doubtless the national attention directed at Teddy Roosevelt and his Rough Riders in May 1898 attracted some newcomers to San Antonio. Tuberculars had continued to come to the city for their health, and by 1901 the local press reported increasing numbers of winter visitors who sought to escape the inclement weather of the North. "Waves of prosperity can almost be felt in the very air," a reporter exulted as he described local architects busily engaged in drawing plans for new homes and buildings.[26]

Building materials for dwellings would change rapidly in the new century. Both hard and soft rock had been popular in residential construction before the coming of the railroad in 1877, after which lumber became increasingly used. Brick structures appeared more frequently after 1900, both in Laurel Heights and the new Summit Place area just to the north. Stucco over hollow tiles would not become a favorite until the 1920s.[27]

One architectural firm announced in March 1901 that it had under construction fifteen homes in the $9,000–$10,000 range, residences that could be afforded only by the upper middle class. Suburbs throughout the city enjoyed a building boom in the spring of 1901, but Laurel Heights exceeded them all in popularity.[28]

Real estate advertisements again appeared with regularity, especially those of Adams and

In the little-mechanized years of the World War I era, Belknap Place received a type of concrete pavement that has since required very little maintenance. This crew was moving past the Koehler estate, enclosed by a $10,000 six-foot iron and concrete fence designed by architect Charles T. Boelhauwe.

Kirkpatrick, who specialized in Laurel Heights homes. Their advertising copy often seemed repetitive: "One of the most beautiful homes in San Antonio . . . never before been put on the market, and probably will never be offered to the public again . . . must be seen to be appreciated . . . artistic treatment . . . leaves nothing to be wished for . . . extensive grounds . . . beautiful flowers."[29]

Regardless of the natural attractions, some prospective residents noted the lack of one amenity—fire protection. Residents had donated property for a fire station in Laurel Heights as early as 1902, and for several years they expected construction in the "near future."[30] When Laurel Heights taxpayers organized an improvement club at San Pedro Springs in August 1903, their primary interest lay in the construction of a sewer system and a fire station.[31]

Atlee B. Ayres drew plans in 1905 for an engine house that would "be provided with a watch tower, where a lookout will be maintained every night."[32] Several years passed before construction began, however, and it would be 1929 before the present fire station would replace the original structure on West Russell Place.[33]

Meanwhile, residents began to landscape their lawns, complementing public improvements such as palm trees to beautify "the aristocratic suburban district," paved streets and sidewalks.[34]

By 1928, Laurel Heights streets were graded and macadamized as far north as Mistletoe Avenue. Two miles of streets with "Callaghan" paving produced a "smooth and admirably rounded surface . . . . almost like asphalt . . . . glistening and white." Described as "the most important civic improvement of the year in San Antonio," they encouraged newcomers to feel justified with their investments.[35] Those anxious to build homes immediately, however, sometimes faced delays.

"We builders have all the work now we can handle," said Laurel Heights builder H. L. Scott, who reported in 1906 that a shortage of skilled labor "has forced our firm to turn away considerable work."[36] Developer Jay Adams declared a week earlier that "real estate activity in this city is without precedent."[37] Six months later, this "phenomenal" demand for property continued. "The high class suburban property, especially in restricted districts, appeals strongly to the San Antonian and likewise to the newcomer."[38]

Hardly any listings of deeds filed from 1905 to 1920 failed to include numerous Laurel Heights sales to well-known San Antonians. Optimism prevailed throughout the realty market in the autumn of 1907. "Laurel Heights, that select and choice spot for the homeseeker, is gaining rapidly in its well-earned popularity. In fact, this gain is so pronounced and its inevitable effect so apparent, that the time is not far off when the prospective buyer will have to cast about for another location."[39] An *Express* writer declared that other than "the fabled cities of California," San Antonio had the most beautiful suburbs in the nation. One stood preeminent.

Laurel Heights, of all the suburbs of the city, has probably made the most uniform strides in the matter of progress and beautification. It is now more than seventeen years since the work of development of this section began. After all that is not such a long space of time when it is considered that at the beginning of these seventeen years Laurel Heights was a waste of cactus and mesquite. Today [1907] it is a dream of loveliness and architectural beauty.

On these Heights are located some of the most beautiful homes in the city and among the city's wealthiest men have selected this spot for their dwelling place. The development here has been of a solid character, and owes its progress to the character of her citizenship. In the seventeen years since it has been an entity, it has either contributed through subscription or general taxation the sum of $76,000 for general improvements in the way of streets, sewers, etc. This suburb is always the admiration of visitors to the city.[40]

Taxpayers on the Heights heard speeches from L. J. Hart, Vories Brown, W. J. Moore, J. H. Kirkpatrick, Thad Adams and C. W. Ogden on the August evening in 1903 when they met to elect W. J. Moore as president and Charles Tobin as secretary of their improvement club. On the

"End of the line" is the label on this 1903 snapshot of the San Pedro Avenue streetcar that ran out to Laurel Heights.

following day, City Engineer John D. Rullmann had men "digging test holes to ascertain the locality and depths of the rock for data on which to base an estimate for a system of sanitary sewers."[41] Three years later, outhouses would become obsolete as the sewer system was extended northward to Woodlawn Avenue.[42]

A resolution at the organizational meeting indicated that residents found satisfaction in their streetcar service. Property owners of the area had donated a sum of $32,500 to the streetcar company whereby it entered into a twenty-five-year contract to provide service to the area.[43] Trolley service into the neighborhood before the general appearance of the automobile raised property values, and the most affluent families built homes along the car lines.

Two years after residents declared their satisfaction with streetcar services, they raised $1,500 and sought more contributions, to lower the grades on San Pedro Avenue north of the springs to Magnolia Avenue. With tracks laid eastward on Magnolia, a loop would be formed with another line that moved northward on Main to Craig Place, west to Howard, and then to Magnolia.[44] Streetcar service would again be extended by 1909 to Kings Highway, as the earliest homes in Summit Place were constructed by that time.[45]

Civic leaders on the Heights did not ignore the overall welfare of the city. Active in the Business Men's Club, which evolved into the Chamber of Commerce in 1909, residents also participated in San Antonio government. Those "most active" in the city charter revision committee in 1907 included John Kokernot, Jot Gunter, T. T. Vander Hoeven and Dr. Frederick Terrell.[46]

Curiously enough, the presidential election of 1908 became associated with the growing American propensity for moving to the suburbs. Previous candidates boasted of their modest beginnings in log cabins, farms, or small towns. William Howard Taft, noted the great Kansas journalist William Allen White, represented a new type of American leader from the suburbs, one "who as a boy knew both swimming hole and pavement . . . . who was afraid of neither cows nor cars." Laurel Heights residents could certainly identify with such a person, and a local real estate reporter used the presidential candidate to illustrate the local "tendency towards the suburban home or rather

The rapid growth of San Antonio that began toward the end of the nineteenth century was a bonanza for the many talented architects who established practices in the city. Here Atlee B. Ayres, left, who became a major Monte Vista architect, stands with C. A. Coughlin in their drafting room on Commerce Street in about 1900.

the home towards the outskirts of the city where country life can be enjoyed impartially."[47]

Diversity in residential architectural plans became obvious as new construction appeared on the northern limits of the city, but this variety was characteristic elsewhere and not just in Laurel Heights. Noted a reporter in 1912:

One of the elements of San Antonio's picturesqueness is found in the variety of styles represented in her residences. Preferences range from the low, spreading bungalow to the massive and imposing. The Queen Anne cottage is found and residences along what is known as "mission" lines and built of concrete are in favor. Then there are the comfortably hospitable looking frame dwellings of two and three stories, and even more.

There is no more apt description of Laurel Heights on the eve of World War I.[48]

Lifestyles reflected in newspaper columns prior to World War I evoke nostalgia for the time when neighbors knew one another and were sufficiently removed from downtown to merit a "Laurel Heights" dateline in the press in the early 1890s. One suspects that promoter Jay Adams was responsible for the social columns, which read much like today's weekly country newspapers. His advertising copy encouraged readers: "To get cooled off go to the best summer resort in Texas. Laurel Heights. Round trip only 10 cents."

While the Adams family left for its customary vacation home in Grand Lake, Colorado, an 1893 Laurel Heights columnist noted that "there are some people, however, who regard the Heights as a summer resort." Mrs. Gregory's house provided rooms for Professor Ramon Guerrero's family (his weak child "improved"), another "downtowner," Miss Mattie Webb, and Miss Orth, "a pleasant young lady and stenographer of the city." Mrs. McArdle also had "her table full of boarders" that summer. August E. Altgelt had just returned from a holiday of several weeks. County Collector José Cassiano, living there temporarily on a "curative mission" because of a persistent case of rheumatism, expressed "himself as much pleased and benefitted and says that if continued residence here renders him sufficiently aristocratic he might be persuaded to buy."[49] He did.

Six months later, the Laurel Heights column informed readers that F. J. Madara had begun a "fine cottage" on East Craig Place near the car line. Streetcar travel was interrupted for two days because the electric line was down on Magnolia. Meanwhile, the electric light company had extended its lines, "making connection with Dr. Smith, Jay E. Adams, and Mr. Beall." Readers may have been curious as to the unidentified possessors of "a carload of furniture and a Grand Piano . . . unloaded at one of our Laurel Heights residences last week, a direct shipment from Chicago."[50]

New Laurel Heights residents seem hardly to have moved in before they began to entertain, but no couples appear to have opened their home as frequently as Mr. and Mrs. E. B. Chandler. Their home, one of the earliest and finest on elegant French Place, was the setting for many large teas, receptions and garden parties. Mrs. Chandler not only demonstrated her talents as artist and woodcarver, she obviously relished her role as hostess.

A garden party in honor of Mr. Chandler's *igeburstag* (birthday) brought together couples and the young unmarried from the Heights and nearby Tobin Hill. "It was intended to be very informal but the ladies came exquisitely gowned" to this party which did not end until midnight. A number of the guests had arrived by streetcars which did not run at that hour, but "Mr. Chandler very thoughtfully chartered a special car to convey them to their respective homes."[51]

According to an *Express* reporter in 1893, "Fair women and brave men battled gallantly for the beautiful prizes offered by the fair hostess, who gave her hospitality in the most inimitable manner" at a Chandler card party. Flowers bedecked the rooms in which "the ladies all looked lovely in beautiful evening dresses and the gentlemen never looked better in their regulation suits."[52]

Many of these guests appeared thirteen years later when Mrs. Chandler entertained at a Progres-

French Place neighbors portrayed about 1900 are, from left, top, financier E. B. Chandler and West Texas rancher Alfred S. Gage, an unidentified man and Mrs. (May) Chandler, center; and, in front, Mrs. (Ida) Gage, daughter Dorothy and Mrs. Seth (Cora) Gage. The portrait was made in the Gages' backyard.

sive Hearts party for "a company of friends." This she did in celebration of George Washington's birthday in 1906. The guest list included such familiar Laurel Heights names as the three Furnish, Moore and McGown-Davis families, as well as the artistic Onderdonks and others from the Gage, Savage and Franklin households.[53]

Less elaborate appointments were found when Dr. and Mrs. Milton J. Bliem entertained in 1903 at their West Mistletoe home for daughter Marion. "The broad galleries outside were lighted up by cheerful jack o'lanterns cut out of large pumpkins."[54] Seven years later, Methodist bishop and Mrs. E. D. Mouzon hosted a similar party at their 126 East French Place home for the Young Ladies Society of the Travis Park Methodist Church and their gentlemen friends. "A large hal-

Organization of neighborhood churches and social groups followed on the heels of Laurel Heights development. These girls, seated before the backdrop of newly completed homes on West Mistletoe Avenue in 1911, were among members of the new Christ Episcopal Church's Junior Auxiliary, sponsored by Mistletoe resident Mrs. DuVal West, first president of the church's Women's Auxiliary.

loween cake of ginger bread was cut with thimble, dime and button found in the slices."[55] That year the Winchester Kelso home at Craig and Main was the scene of a gala lawn party to which daughter Ruth had invited almost all of the young people on the Heights.[56]

Developer Jay Adams and his wife also entertained frequently during the 1890s at their grand home on Belknap. Members of the Laurel Heights Euchre Club gathered, apparently twice a month, in the Adams home and in those of other members over a period of years.[57] Alcoholic beverages were not served at the Adamses parties. As members of the Disciples of Christ, they abstained, as did many of their friends, who were among the organizers of today's Central Christian Church.[58]

Even though they did not drink alcoholic beverages, card playing for prizes increased among members of the Christian Church. First Presbyterian Church elders felt compelled to call to the attention "of its members [many of whom lived in Laurel Heights] the prevalence in our community and even among the members of this church of playing of games with gambling tendencies. As a Session we are disposed to make no tirade against card playing in general, believing that this is a matter for each individual conscience, but we do single out the phase of card playing known as Progressive Euchre . . . . and without fear of contradiction assert that as now played they have a direct tendency to gambling."[59]

Regardless, the Progressive Euchre craze continued on Laurel Heights with both ladies and gentlemen participating. After the turn of the century, however, other types of card games attracted the attention of an increasing number of affluent ladies on the Heights. No social change escaped the watchful eyes of Marin B. Fenwick, society editor of the San Antonio *Express*, who by 1911 had the most influential newspaper column for women the city has yet known. Readers perused several paragraphs of didactic social instruction before they reached the social tidbits in "Facts and Fancies About People Here and Abroad":

To play cards well requires mental exercise that is wholesome and refreshing, so if the players but be firm against the evil tendencies of the game, the pastime will not be so discredited and a splendid mode of entertainment will be the outcome.

Now that the formal season has closed, society has given herself up to this form of pleasure. In every direction there are clubs of bridge, five hundred and even high five. Some of these gatherings are on an elaborate scale of entertainment, each hostess vying with the next to do so just a little more than is expected.

On Laurel Heights the card fever runs up to the danger mark, for housewives have to be very watchful of their happy homes or card-orphaned children will suffer from the constant absence of mothers at one or another of the club meetings. There are two Tuesday Card Clubs, a Wednesday afternoon Bridge Club, Wednesday Evening Card Club, and a Friday Bridge Club on the Hill.[60]

Even though it might be a waste of time, Miss Fenwick later recognized one socially redeeming aspect of card playing. Conscientious players would find little time "left for idle gossip, which is ten times more harmful recreation than card playing." Indulgence in idle talk seemed to be indigenous to an "over the teacup" setting. While Miss Fenwick might abhor any form of gossip, she frequently ignored the fact that she herself was the leading local purveyor of idle talk that some might regard as a private matter.

That reminds us that we heard a shocking bit of news yesterday which was told us in dead secret. "Dead secrets" are always more interesting. It seems that some of the members of the bridge clubs—yes, we'll tell it all; Laurel Heights Bridge Club—smoke. Not that time honored cob of their grandmother's day, but the devilish little cigarette. We have been hearing for some time of women who smoked and did various up-to-date stunts, but they don't live on Laurel Heights and they are not suffragists, and did not learn their

As tennis, golf and bowling grew to be popular sports on Laurel Heights, ladies' teas became an enduring social ritual. Here, from left, Mrs. Arthur Seeligson, Mrs. Gilbert Denman and Mrs. John Meusebach plan a benefit event for the opening of the Majestic Theater downtown in 1929.

tricks at the polls. Whether society is going to establish a quarantine against these women will be announced later.[61]

More to be praised that month were the dozen young ladies, more than half of whom lived on the Heights, who organized for the season of Lent the Debutantes' Bible Class at the newly constructed Young Women's Christian Association. Studying the Bible as literature seemed an eminently desirable expenditure of time, but a weekly class during the forty days of Lent did not intrude inordinately upon one's time.[62]

Four years later, also during Lent, Miss Fenwick described some young ladies as going "madly after tennis or still more exclusive, golf. There are many expert tennis players in the city and quite a few splendid courts, among them one at the Woodhull home in West French Place. Just down the street a stone's throw is the court at A. S. Gage's home and just a few blocks on down West French Place one comes to the McGowns' court, while the Lipscomb court is very seldom idle."[63]

Young people had become devotees of a new sport by the turn of the century at the Laurel Heights golf links, located to the northwest of the San Pedro and Summit intersection. Matches for young ladies and gentlemen occupied much of the 1901 Christmas holiday season.[64]

Another recreational activity involving both sexes of varying ages had become popular during the first decade of the century. Members of the Laurel Heights Bowling Club frequently invited their friends to join them in this fashionable recreation.

Some of the gatherings, such as on the evening of December 23, 1904, provided opportunity for a festive celebration when "Christmas colors prevailed in the decoration and a merry game of bowling was indulged in." Ladies rotated as hostesses, and Mrs. D. K. Furnish and Mrs. T. T. Vander Hoeven served that month.[65]

Men of all ages participated in organized recreational activity. A group of the very young appeared in the 1893 Battle of Flowers parade:

The boys rode heavily trimmed and flowered machines notable among which were two little fellows with gold papered bicycles and carrying a banner with the inscription "Laurel Heights World Beaters." A Gabriel disguised in mask as a monkey closed the wheelmen's division. The wheelmen kept well together and turned about in graceful curves, it being the first well-managed cycle parade ever given here.[66]

By the time the golf links were completed, however, men on the Heights turned to that sport or to the gun club. By 1904 players on the Laurel Heights golf links had formed an organization under the leadership of E. B. Chandler. With membership at $25 and annual dues at $20, twenty-five charter members formed the Golf and Country Club of San Antonio and built a $1,600 clubhouse. Onlookers viewed the undertaking as "preposterous" as there would be insufficient local interest, but the clubhouse opened with a gala affair in April 1904 with the "crack Dallas golf players" as guests for the occasion.

Let it be known that the Golf and Country club is not altogether a coterie of golf cranks. Rather it is a country club in the truest sense of the term. It is meant as a headquarters for the best people of San Antonio, either residents or visitors. The society ladies of the city have taken on the idea of serving tea and light refreshments every Saturday afternoon and to keep pace with the demands of the society the officials are planning lawn tennis courts to be laid out so that play can be seen from the clubhouse verandas.[67]

Considerable jocularity could be observed among the golfers: "Lewis Maverick turned up Friday with a stick that he feels he can do wonders with. There is a rumor out that he has challenged a certain man who put him out of the game last Saturday."[68] This course continued as the local golfing center until construction of the San Antonio Country Club north of Fort Sam Houston.

"George," a horse stabled behind sculptor Pompeo Coppini's rented home on West Woodlawn Avenue, became the model for the mount in Coppini's winning entry for a statue memorializing Terry's Texas Rangers, a Confederate Army cavalry unit. The sculpture, in front of the state capitol in Austin, was dedicated in 1907.

While golfing interested an increasing number of recruits, dozens of local men continued in the shooting tradition of their Texas forefathers. Joe Shiner and H. L. Wagner founded the Laurel Heights Gun Club in the spring of 1906; within two years, eighty-nine members joined to make it the largest gun club in southwest Texas. Trap shooting, however, represented a new experience for some of these men, who had recently become frustrated by a lack of game birds in the area. Shiner and Wagner first set their traps up on Laurel Heights but then moved "north of the hill" as new homes appeared in the neighborhood. Joe Frost became president, and the legendary Mrs. Adolph Topperwein encouraged a dozen ladies to take up the sport.[69]

A grand shoot of July 4, 1908, attracted scores of people to the club at the streetcar terminus of Summit Addition. "This line connects with San Pedro cars at the corner of Magnolia and Howard streets . . . It is further announced that a grandstand has been erected from which spectators may view the shooting from grateful shade. Lunch will be served on the grounds all day."[70] Residential encroachment, however, led to an increasing

number of shoots being held at Scheuermeyer's Park on New Braunfels Avenue.

Sports attracted Laurel Heights men more than any other outside endeavor, but a small group of residents sought more bon vivant company among the Chili Thirteen. Organized in 1905, these witty intellectuals planned monthly Mexican suppers "where hot tamales of wit and chili con carne of soul shall pass back and forth across the festive board, properly irrigated by the brew Plerian that has made San Antonio justly famous."

The first such gathering took place at the Original Mexican Restaurant on Losoya Street where "bon mots were sauce to enchiladas and seasoning to frijoles, while digestion waited on appetite and good fellowship flowed upward in the incense Havana." Laurel Heights personalities in this group included architects Harvey L. Page and Atlee B. Ayres, artist Robert J. Onderdonk, bookseller George Roe, realtor and orator J. H. Kirkpatrick and sculptor Pompeo Coppini. Coppini later recalled the role of the Chili Thirteen in establishing the Order of Omala and constructing the float for King Selamat I (David J. Woodward) in the first Fiesta night parade.[71] Sculpting "Terry's Rangers" also occupied Coppini during his Laurel Heights residence:

I started my sketch for the Terry's Texas Rangers for the competition that was to take place in Austin in May 1905. I worked a small model of the pedestal and of the horse in the backyard of the home I had rented from Mr. Norval J. Welsh on Woodlawn Avenue, as I had bought to serve me as a model a horse not a thoroughbred, but just the type of cavalry horse the poor Confederates had, or any cowboy, as a matter of fact—and a horse that we used for our first carriage. His name was George. I bought a real Texas saddle, and I used to ride him almost every day.

For the model of the rider I used Mr. Jim McNeel, a former Ranger himself and son of a well-known captain of the Texas Rangers. Jim, as I have already told, was my neighbor on Locust Street and the son-in-law of Albert Maverick, Sr., then living in his home in front of the Post Office, and facing Alamo Plaza, across the way from the Hugo-Schmeltzer Building. On May 11, 1905, I won the competition against sixteen artists and some bold monumental granite and marble dealers of the State, who had artists make the sketches for them.[72]

The Ancient Order of Hibernians also included a number of members from the Heights. Most San Antonians would have regarded this as an "Anglo" neighborhood, three being also very fine residents of German or Mexican heritage. Even so, such en-

San Antonio's most distinguished family of artists, the Onderdonks, posed on their French Place lawn in 1912. From left are, top row, Gertrude (Mrs. Julian), Eleanor, Emily (Mrs. Robert) and Robert Onderdonk. In front are Julian and his children Bob and Adrienne Onderdonk.

trepreneurs of Irish ancestry included L. J. Hart, Michael Goggan and J. H. Kirkpatrick, who was Scotch-Irish but allegedly had "so much good Irish blood in his veins" that many credited his great speaking ability to his Irish background [73] Kirkpatrick's oratorical powers became legendary after his welcoming speech to President Theodore Roosevelt when he returned to San Antonio for a reunion with his Rough Riders of Spanish-American War fame.[74]

Life on the Heights involved less organized activity as well. Emily Gould Onderdonk's diary of the years 1891–1910 reveals the extraordinary amount of time ladies spent visiting and shopping and their delight in the festivities associated with holidays, especially Christmas. Son Julian Onderdonk spent the 1891–1892 winter with his grandparents, the Nathan Goulds on French Place, and "attended school to a Miss Nora Franklin on Laurel Heights." Fireworks, a scroll saw and candy stuffed in stockings and a bureau drawer in an unoccupied room were among the gifts for nine-year-old Julian. A year later, the gifts were "ar-

ranged on table and divans" as well as in the stockings. There was no Christmas tree in the home until 1909, after the arrival of great-grandchildren.[75]

Children's parties flourished on the Heights. Guests named in local newspapers suggest that almost everyone in the neighborhood received invitations to affairs hosted by their peers. Mrs. W. W. Lipscomb's Christmas party in 1902 at 123 East Craig provided such a setting. As in other spacious homes during this era, festivities often took place in the attic. "Mistletoe, holly, palms and bunting and the soft lights from the Japanese lanterns made it an ideal and beautiful place." A Christmas tree hidden in an alcove provided candy-filled Mexican baskets for seventy children representing most families on Laurel Heights.[76]

Young people likewise gathered for cards, trolley parties, punch parties, croquet on the lawn, porch parties, bicycling and picnics. San Pedro Springs was the most convenient destination for excursions, but sometimes chaperoned groups went by streetcar as far as the Argyle in Alamo Heights or the missions below town.[77]

The automobile began to facilitate the mobility of these affluent youths by World War I. By that time, it had become something of a status symbol for young married ladies to own their own cars. When the war broke out, a number of the post-debutante set began to learn the fundamentals of automobile mechanics. Students in the International Motor School, "all well-known for their patriotism and energetic determinations," included Katherine and Marjorie McGown, Juanita Hopkins, Jean Aubrey, Elizabeth Kokernot, Clara May Brooks, Constance Ball, Gertrude Negley, Jeannette Hagelstein and Estelle Staacke.[78]

Even before World War I, Laurel Heights had begun to take on a new appearance. Few vacant

Growing popularity of the automobile aided the mobility of entire families. Here Atlee B. (Jr.) and Robert M. Ayres, sons of architect and Mrs. Atlee B. Ayres, drive south down Ashby Place past Otto Koehler's carriage house in about 1915.

West Woodlawn, boasting several "solid blocks of fence-less houses," came in for particular praise. When residents tore their fences down, they planted roses and shrubs between the sidewalks and the street.[79] Rather than waste the material, one could use the old fence "in the rear to keep the chickens at home or for a barnyard of any sort . . . . Summing up the whole proposition, a fence may be useful in the backyard, but is an offense in the front yards."[80]

Annual contests for "most beautiful yards," inaugurated in 1911 by the San Antonio Real Estate Exchange, attracted many entrants. Few could match the two century plants and other plantings in the gardens of Mrs. Chandler and those other grand homes along French Place, but neighbors vied with one another in adding to the beauty of their streets.[81] These contests, revived after the war years, afforded particular attention to lawns of such residents as F. L. Hillyer at 111 East Craig.[82]

Each spring on the Heights, the profusion of blossoms on the laurel trees and "the flowers of the wild verbena and primrose" attracted press notice.[83] Much to the surprise of residents, the peach blooms produced excellent fruit by late summer, as one resident put it, "on 1000 feet of rock and one inch of soil." W. J. Moore, who lived on West French Place, produced a "perfect" peach ten and a half inches in diameter.[84]

Anything out of the ordinary, peaches or people, provoked conversation. Among the newcomers to San Antonio in the winter of 1902–1903, a "divine healer" made his residence in a home he rented from Colonel W. T. Way at 202 West Woodlawn Avenue. One Francis Truth, late of Boston, received a visit from a reporter who noted that Truth allegedly could "cure all diseases by the laying on of hands." Truth claimed that his visit came at the behest of a prominent San

lots could be found, and trees planted by the earliest residents had spread their branches. Considerable publicity had been given to the development of beautiful lawns, and the removal of fences, many of which had fallen into disrepair, was a desideratum.

By 1917, antagonism to fences was so strong that no fence-enclosed lawn would be permitted in the annual "beautiful yard" contests. Stockades had been a necessary protection when San Antonio was "a scrawny frontier town in the midst of a wild and lawless country." They had come down and since the Civil War fences of board and wire had taken their place. Inasmuch as cattle no longer roamed the streets and it had become illegal to keep unpenned chickens in the city, "to hide a beautiful lawn behind an unsightly fence is little short of a crime . . . Fenceless yards encourage civic pride . . . . The laggard in a neighborhood will be shown up in his true colors when there is no fence to hide his lack of civic pride. Civic pride is merely a form of patriotism."

Antonian who needed his services, friends of whom "besieged" the healer to remain in town throughout the winter months. Faith healer Truth offered his "services to a limited extent to all those affected."[85]

Occasional waves of excitement erupted, usually prompted by a somewhat traumatic experience. "Several days since we had a sunstroke matinee. A horse attached to a wagon and engaged in the laudable undertaking of removing a load of evening earth to remote parts suddenly fell to the ground." In spite of ministration from a nearby veterinary surgeon, Dr. James C. Talcott, the horse succumbed the following day.[86]

Runaway horses could also cause distress, as did one "attached to a laundry wagon having taken fright and French leave. It executed a brilliant dash . . . and decorated the Heights with a promiscuous shower of miscellaneous wearing apparel."[87] Residents complained occasionally about "loose stock running at large nightly in that neighbor-

Once cattle no longer roamed city streets and it became illegal to keep unpenned chickens, many thought that "to hide a beautiful lawn behind an unsightly fence is little short of a crime." This ornamental fence at Belknap Place and French Place once allowed views of the D. S. Combs family house and grounds but now encloses a parking lot.

hood."[88] It is not clear what unpleasant conditions plagued the neighborhood to such an extent in 1903 as to cause twenty representative citizens to meet at the Laurel Heights grocery to take "steps for better sanitary measures. L. J. Hart was elected chairman and R. M. J. Bliem, secretary."[89]

Gatherings of boys could lead to disturbances, more often in the summer months—except at Halloween. An especially noisy group playing on the pavilion near the Gregory school offended some nearby elders who gave chase, leading to little Willie Green's broken arm. "In accelerating the somewhat tardy retreat of Willie from the pavilion, a slight manual encouragement was given him, which eventuated in a fall down the stairs."[90]

Destruction of property could produce greater chagrin. "Residents of Laurel Heights are complaining of boys throwing rocks at chickens and turkeys in that vicinity. Many of the chickens are crippled in this manner and one family has lost about $40 worth of fine chickens, which were killed by mischievous boys."[91]

Laurel Heights appeared to be a safe area in which to reside, though police surveillance proved inadequate in 1907 when a burglar entered the home of J. H. Kirkpatrick and choked his niece "into insensibility," provoking the wrath of San Antonio's foremost orator. "I have not seen a policeman on Laurel Heights for three months prior to last night, when three came in response to a call . . . . We people in Laurel Heights pay a tax for protection but do not receive any police protection whatever and it is surprising to me that half of the houses up here are not robbed."[92]

Shocking experiences such as those suffered by the Kirkpatrick family were few. Memories of an idyllic neighborhood are more common. Mrs. E. S. (Ruth West) Emerson pleasantly recalled her pre–World War I childhood days on West Mistletoe when it was safe for a six-year-old to travel to downtown alone by streetcar.

For all classes of people, the streetcar offered a common denominator for transportation in the first decade of the century. From town, the streetcar came out San Pedro Avenue, turned east on Locust to Main and headed up to Craig. There, to avoid the excessive elevation of two hills, it turned west one block to Howard and up to Magnolia, where it turned west to San Pedro and back downtown. One could transfer to another car—

known as the Toonerville Trolley, after a popular cartoon—which moved north and south on Howard between Magnolia and the terminus at Kings Highway.

Before the advent of the automobile, for most Laurel Heights families during the beginning of World War I, Mrs. Emerson recalled that business and professional men rode the trolley to their offices; their wives took it to downtown shopping, and the children took it to distant schools. There were the exceptions for those who walked to St. Anthony School, down to Travis School on Main Avenue, to San Antonio Academy just across San Pedro Park, and, for several years after World War I, to Saint Mary's Hall in the former D. J. Woodward mansion on San Pedro at Woodlawn, before it moved to French Place between Main and McCullough. As there were no crosstown streetcar lines, some of the boys rode their ponies across to West Texas Military Academy (now Texas Military Institute), located on Grayson Street until 1911.

For those who chose to range afar from San Pedro Avenue, it was necessary to go downtown and transfer to another line. One could go north on River Avenue (Avenue C, later Broadway) to Alamo Heights. Families from Laurel Heights would sometimes alight from the Alamo Heights trolley at what is now Hildebrand and tread a wooden walkway up to the new country club, which for most had supplanted the Laurel Heights golf course. This Laurel Heights site, however, did continue for a number of years as an athletic center. Mrs. Emerson remembered walking over to football games there, perhaps as late as 1918. Prior to World War I, a number of Laurel Heights girls attended Saint Mary's Hall downtown, the Mulholland School on Brooklyn Avenue, Miss Wasson's School on Oakland, or, later, the Bonn Avon School.

As today, some moved back and forth between public and private schools. Should one opt for a public institution at the junior level, for all San Antonio children it meant journeying to the "seventh grade school" on Avenue E or the "eighth grade school" at what had been the German-English School on South Alamo.

Among Mrs. Emerson's early childhood recollections were of those days when her mother's friends, grand ladies from French Place, arrived with carriage and driver to take the Wests on a drive through Brackenridge Park, where buffalo roamed as far south as Josephine Street. Mulberry Street did not yet bisect the park, nor were there any bridges. The little girl seated on the carriage steps delighted in treading her bare feet in the river water. Gates at the park entry closed at 6 P.M. and on days when it had rained, to prevent deep ruts on the unpaved roadways.[93]

Such memories may seem wistful to a younger generation, but they can be shared in a realistic manner by those who grew to maturity toward the end of the Gilded Age in San Antonio—and indeed, elsewhere in America.

"The Paradigm of Residential Districts"

2. Development Expands

By the turn of the century, Laurel Heights had fulfilled most of the prophesies made by developer Jay Adams. Such traumatic experiences as theft, fire and physical assault occurred infrequently in this convivial neighborhood, and newcomers continued to build to the north. By 1906, the city limits had reached Summit Avenue.[1]

Appropriately, this was the year in which public attention was directed to yet another residential development—the Summit Place subdivision, touted as "the paradigm of residential districts." Summit Place Company assured prospective buyers that no other neighborhood in San Antonio could offer an installed "indispensable sewer . . . ample water service . . . handmade Macadamized streets . . . all utilities . . . deliveries to the rear of your residence . . . wide and properly kept alleys . . . sales of all sites are restricted . . . no business houses . . . seven minute car service."[1] Furthermore, the company assured an inquiring public that Summit Place, contiguous to the northern boundary of Laurel Heights, would be "the only residential district developed exclusively for families of refinement and social prominence."[2]

During the ensuing year local papers announced that "fairyland itself" could be found in Summit Place, where on lots two hundred feet deep "the home-loving and appreciative father and husband may now surround his family with rare blessings of ideal comfort and classic environment."[3] Company officials hoped for an "invasion by the Home-Loving American Accumulator of Wealth and Influence."[4]

Unfortunately, the Summit Place promoters faced a legal suit in 1907, just before local courts went into recess for the summer. Not until March of the following year did the project actually open, at which time two "fine residences" had been completed and occupied."[5]

Development in Summit Place followed the pattern encouraged by women's clubs throughout the nation. Beautification and civic improvement in urban life found support among an increasing number of vocal, well-organized, upper-middle class women.

Keeping pace with the onward march of events, citizens in San Antonio, who would live where there are liberal plots of ground for the proper home development and nature's green is allowed to hold sway, where one's neighbors' promiscuously located improvements do not offend the eye, and banding together in what is known as restricted residence districts. Of these, Summit Place is perhaps the most nearly ideal in the matter of natural advantages and completed conveniences . . . . and entirely aloof of the boom methods, which never raise the character of a neighborhood [6]

Occupying the crest of the hill, Summit Place was identified by developers as "of Laurel Heights yet not in it."[7] Street poles were not permitted on east-west avenues, along which all residences would face; indeed, the "ancient roadways of Rome" were "no more perfect" than those on Summit Place. A path of palms and roses was planted near the streetcar terminus at the head of Howard Street, the main entrance for the development.

Actually, Summit Place had three entrances, each "defined by a magnificent cut stone and ornamentally fixtured gateway. On the massive pillars are immense bronzed lamps and tablets and plates bearing the name of the thoroughfare . . . The arch on Howard Street is of a special New York design, where it was manufactured by the William H. Jackson Company."[8]

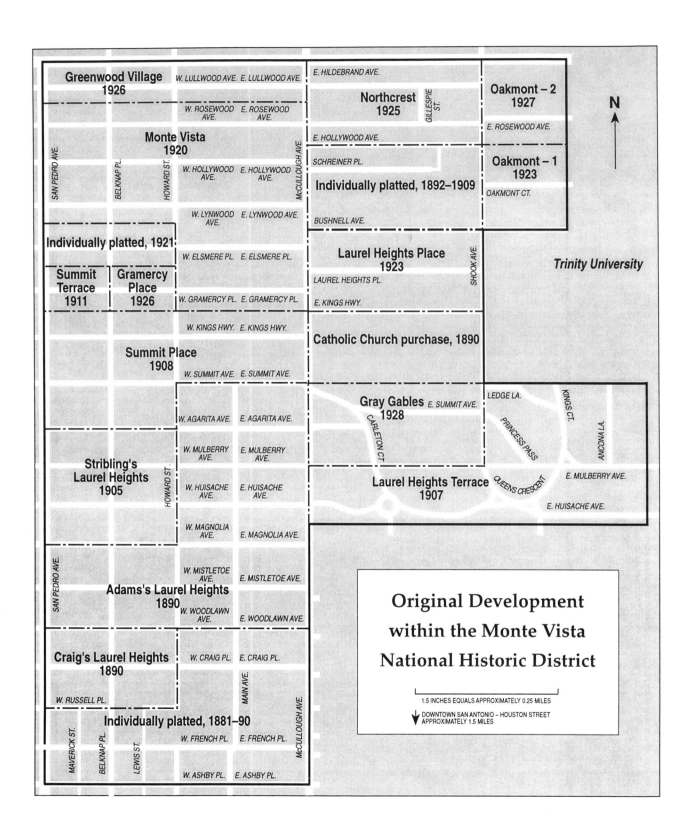

Greenwood Village
1926

W. LULLWOOD AVE. E. LULLWOOD AVE.

E. HILDEBRAND AVE.

Northcrest
1925

GILLESPIE ST.

Oakmont – 2
1927

W. ROSEWOOD AVE. E. ROSEWOOD AVE.

E. ROSEWOOD AVE.

Monte Vista
1920

SAN PEDRO AVE.

BELKNAP PL.

HOWARD ST.

E. HOLLYWOOD AVE.

Oakmont – 1
1923

W. HOLLYWOOD AVE. E. HOLLYWOOD AVE.

McCULLOUGH AVE.

SCHREINER PL.

Individually platted, 1892–1909

OAKMONT CT.

W. LYNWOOD AVE. E. LYNWOOD AVE.

BUSHNELL AVE.

Individually platted, 1921

W. ELSMERE PL. E. ELSMERE PL.

Laurel Heights Place
1923

SHOOK AVE.

Trinity University

LAUREL HEIGHTS PL.

Summit Terrace 1911

Gramercy Place 1926

W. GRAMERCY PL. E. GRAMERCY PL.

E. KINGS HWY.

W. KINGS HWY. E. KINGS HWY.

Catholic Church purchase, 1890

Summit Place
1908

W. SUMMIT AVE. E. SUMMIT AVE.

Gray Gables E. SUMMIT AVE.
1928

LEDGE LA.

KINGS CT.

W. AGARITA AVE. E. AGARITA AVE.

CARLETON CT.

PRINCESS PASS

ANCONA LA.

W. MULBERRY AVE. E. MULBERRY AVE.

Stribling's Laurel Heights 1905

HOWARD ST.

W. HUISACHE AVE. E. HUISACHE AVE.

QUEENS CRESCENT

Laurel Heights Terrace
1907

E. MULBERRY AVE.

W. MAGNOLIA AVE. E. MAGNOLIA AVE.

E. HUISACHE AVE.

SAN PEDRO AVE.

W. MISTLETOE AVE. E. MISTLETOE AVE.

Adams's Laurel Heights 1890

W. WOODLAWN AVE. E. WOODLAWN AVE.

Craig's Laurel Heights
1890

W. CRAIG PL. E. CRAIG PL.

MAIN AVE.

W. RUSSELL PL.

McCULLOUGH AVE.

Individually platted, 1881–90

MAVERICK ST.

BELKNAP PL.

LEWIS ST.

W. FRENCH PL. E. FRENCH PL.

W. ASHBY PL. E. ASHBY PL.

N

Original Development within the Monte Vista National Historic District

1.5 INCHES EQUALS APPROXIMATELY 0.25 MILES

DOWNTOWN SAN ANTONIO – HOUSTON STREET
APPROXIMATELY 1.5 MILES

SUBDIVISION BOUNDARIES RESEARCHED AND DEFINED BY
MARIA WATSON PFEIFFER AND SUE ANN PEMBERTON-HAUGH

An architect's rendering shows one of three monumental arches designed for Summit Place.

Full-page promotional pieces in 1910 sought to identify the new contiguous development to the west of Howard, facing on San Pedro, with Laurel Heights and Summit Place.

Laurel Heights for several years has been conceded by every honest real estate man to be the most attractive residential section of the city, but Laurel Heights is not on the market. The extension of residences in this direction has been stopped for several years by the fact that every lot has passed into private hands and is being held at prohibitive prices. . . . Men who have built in Laurel Heights district have spent money on their homes to make them the most attractive of any in San Antonio. This is not a district of inexpensive bungalows, but of stately mansions, of homes that represent the culture and wealth of San Antonio's most exclusive, aristocratic circles.[9]

Developers suggested what was said of Summit Place would later be said of Summit Terrace.

Summit Place during the week has . . . made splendid strides . . . . Some of the larger residences to be erected are the following: John W. Kokernot, brick and stone mansion to cost about $40,000; Chris Hagelstein, beautiful brick residence, for which he has just paid $20,000; R. B. Cherry, brick residence, to cost about $17,000, and will, within two or three weeks, begin the construction of a stone mansion on the Kings Highway. H. L. Kokernot is now maturing plans for a mansion on the upper eastern end of Kings Highway, the cost of which will be in the neighborhood of $100,000.[10]

Summit Place construction did not equal promoters' enthusiasm. Speculators for two decades purchased lots north from French Place, but ownership of these divided properties could change

hands more than once before a home went up. Extensive advertising by Commercial Loan and Trust Company, Summit Place's exclusive agent by 1917, led to construction of no more than twenty homes on Summit and Kings Highway between McCullough and San Pedro prior to World War I.

Residential construction did not cease during the war years in the city, which was so closely tied to the military. During the nine months from June 1, 1917, to March 1, 1918, homebuilding permits exceeded those of the previous year by 57 percent. Higher labor and material costs were no deterrent, as demand forced rental prices upward. Huisache Avenue, perhaps more than any Laurel Heights street, became the scene of exceptional activity. Frame dwellings were still favored, but discussion of "fireproof" construction led to more brick, tile and stucco, characteristic of new homes in Laurel Heights and Summit Place and the Monte Vista subdivision in the decade to come.[11]

In regions with a mild climate, the bungalow, a structure endemic to India and with lower construction and maintenance costs, was coming into favor among families of modest means, especially young families. San Antonio bungalows were generally frame, though brick, stucco and hollow tile appeared in this neighborhood.[12] Builder W. D. Syers acquired four lots on Woodlawn, six on Mistletoe and another on Summit Place, where he planned eleven $5,000 to $6,000 bungalows.[13]

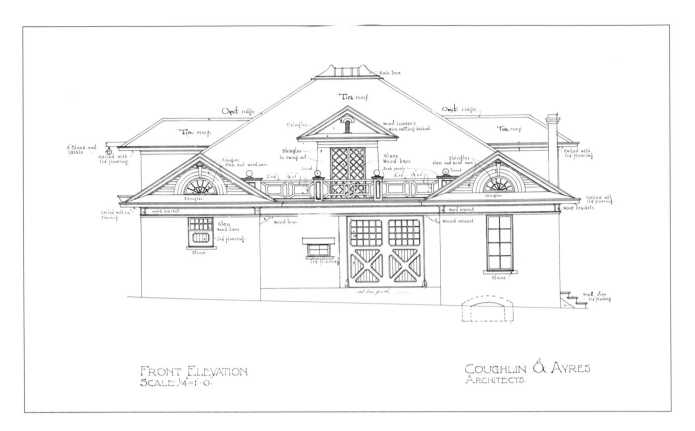

FRONT ELEVATION
SCALE 1/4"=1'-0"

COUGHLIN & AYRES
ARCHITECTS.

An elegant carriage house was considered essential for Monte Vista homes until World War I, when popularity of the automobile dictated a change to a "motor car house," or garage. This carriage house design by Coughlin & Ayres was carried out in 1899 for the Alfred Gage home on French Place.

Quite another change occurred in home planning in this period. Elegant stables and carriage houses were no longer built behind fine homes, following demand for a motor car house or garage. When the motor car first appeared, "it was housed in temporary and usually unsightly structures." By war's end, many prospective buyers refused to look at a property without an attractive garage.

Latticework or an arbor gave camouflage for some garages; space beneath hillside homes could offer parking in a basement with heating and laundry facilities. In Laurel Heights, a detached garage more likely was at the rear and also housed servants' quarters. As one commentator put it, "the motor car problem is a small one compared with the servant problem in San Antonio."[14]

Meanwhile, new interests took over Summit Place development. Rogers-Hill and Company became the sales agent for remaining vacant lots in March 1919. Homes ranged from $10,000 to $75,000, homesites from $2,800 to $15,000.[15]

Wallace Rogers and Russell C. Hill became the two most associated with Monte Vista develop-ment. Rogers touted the qualities of San Antonio and insisted its welfare depended on factors other than the "soldier population." As "a gateway to the widest contributory territory of any city in the United States," San Antonio would, he prophesied, see unsurpassed homebuilding.[16]

Both Rogers and Hill continued with Monte Vista, along with other well-known local real estate investors, following organization of the San Antonio Development Company in 1920:

A tract of land consisting of 94 acres representing a part of the original estate sold by the City of San Antonio in 1852 at auction to David Alexander, father of the late Mrs. Eleanor A. Stribling, was sold yesterday by Ben Stribling to the San Antonio Development Company for a consideration of $160,000, and arrangements are being made by the new owners for the immediate opening of a thoroughly modern and high-class exclusive residential subdivision.

Wallace Rogers, secretary and treasurer of the company, stated last evening that in taking over the property the company will make special effort to dispose of the lots direct to builders themselves who plan to reside in the addition and who can afford to spend between $10,000 and $30,000 in the construction of their homes. It will be one of the aims of the company to avoid selling any part of the land to investors or land speculators. H. L. Kokernot is president of the San Antonio Development Company and J. E. Jarratt is vice president. Stockholders and members of the board of directors are as follows: H. L. Kokernot, J. E. Jarratt, Wallace Rogers, Russell C. Hill, Ed. Rand, F. L. Hillyer, Ed. S. Fomby, Lee B. James, Robert O. Huff, Ralph Cameron, Jack Locke, Lane Taylor and Will Fordtran.

The new addition is considered one of the most ideal locations for the establishment of a residential section. Sixty acres of land is located on Antelope Hill, considerably higher than either Summit Place or the Kings Highway section. The entire addition of 94 acres is bounded on the east by McCullough Avenue, on the west by San Pedro Avenue, and on the south by Kings Highway and Summit Place, extending north beyond the city limits.

A staff of surveyors is already at work laying out the addition and planning street locations, and Mr. Rogers states that no time will be lost in making the addition ready for an official opening. Bids for the street work including paving, will be let as soon as the surveyors have completed their work. All modern improvements will be made to the addition. Streets will be paved, a modern sewage system installed and the addition will have an especially ornate and thoroughly equipped electric lighting system. Natural gas will be arranged for and an up-to-date water system will also be installed as soon as work is started on the improvement.

In connection with the transfer of this particular tract of land, it is of interest to many to recall the late David Alexander as the original owner of the property. Mr. Alexander was known as one of the brightest financial men in the entire South and was an authority on the world's finance during his period. At his death, the property reverted to his daughter, the late Mrs. E. A. Stribling, and since that time has been known as the Stribling estate.

Unusual interest was manifested yesterday in local real estate circles over announcement of the proposed new addition and unlimited inquiry leads to the belief that the company back of the addition will have an early building program. The first new home to be erected in the new addition will be started almost immediately. Lee B. James, who according to announcement made yesterday plans to contract a beautiful residence at a cost of more than $30,000. Work will be started on the building within the near future.[17]

Within two weeks, Development Company deeds were recorded with the County Clerk.[18] Public attention turned readily to the new area when promoters Rogers and Hill announced a $100 gold prize to the individual suggesting an acceptable name for the development.

Approximately 5,000 contestants from around the state made suggestions. Two submitted the name "Monte Vista." Both Mrs. N. B. Love of 412 West Myrtle Street and a Galveston courthouse employee, Mary E. Wood, selected Monte Vista "as most nearly carrying by word the impression of the site which is the highest north and the culmination of the series of heights that rise in succession to the north from the business section of the city." To reach this commanding residential terrain from downtown, "one need not encounter a railway crossing or disagreeable block." Whether on Howard, Belknap or San Pedro, in going to or from the business district "the tires of a car never leave smooth paving."

Monte Vista itself would be paved primarily of Uvalde Rock asphalt, and its streets would boast ornamental lighting and plantings of palms and shrubbery. Unsightly utilities would be built along the alleys behind lots ranging upward from 100 feet by 150 feet.

"Monte Vista" was the winning name submitted by two of the 5,000 entrants in a statewide contest sponsored by the subdivision's developers in 1920.

Maintaining families in large homes with few labor-saving devices required domestic help. Here Patricia, who was of American Indian descent, sits in uniform with her charge Frank C. Davis Jr. and his toy dog on the upstairs gallery of the Davis home on French Place in about 1915.

Planning for Monte Vista reflected the extensive investigations the promoters conducted in exclusive residential areas of other cities. Obviously, most major investors intended to live in the neighborhood.

Many building sites already have been secured by those who contemplate building at Monte Vista in a short time. Dave Straus, president of the L. Frank Saddlery Company has secured 300 feet at the north of Belknap Street, upon which he expects to build a $100,000 home. Lee B. James, who had been living in Kansas City, has 125 feet at the northeast corner of the same thoroughfare, and now has a $65,000 home under construction there. John Kokernot has 500 feet on Lynwood Boulevard and Herbert Kokernot has 250 feet on Gramercy Place, another of the beautiful thoroughfares in Monte Vista, running east and west. They expect to build this fall. J. E. Jarratt also has a 250 foot site on Gramercy Place and McCullough. Frank G. Huntress has a 200 foot

home-site on Elsmere Place, facing south, and Holman Cartwright 150 feet on Elsmere Place, also facing south. E. C. Munday of Eagle Pass has secured a beautiful 225-foot site at Gramercy Place and McCullough, facing north.

Among others who have already secured home sites in Monte Vista are Russell C. Hill, who has 175 feet facing Elsmere Place; Wallace Rogers, who has 175 feet facing north on Lynwood Boulevard, and Gerald Melliff, who also has 175 feet facing north on Lynwood Boulevard.

An interesting feature of the development of Monte Vista are the inquiries that have been made for sites by groups of friends who are desirous of building in a section where they will be neighbors, at the same time making their own associations more convenient and protecting themselves from neighboring with uncongenial persons. The insistence that all buildings be on 100-ft. lots or more does away with danger of undesirable neighbors.[19]

Desirable neighbors, of course, would be those who could afford a sufficient number of servants to maintain homes fit for San Antonio's elite. Most of the homes in this historic district, including many that today would be regarded as dwellings of modest pretension, were constructed with servants' quarters on the premises. The 1900 census of the Laurel Heights area indicates that live-in servants were of diverse ethnic backgrounds, but very few were of Mexican birth or Spanish surname. Some families had only black servants, others white, some both races. As the years passed, white servants began to be less apparent. Following the Mexican Revolution, an increasing number of nationals from that country were found in domestic service.[20]

Live-in servants customarily received "time off" only on Thursdays and Sundays after the noon meal. As stores were closed on Sundays, they did most of their shopping on Thursday afternoons. Streetcars were their only transportation, so they were often seen along Howard Street. In addition to their jocularity, Mrs. Emerson remembered their communicative whistles at a time when neighborhood boys home from the University at Austin had their own fraternity whistles. But there was a difference. Whistles of the Negroes ended with a very "mournful sound."[21]

Racial segregation, whether in housing or on streetcars, was an expected way of life from the outset in Laurel Heights. Indeed, the traditional southern way of life seems to have been transplanted and to have flourished in what had been Mrs. Kampmann's goat pasture. The pattern of noblesse oblige or paternalism remained intact in

As San Antonio residents and institutions left downtown, they sometimes took familiar artifacts with them. Ike S. Kampmann, his 1880 home doomed for the Scottish Rite Temple, had architect Henry Phelps incorporate its arched Richardson Romanesque stone entry as the focal point of his new home (1921) out on Kings Highway. The Episcopal girls' school Saint Mary's Hall brought five Class Day stones (1910 to 1914) from the old school downtown to mount on the French Place campus, where the school had moved in 1925. Shown with the stones are Mrs. Charles Armstrong and Bishop William T. Capers.

in some families past the mid-twentieth century. Servants as well as homeowners contributed to the sense of continuity in the neighborhood.

Mrs. Emerson, along with other residents of the Laurel Heights–Monte Vista area, regarded longtime family retainers as a very special part of their lives. Robert Brownlow became employed by Judge DuVal West and other neighbors such as the Ed Dumas family on West French in 1932, and remained with the next generation of the West-Emerson family on West Mistletoe until 1973. Brownlow's association continued thereafter with the Emersons and Dumases on a limited basis.[22]

Annie Johnson, as a child of eight in 1895, joined the Walter Evans family in Kentucky and traveled with them to San Antonio in 1914. Apart from the family for only the first decade of her married life, she returned to San Antonio in 1933 in the service of the Evans daughter, Mrs. Edward Fitch, at 314 West Summit, and remained with the next two generations of Fitch descendants, the Frank L. Churchill family. Members of the Evans-

Fitch-Churchill connection joined in celebrating Annie Johnson's ninety-fifth birthday in 1982.[23]

One block north on West Kings Highway, two longtime retainers came to be well known in the neighborhood. Agnes "Aggie" Robinson joined the Thomas Goggans prior to World War I and served two succeeding generations of the family at 315 West Kings Highway. When she was debilitated by a stroke in 1976, her duties were taken over by daughter Clara Barnes. Monte Vista residents recall Aggie Robinson in her starched uniform in a wheelchair, waving an American flag at the July 4, 1981, parade, and her front-page photograph in the San Antonio *Express* the following morning. She continued to reside with Jean Goggan Kuntz until her death the next year.[24]

Nearby, at 234 West, Annie and Homer Keys joined the General Thomas H. Slavens family in 1942. Though she died in 1976, Keys continued in service with the Slavens family.[25]

For more than five decades, Elsie Routh witnessed the transformation of Lynwood from her vantage point at 242 West. She joined Dr. and Mrs. Thomas J. Walthall there on September 1, 1924, where she continued sixty years later. Jess Esquivel, who began lawn service for the Walthalls in 1934, likewise continued his weekly duties a half-century later.[26]

Family continuity was expressed in heirlooms as well as in long-time servants. This characteristic of gentility was found abundantly in the Luther B. Clegg residence on French Place, where the furnishings were among the most admired in town. A feature story in 1928 by Etta Martin also revealed that other friends and neighbors, most representing older families on Laurel Heights than in Monte Vista, also collected such furnishings.

"When I moved into this house," Mrs. Clegg said, "I had colonial furniture and people told me that it would be 'all wrong' in a Spanish home. But I have found that any good furniture may be adapted to any good architecture just as one may combine any old lace, old jewels or old fabrics. All good things harmonize. Period furniture may be artistic and satisfactory but it is faddish. . . .

"I have no patience with those aptly called 'interior desecrators' whose weakness is to let a Martha Washington sewing table play 'Pussy Wants a Corner' with a winged chair across the room and one piece of Chinese embroidery that could mean anything or nothing.

"My most treasured heirloom?" Mrs. Clegg repeated. "It is a grandfather's clock that has seen seven generations of my family counting little Billy Clegg, my grandson. And it is still keeping good time." Mrs. Clegg's rare possessions are almost countless. There are books, tables, chairs, beds, dressers, silver, lusterware, and many other things to delight the heart of lovers of art. Chief of all there is Mrs. Clegg, who knows how to combine and blend and arrange to the best possible advantage. . . .

"No need to be rich to collect. We need only be discriminating and preserving. Close friends and relatives are very apt to give their best things to those who cherish them. I have been fortunate in that respect. No need to travel to distant countries. The shops here have things as good as I have seen in shops anywhere. San Antonio was settled by people from mostly every state and foreign country, and many of them brought their household goods when they came . . . . Rare pieces of furniture are being faithfully reproduced here.

"But one must be careful in purchasing from shops. All that is dirty is not old, and long histories are easily invented. Not many of our things have come from shops. Some of them are really rare and have come to us in such a way that we know they are well authenticated."

For some years Mrs. Clegg has been interested in the collection of garden books. One of them, old Geroude's Herbal, is 300 years old.

"There are so many wonderful things in San Antonio that nearly every home has charming things," Mrs. Clegg went on. "Mr. and Mrs. Harvey Page probably have the handsomest collection of intrinsically valuable things at their home called Valley Vista. Mrs. Albert Maverick of Sunshine Ranch and every one of her fascinating children are discriminating connoisseurs of things beautiful. Mrs. Eugene Fellows cherishes the household treasures accumulated by her distinguished parents, who brought many things from France in 1854. Mrs. Bruce Martindale has a notable collection of silver; Mrs. P. J. McNeel has rare lustres; Harry Hertzberg, a fine library; Mrs. Wallace Robinson, lace handkerchiefs; Mrs. D. K. Furnish, old Dresden; Mrs. John Covington, rare family portraits; Mrs. Perry J. Lewis has 30 rooms full of fascinating belongings, indeed many rare rugs and lovely rosewood furniture. Mrs. H. O. Thomson, Miss Alice O'Grady, Mrs. Mary Aubrey Keating, the Onderdonks, Miss Jean Cunningham, Mrs. Will Rote and Mrs. Weakley are a few more of the many who have charming things."[27]

Express columnist Etta Martin was succeeded some four decades later by Bonnie Sue Dilworth Jacobs, whose research on French Place for the *North San Antonio Times* led her to record another role of its residents in local society.

French Place was called the "Street of Queens." Among the Fiesta royalty have been Queens Catherine Franklin, Katherine McGown, Martha Lewis, Elizabeth Kokernot, Beatrice Stribling, Katherine Hart, Josephine Woodhull and Molly Denman and Princesses Mary Davis, Eleanor Stribling, Cornelia Vaughan, and Emily Denman.[28]

What becomes increasingly apparent through the years is that a number of families, albeit in succeeding generations, were identified with both Laurel Heights and Monte Vista. Family names, heirloom furniture and even servants followed the progression of people who ascended Antelope Hill to build their homes.

"A Neighborhood of Culture, Refinement and Good Breeding"

3. The Monte Vista Area Matures

San Antonio, and Monte Vista in particular, offered promising investments in the years following World War I. There was a concerted real estate effort to encourage local businessmen to live in their own homes—a symbol of success.

Status might also be attained by following another recent trend. Unsightly fences were not to appear in the new suburb where the flow of Bermuda grass from lawn to lawn added to the parklike atmosphere. Back lawns, often not much more than a chicken yard in yesteryear, were enhanced by homeowners' landscaping talents. Outsiders were also welcome to participate. Tourists, in increasing numbers, began to return to San Antonio and real estate investors were urged to "build it now."[1] Monte Vista developers Wallace Rogers and Russell Hill made presentations to local civic groups, and in interviews with newspaper reporters touted the future of the city.[2]

When results of the 1920 census were made public, San Antonio's realty fraternity had reason to be jubilant. Once again, as in 1910, the city surpassed Dallas and Houston in population. "If in 1910 the citizens of San Antonio felt justified in rejoicing over gaining supremacy among Texas cities in population, have they not greater reasons to be elated over the city retaining supremacy?"[3] Land investments appeared more profitable in San Antonio than in communities that suffered from the postwar recession.[4]

"San Antonio is the busiest city in the country, according to salesmen of building materials and equipment," a prosperous situation abetted by modest new bungalows in other neighborhoods as well as the finer homes in Monte Vista.[5] Some claimed that for "ten years San Antonio" had "been leading every city of Texas in residential architecture."[6]

Rogers and Hill could well be satisfied with their successful development, so recently pasture land. By the end of 1922 they prepared for further expansion of Monte Vista.[7] Announcement came of plans to develop the thirty-five acres just north of Hollywood Boulevard. While "a high class of bungalows" would be built, restrictions would be lower than the minimum improvements required on Hollywood ($8,000), Gramercy ($12,500) or Lynwood ($15,000).[8]

A total of $60,000 worth of new improvements for the Monte Vista residence section are now underway and will be completed within three months, according to Wallace Rogers of the Rogers-Hill Company. All improvements necessary for the opening of 180 homesites will be made, including laying out and paving two streets, making sewage, gas and electric light connections. When this work is done the entire subdivision of Monte Vista will be complete.

As announced by Mr. Rogers, work underway is not that of extending Monte Vista but that of completing the development of the original home section. Two streets [Rosewood and Lullwood] will be opened north and parallel to Hollywood Boulevard, extending from San Pedro to McCullough avenues which is a distance of more than 3,000 feet. The entire paving project underway calls for more than a mile of pavement on both streets. Plans have already been announced for the beginning and erection of 10 new dwellings in the newest part of Monte Vista before the completion of the improvement work. Those homes will go under construction within two weeks.

Also, with the paving of the two new streets, Howard and Belknap will be extended through to the north boundary of the addition. The Rogers-Hill Company has spent more than $250,000 in improving Monte Vista since the addition was opened. All the streets have been paved. Water, sewers, gas and lights have been installed. The Summit streetcar line has been extended into Monte Vista and service was inaugurated several weeks ago over the shuttle line.[9]

Rogers and Hill conducted one of the most extraordinary advertising campaigns in local real estate history for two years, from late 1920 through 1922. Superlative adjectives in both Sunday papers produced verbal imagery that Monte Vista founders had designed an elitist park such as could be found elsewhere only in Pasadena or Hollywood, Highland Park or Munger Place in Dallas, or in Kansas City's Country Club District. Prices for building sites here would be cheaper, but original purchasers would know that their investments would endow them with the "greatest promise for the future." A sound investment, San Antonio's best people as neighbors and the most beautiful natural setting in the city—thematic expressions repeated a diverse phraseology—did not go unnoticed by the local elite.

Monte Vista's "natural beauty" became a favorite slogan of developers. They encouraged prospective buyers to conjure up images of a home which would "command a magnificent view" or where one could enjoy "healthful breezes that circulate through those hills and dales." One could even expect "a mountain view ever before his eyes, stretching to . . . the hills of Blanco and Bandera."

Visitors should readily understand that they could enjoy the "sweeping, magnificent view" of downtown to the south, but one wonders how many had such extraordinary imaginations as to look northward and find that "veiled in a lazy, purplish haze stretch the foothills of the Rockies." A well-known landscape artist declared, "The eye is flattered wherever it wanders." Monte Vista "is not merely a commercial venture it is an artistic achievement," ran other copy.

Admittedly, the neighborhood— to "always be the show place of the city"—was not without help from artists, artisans and architects. "The superb skills of Nature and ingenious minds of men have joined forces in making Monte Vista one of the most delightful residential parks in the South." Seemingly, nowhere else would one find such a perfect site for the ideal home. "A whole volume

of words can't create the same impression gained by a ten-minute visit. You need to be there to feel the coolness, to see the fine, sweeping view, to sense the air of dignity and exclusiveness in the aristocratic homes under construction."[10]

Not only would visitors be immediately captivated by Monte Vista, they could be reassured that here lay a secure, long-term investment. "Have you ever looked frankly into the Future—that mirage-land of vain longings and gayly masqueraded disappointments—in an effort to catch a glimpse of yourself in the years to come?"

Monte Vista homes had "character that will improve with age . . . it is not one-tenth as beautiful as it will be in ten years." Nowhere else could one find such a sense of security and permanence as in a magnificent setting 165 feet above Houston Street with exclusive restrictions, a solid rock foundation, three attractive thoroughfares from downtown, ornamental lampposts and the best in street construction and public utilities.[11]

Even before San Antonio's most catastrophic flood in more than a century descended on September 10, 1921, Monte Vista developers, as had those in Laurel Heights a generation earlier, emphasized the advantages of the neighborhood's underlying rock foundation. A solid rock undergirding, from three to five feet deep to the east and from seven to twelve feet to the west, enabled Monte Vista builders to save several hundred dollars on each foundation. Four months before, the flood developers would offer a viable argument.[12]

"He is like a man which built a house and digged deep, and made the foundations out of rock and when the flood rose the stream beat vehemently upon the house and could not shake it, for it was founded upon a rock."—Luke VI, 46.

In Monte Vista, underlying a thin but fertile top soil, is a layer of hard, firm stone. You needn't worry for a moment about your foundation. In ten, twenty or thirty years, your home will stand as firmly and solidly on Mother Earth as it did that proud day when you first "moved in." In other locations you must spend four or five hundred dollars to establish a firm foundation. In Monte Vista, nature herself has provided this, free of charge.

No long, jagged cracks in the walls; no uneven, sagging floors; no doors that refuse to open or close many times daily; no exorbitant repair bills that pour in month after month. Freedom from worry of this kind is worth something, isn't it?[13]

After the flood, advertising copy could offer an "eloquent argument" for a neighborhood "untouched by the swirling waters" and where "a cloud

---

Facing page: As if to verify developers' claims of the magnificence of life and leisure possible in the Monte Vista area, Mrs. Luther B. Clegg in the late 1920s relaxes with a book in the comfort of her home, a Moorish-style villa at 510 West French Place.

burst could do no harm." Altitude and the "limestone stratum of great strength and solidity" likewise added to the credibility of developers' contention that "a fine home upon a weak foundation is worth less than a cheap home upon a strong foundation." Another variation on this theme advised that "a mansion on an undesirable lot is actually worth much less than a more modest home on a desirable lot." With the opening of streets north of Lynwood, potential purchasers were reminded that some lots could be had for as little as $2,000.[14]

Considerable advertising copy focused on the "exclusive environment" of Monte Vista, where early on such distinguished citizens as Herbert L. Kokernot, O. J. Straus and Lee B. James purchased homesites on which to build. One would surely want a home "in a spot that is destined to grow famous," especially if one were aware that it was his "duty to live in a neighborhood of culture, refinement, and good breeding, where your loved ones will be carefully shielded from harmful and degrading influences." One should also heed "a certain wise man's declaration that what your children will become depends very much upon what kind of neighbors you have." It would be a "tragic mistake" to select "a poor or indifferent location," certainly for those who planned to build permanent homes "for themselves, their children, and their children's children."

In Monte Vista, one could surround his children's "tender thoughts and susceptibilities with the best." One could also be assured that "a home in Monte Vista is the ultimate goal of every ambitious San Antonian." Monte Vista residents could never be embarrassed when asked, "Where do you live?" Status seekers could be reminded of the old adage, "Birds of a feather flock together."[15]

How important is it that your home be situated in the right neighborhood? You owe it to your children to see that their friends shall be the sons and daughters of interesting, worthwhile families. You owe it to your wife to provide her with a home surrounded by beauty, dignity and culture. You owe it to yourself—for your intellectual, social and business advancement—to live in a neighborhood where you will know intimately successful, accomplished men of affairs. You may pay these debts to your children, your wife and yourself if you building in charming Monte Vista.[16]

The most pithy of a series of personal testimonials in 1924 came from Herbert L. Kokernot: "The fact that I own property in Monte Vista is

By the mid-1920s, the cool, whitewashed walls and rounded arches of Spanish Colonial Revival made the style a favorite in sun-drenched San Antonio and Monte Vista. This photo at the Percy Mannen home on Bushnell Avenue was apparently snapped by architect Atlee B. Ayres himself.

sufficient evidence of my complete faith in it." With an investor's eye, O. W. Stapleton believed "that property values will increase more rapidly here than in any other part of the city." George D. Campbell sought future insurance in a neighborhood with "no stores, apartment houses, shops and very cheap unsightly houses." Kenneth C. Perry appreciated the cooling breezes and utilities in the alley for a home close to the business district. Other testimonials came from such local notables as F. F. Stauffer, Dr. Thomas J. Walthall, Leo Brewer, Lee B. James and Harry L. Benson.[17]

Time and again, in news stories and advertisements, names of well-known San Antonians appeared as purchasers of homesites in Monte Vista. By mid-1923, a partial list included Walter Nolte, Everett Love, Ed Rand, Henry Hart, R. B. Cherry, Fidel Chamberlain, William Fordtran, Hull Youngblood, W. W. McAllister, David Straus, F. G. Huntress, John Kokernot, Randolph Carter, Mrs. Mary Stowers, Dr. J. L. Felder, A. J. McKenzie, Frank G. Huntress, Jr., Winchester Kelso, Porter

Loring, Henry M. Hart and P. H. Swearingen. Within six months more than $500,000 had been spent on homes ranging in value from a bungalow at $8,000 to three homes costing $62,000 each, according to one account.[18] Actually, prior to inflation in the latter part of the decade, the finest homes represented an expenditure in the $40,000 range for the self-styled "pioneers" in Monte Vista.[19]

San Antonians had become increasingly proud of their fine homes and diversity of architectural styles appearing throughout the city. Particular attention had come to focus on doorways; Monte Vista residents expressed their individuality in that feature. Although descriptive of the city in general, the following observations were especially characteristic of Monte Vista:

In the home under construction in San Antonio at the present time it is safe to say that the Colonial entrance is the most popular. This probably comes from the way home builders in the United States are adopting the Colonial type of architecture. But it is also safe to say that the Colonial entrance is one of the most beautiful. It immediately bespeaks the hospitality of the home. It offers the visitor a cordial welcome. People are finding this out and as the doorway is now receiving a greater part of the attention of the home builder, it is estimated that every tenth house erected recently is either entirely colonial or has windows, doors and mantels in that style.

Then there are the modified Spanish types of architecture and the extreme Spanish types of architecture and the extreme Spanish lines. During the recent years Italian designs have been mixed with Spanish and Moorish and the result, so far as the entrance is concerned, is pleasing to the eye. . . . If there be still a man who insists upon originality in his home—the kind of the originality which expresses a part of his history, he can do it the easiest, in designing his doorway. There are only a few doorways in San Antonio alike. The same is true of people. A neighbor's house is hardly ever copied, nor are any part of its architectural designs duplicated in the grounds or outhouses.[20]

Similar pride in San Antonio residential architectural styles was expressed in press statements, including an overly enthusiastic declaration that approximately three-fourths of the local citizens owned their homes in 1926. It is true that local real estate agents had worked out financial arrangements of lower down payments than perhaps could be found elsewhere in the country. Favorable terms encouraged purchase of four- to six-room "utility homes" in the city, especially of those dwellings of superior design and construction found on Lullwood and Rosewood. Two well

known local builders in 1923 became active in the "new era of small home building."

W. A. Baity began construction in 1923 of ten bungalows on Rosewood in the $6,750 to $7,250 price range. These homes required a 25 percent down payment. Baity had a well-established reputation as he had constructed "hundreds" of homes elsewhere in the city. These bungalows, some of which were two-story, included "modern" conveniences.[21]

Shown here are pen sketches by C. B. Schoeppl Company of small two-story houses, which are rapidly coming into great favor over the commonplace bungalow. They offer the conveniences and comforts of the large home at no greater cost than the cottage. The most practical low priced home yet devised. The small two-story house is more practical for the small lot. There is less roof area—less roof trouble. The bedrooms, being on the second floor, afford greater privacy and are cooler. The two-story is more economical to heat than the cottage or bungalow—larger rooms—more airy and comfortable.

By careful planning and study C. B. Schoeppl Company have worked up designs and drawings for small, conveniently arranged two-story homes. We have reduced the costs of building these homes to a point where they cost less than the average bungalow of equal size, with more porch space a desirable feature for the San Antonio climate. Less ground space utilized by the building leaves more yard for landscaping and gardening.[22]

In 1925, before all building sites on Rosewood and Lullwood in Monte Vista had been filled, B. G. Irish, a well-known subdivision developer, announced plans for "Northcrest," defined as Rosewood and Lullwood between McCullough and Shook Avenues. Fifty-foot lots with utilities in place sold for $990 to $1,990. These 112 homesites required a down payment of only $15 to $25, without interest on the remaining principal. Such flexible financing could not be found elsewhere in preferred northside residential areas.[23]

Interestingly enough, perhaps because the area had become well established, Robert McGarraugh's advertisements never mentioned financing possibilities in Greenwood Village, his later development on Lullwood west of McCullough.

Not only did Monte Vista succeed because some outstanding developers and builders lent their entrepreneurial skills to the task, but several of the Southwest's most reputable architects exercised their talents throughout the neighborhood.

Atlee B. Ayres, perhaps best known, was joined by his son, Robert, in 1923, when Monte Vista

Architect Atlee B. Ayres took his leadership role in popularizing the Spanish Colonial Revival style seriously. He had designed his new home at 201 Belknap Place in 1909 in the Craftsman style then in vogue, with a living room, top right, that was a classic in that decor. In the early 1920s, however, he stripped the exterior and remade it in the increasingly popular Tudor style. Moving chimneys, fireplaces, and partitions, he transformed the interior, lower right, as a paradigm of Spanish Colonial Revival.

was well under way. Atlee Ayres's designs include some of the outstanding homes in Laurel Heights, but by the 1920s he had become renowned for his institutional (notably on the University of Texas campus) and office buildings, and other structures ranging "from courthouses in the Valley to mansions in Kansas City." Trained at the Metropolitan School of Art, an adjunct to Columbia University, Ayres spent some years in Mexico prior to his return to San Antonio and his association with C. A. Coughlin at the turn of the century.

Noted a University of Texas School of Architecture exhibition commentary: "Ayres' complete mastery of the Spanish Revival Style, so appropriate to the San Antonio region, may be seen in large civic commissions such as the San Antonio Municipal Auditorium [1924], in association with George Willis and Emmett T. Jackson."[24]

Ayres, fellow of the American Institute of Architects, praised extant evidence of the finish in Spanish architecture found nearer to him in his volume on Mexican architecture (New York, 1926) and in statements to the local press. He contended that a city such as San Antonio should be structurally distinctive and could readily be so if "local designers should follow more closely the Italian and Spanish types of architecture, which are more adapted to the Southern climate."

Mr. Ayres pointed out the fact that lamp posts on Losoya Street with flower boxes placed on top is one of the small features that will make San Antonio distinctive. When a visitor comes to San Antonio for the first time, he leaves with one impression on his mind, gained from the most striking thing brought to his attention. . . . Also when a visitor enters a city he expects to find the things which uphold the old customs and traditions of other years. Spanish and Italian types of architecture are expected to be found here as they would be expected in California, and a fine array of such distinctiveness will impress the visitor.[25]

To another reporter, Ayres praised "Italian architecture in finer home construction [which] is increasing [in] popularity here." He indicated there was a "noticeable, although not a radical, difference between Spanish and Italian types of architecture." Unfortunately, Ayres did not delineate the difference, and an untrained eye in Monte Vista today is unlikely to distinguish between the two styles. Current observers might well use the term "Mediterranean" rather than "Italianate," the description commonly used when these 1920s structures were built.

Ayres noted that Italian and Spanish architects have since exchanged designs, hence similarities in architecture which have been "modified in America." He encouraged "white stucco walls with the green foliage around the house and the bright blue sky as a background constitute a beautiful combination."[26]

Son Robert favored a style of architecture similar to that of the father. This is evident in Robert's own home, the prize-winning "Spanish farmhouse" on Laurel Heights Place. Unfortunately, designs in the Ayres collection at the University of Texas do not indicate which designs are the son's after the father included the younger man's name in the firm title. Robert Ayres indicated to this writer that a number of alleged Atlee B. Ayres–designed homes actually represent work of the son. The University of Pennsylvania School of Architecture and an architectural firm in New York City served as the training ground for the son before he returned to San Antonio in 1923, when the firm became "Atlee B. and Robert M. Ayres, Architects."[27]

Ayres and Ayres were not the only architects in San Antonio who found Spanish and Italian designs well suited to the city. Carleton W. Adams of Adams and Adams (Carleton C. Adams had died in 1919) applauded the revival of these styles in the twenties. A son of Jay E. Adams, who developed much of Laurel Heights and purchased property in Monte Vista prior to his death, Carleton Adams also acquired holdings in that neighborhood. This architect noted that he and other colleagues "are going back to direct Spanish and Italian influence for their building designs instead of to the missions." Architects found that earlier styles proved "better to work with and develop" than the mission architecture.[28]

More residential designs can be attributed with certainty to the Ayres and Adams firms than to any other in Monte Vista. It is difficult to know whether their numbers might have been matched by architect Robert B. Kelly, vice president of the Kelwood Corporation for several years after its founding in 1924. Prominent attorney Arthur A. Seeligson served as president and H. C. Wood as secretary-treasurer of the new company, which offered architectural, construction and financial services to purchasers of Monte Vista homes in the $15,000 to $20,000 class.

This 1927 aerial view was taken toward the northwest above a rock quarry (foreground), later part of the campus of Trinity University. The partially-paved Shook Avenue runs from lower left, past the new high-rise Bushnell Apartments to (upper right) the newly-developing subdivisions of Oakmont and Northcrest and Hildebrand Avenue, which would be extended two years later to Broadway and become a major east-west artery.

Although Kelwood acquired much of its reputation for design of the Aztec Theater, Bushnell Apartments, and Julius Seligman mansion, many of its homes were on Elsmere, reflecting Kelly's argument that "the time has come" when the city should be of permanent construction. Initial costs of brick veneer, hollow tile or stucco exceeded those of a frame home, but he contended that, with upkeep and depreciation on the cheaper construction, total investment would be equal within a decade. Kelwood would thus "render a service not only to the individual who is building, but also to the city," as its appearance improved with more substantially built neighborhoods.[29]

Oilmen contributed to the increase in "pretentious" homes in San Antonio. One commentator noted: "Oil men make their money in that business and as a matter of sound investment of profits place it in real estate investments in addition to building for themselves comfortable homes."[30]

Most homes in Monte Vista at the outset were built by individuals who purchased a particular site

and sought an individual architect such as Harvey Smith, Richard Vander Stratten, Beverly Spillman, Henry Phelps, John Marriott or Ralph Cameron.

A number of later, less expensive quality structures were built for speculation by Kelwood and other firms that were architect/builders. Frost Carvel and Company by 1925 had begun construction of more than a dozen homes on West Hollywood and several on West Rosewood. Robert McGarraugh built extensively on Rosewood and Lullwood. C. B. Schoeppl's homes could be found from Huisache to Hollywood. Ellis Albaugh, singly or with a partner, also served as architect/builder of several Monte Vista homes.[31]

Most homes built on speculation were in a lower price range than individually constructed residences. As in purchase of other major items during the 1920s, easy installment buying was increasingly a factor in local real estate. It was now possible to buy homes from $9,000 upward in 144 monthly installments from about $100 at 7 percent interest.[32]

Plans were announced in 1928 to develop sixteen acres in "the last vacant piece of land in [the] thickly settled fine home section of Laurel Heights." Robert McGarraugh, following success in the Rosewood–Lullwood area, planned to develop the Phil Shook and Vander Hoeven property as "Gray Gables" in a belt of stately oak and other native trees by extending Agarita and Summit east from McCullough to Shook Avenue. His plans were delayed by depression and war. Thus only in this section of the Monte Vista Historic District do most homes date since World War II.[33]

Another development within the Monte Vista Historic District came earlier than Gray Gables but well after failure of a City Council plan in 1910 to establish a forty-acre San Jacinto Park. This acreage, now part of Trinity University campus, would have been turned into a park while the remaining 260 acres of publicly owned property continued as a rock quarry "adequate to supply the city with stone for many years to come."[34]

Twelve acres to the north bounded by Bushnell, Shook and Hildebrand were purchased by Thomas H. Masterson in 1923 and divided into twenty-one building sites known as Oakmont. "A quiet exclusion of all that is ordinary establishes a background for the individuality and personality which the smart world demands of its leaders," ran a promotional piece. Once again, the site focused on "one of the best foundations that may be found in San Antonio. It is necessary to blast every inch of the way into solid rock when building a foundation. This is covered with a rich soil and the beautifying of the grounds around a home with trees and shrubbery is insured."[35]

Another 11.75 acres, extending northward to Hildebrand, was added to Oakmont in 1927. Robert S. Yantis, who purchased this tract from Mrs. Eva S. Vander Hoeven, declared that Oakmont "ranks very high as a subdivision. It has all the qualities which count in making a first-class home community—environment, elevation, rock foundation, trees, all modern conveniences, careful and rigid building and ownership restrictions." Property facing the 400 block of East Rosewood had the following restrictions:

The property shall be used for residence purposes only, and not apartment house, double-house, flat, lodging house or hotel, nor any structure of any kind whatsoever other than a first-class private residence, and the customary out-buildings, shall ever be erected, placed, or permitted on said premises. Such residence shall cost and be reasonably worth not less than $15,000 and must be constructed of rock, brick, tile or stuccoed exterior. Not more than one residence shall occupy each 100-foot lot.[36]

Other construction on Bushnell between McCullough and Shook, as well as on Laurel Heights Place, took place primarily in the mid-1920s, homes not part of the Oakmont development.

Meanwhile, San Antonio and Monte Vista shared in the national prosperity of the twenties. Local headlines proclaimed a "1925 Record Year for S.A. Builders," "$29,527,886 New Record in 1928" and "Deals Show Large Gain in 1929." While the first six months of 1929 were "the most prosperous in the history of San Antonio"— the city ranked eighth in national building that year—the stock market crash contributed to a general decline in construction.[37] Realtors blamed speculative stock market investors. Arthur E. Baird, well-known local sales manager, continued to express optimism:

Millions of dollars of Texas money . . . could have been invested safely and profitably in Texas where a handsome return would have been paid the investor, in addition to building up the community and making more money for us all . . . . San Antonio real estate (is) one of the safest and most profitable investments to be found in America. . . . The world is not coming to an end. . . . So, now is the time to get in.[38]

A mid-1920s Spanish Colonial Revival Monte Vista landmark, the Harry Landa home with its shaded patio, is now a branch of San Antonio's public library system.

4. French Place and Ashby

San Pedro Place, renamed Ashby Place in 1914, marked the northern boundary of Tobin Hill, San Antonio's most elegant residential district prior to Laurel Heights. It was no surprise that the next development to the north was on the hills beyond. French Place became the most fashionable street in Laurel Heights. In the decade after Nathan Gould built its first modest bungalow, mansions began to appear.

Nathan Gould of Rhode Island, who with his wife and daughter followed son Stephen to Texas in 1876, tried farming in the environs of San Antonio before he built "Bella Vista," 128 West French Place, in 1882.[1] Originally it faced south; later (1892) additions and alterations converted the French Place doorway into the entrance. Problems the family encountered, reported by daughter Emily, are not unfamiliar to today's new homeowner.

The carpenter backed out of nearly everything, besides not delivering up the house when he promised, which put us to an additional expense of a pretty blue and white matting for our room. Mother has a red and olive for hers and a new Brussels for the parlor. The view is very fine and only for the lack of water for which we have to pay 20 cents a barrel, the place would be just what we need, near town, but very retired.[2]

Gould's granddaughter, miniature painter and curator Eleanor Onderdonk, recalled the home in which she spent her childhood.

Our house stood on the slope of a hill all alone. It was a simple cottage of the conventional type painted a light blue grey. It overlooked the town a distance of two miles away, across the prairie to the south, and to the east the government post. . . . The house was built on a rocky ledge that ran in a northeasterly direction rising sheer from the spring, far out to the heights beyond the head of the river. On a still night a wagon passing along gave a hollow sound which indicated a cave far below. The southeast wind in summer swept unbroken across the prairie and sometimes felt as if it came from a fiery furnace, but at night it was soft and cool; the white moonlight gave the land a ghostly brilliance, and the coyotes howled, taking up the mournful note of the train whistle.[3]

A year after their marriage, Emily Gould and Robert J. Onderdonk moved into her parents' home. Here future artists Julian and Eleanor, as

When the Gould–Onderdonk home, first on French Place, was built in 1882, the family could look across the prairie toward downtown San Antonio and hear coyotes howling in the white moonlight.

well as their brother Latrobe, were born. Not only did the house sit on spacious grounds, enabling Robert to construct a studio, but the vistas served a family of artists well indeed. Moreover, wealthier families who soon built nearby came to be both personal friends and patrons of the talented Onderdonks. Members of the family lived in the home for nearly a century. A Texas Historical Commission marker is placed on the structure, the oldest in the Monte Vista Historic District.

Following the Gould-Onderdonks into the area known as San Pedro Hill by the late 1880s were the veterinarian Dr. James C. Talcott at 105 and Dr. Daniel W. Talcott at 115 East San Pedro Place (Ashby).[4] Four homes were built in the traditional opulence of the period during the remainder of the decade, but those of Judge Leroy G. Denman, Colonel Augustus Belknap and Josiah Townsend Woodhull have been razed. Each of these French Place residences appeared in a 1914 pamphlet of outstanding San Antonio homes.[5]

The Belknap home (205 West), by that time purchased by the Perry J. Lewis family, "was built 27 years ago [1887] by the late Colonel August Belknap and is the second house erected on Laurel Heights." Responsible for supplanting the old mule-drawn streetcars by those powered with electricity, Colonel Belknap had become a local hero. Little wonder that his grand residence attracted attention. Boasting twenty-two rooms, the home commanded a magnificent view in what briefly was known as the new suburb of "Belview, this nomenclature being derived from the name of the originator of the suburb and the splendid view obtainable from it of the city." More extensively covered by the press than others of that day, it suggests the tastes of the affluent in San Antonio.

Col. Belknap's residence is two and a half stories high and built entirely of Eagle Pass pressed bricks, which are susceptible of being lined and dressed until the structure is given the appearance of having been made of tiling. The architectural design of the building is an adaptation of the old English Gothic to the new Queen Anne. The edifice is so constructed as to give each room an equal exposure to the delightful south and east breeze and to catch as little as possible of the chilling norther. . . . The rooms on the ground floor are all capable of being converted into one by means of handsome folding doors. . . . In keeping with the most modern fashions, the floors are not to be covered with carpets, but in their stead are to be substituted the richest and most magnificent mosaic and marqueterie. The casing and finishing are all done in Texas mesquite, which perhaps is the first time this

The 1880s Leroy Denman house at French Place and Main Avenue, with its spacious grounds and commanding view, seems to have been of Victorian Second Empire design until apparently later addition of the unusual classical double pediments and columns. Its razing for an apartment complex in 1973 galvanized Monte Vista residents into organizing and forming a district with protective historic zoning.

Texas product has ever been used for such purpose. The mesquite shows a polish considered by many to be superior even to the conventional mahogany or black walnut.[6]

Judge Denman's home (109 West) was praised for "wide galleries and massive columns set in the midst of a grove of native trees, [which] fittingly crowns an eminence which overlooks a splendid sweep of lawn, unmarred by shrub or tree, extending from the terrace near the house to French Place, a distance of about three hundred feet."

Stockman Josiah T. Woodhull, later vice-president of Frost National Bank, had married Miss Lula Frost in 1885. Their home (115 West), "picturesque in its Southern style of architecture," likewise attracted attention. It had wide galleries and a spacious lawn extending down to the street.

All three homes featured gardens of distinction, as did others later on French Place.[7]

The absence of fences along French Place added to the feeling of spaciousness and enabled passersby to enjoy the lawns. A few older homes such as the Chandlers' had ornamental fences, but

The wide verandas on the 1880s Josiah Woodhull house that stood at 115 West French Place mark it as having been designed for the Texas climate, rather than for style considerations alone. Set well above ground level to catch the prevailing breeze, and with an arched Richardson Romanesque entry, the home seems a precursor both to the bungalow and to the shingle style becoming associated with resort homes in the northeast.

most residents supported the public campaign to rid San Antonio of this plague. Laurel Heights apparently served as a role model in a 1912 diatribe against fences, featuring a photograph of the French Place block just east of San Pedro:

To get a fair conception of what the no-front-fence campaign is accomplishing, compare the street shown above with any other in the city, on which the front fence is still an institution. The front fence, except it be ornamental in good taste, is on a par with the town cow and smacks of more provincialism than San Antonio can stand for.[8]

Spacious lawns and grand homes characterized French Place and Ashby for a generation, but others than the Denman, Belknap and Woodhull residences also suffered from the bulldozer. "Laurelia," G. Bedell Moore's 202 West French home, completed before the turn of the century on the grounds of the present Bexar County Medical Society, boasted extensive floral plantings and a pergola that suggested an Italian garden.[9] Fabled cattleman and landowner Alfred S. Gage's carriage house, designed by Atlee B. Ayres and put to adaptive use by Christ Episcopal Church, remains.[10] The church razed the turn-of-the-century home, its construction so graphically described in Gage's letters to his absent wife, Ida, which were found by architect Fred Buenz before its razing.[11]

Next door, in a house built at about the same time as the Gage home but now a church parking lot, the D. S. Combs family lived until they sold the home to A. J. Vick, whose extensive improvements gave the house "a distinctive air of stately elegance combined with real comfort."[12] Others razed on West French Place include those of prominent San Antonians J. K. Burr (115), W. H. Weiss–Perry J. Lewis (205), William C. Lott (314), H. L. Kokernot–J. K. Beretta (404) and Michael Goggan (405). On East French Place a similar fate met the homes of the Leon N. Walthalls (135) and J. H. Savage (147).

A block south, the greatest loss on Ashby was certainly the Atlee B. Ayres–designed home of Charles Zilker at the northeast corner of San Pedro. This spacious 1913 two-story, with four servants' rooms in the attic, featured handpainted decorated paneling and a slate roof, and was constructed of "a selected pattern of pressed brick . . . . with white stone trimmings."[13] This home was at the site of an earlier home constructed by Charles W. Ogden in 1901.[14]

Happily, a number of fine homes remain on Ashby. The grandest of them all, the Otto H. Koehler house, is on the south side of the street; the southern boundary of the historic district is on

West Texas rancher Alfred S. Gage's family gathered along the lower gallery of their French Place home (1899, Coughlin & Ayres, architects) shortly after its completion. Its Beaux Artes style includes elements of neoclassic and, with its Richardson Romanesque entry arch, of contemporary decor.

the north. Built in 1901 from plans by architect Carl von Seutter, the home was "a perfect palace and a picture in dressed white limestone."[15]

Just as there was a move to rid the neighborhood of fences, the beer baron built a $10,000 six-foot concrete and iron fence designed by Charles Boelhauwe. But, "When a property owner puts up a fence that costs him $10,000, he immediately puts himself out of reach of the 'down with the front fence agitators.'"[16] The 12,655-square-foot Koehler mansion, owned by San Antonio College, has a state historical marker.

At 415 West Ashby is the Herman G. Staacke home (c. 1910). The city's best–known wagon dealer sold it to the city's first physician to use an automobile, Dr. William Wolff, whose extensive 1924 remodeling used Ayres and Ayres.[17] It was the home to San Antonio College's president before restoration by Heather and Greg Letterman.

The Gage carriage house, rebuilt after a fire (1908, Atlee B. Ayres, architect), was restored for classroom use in 1961 by Christ Episcopal Church. Its style influenced design of a facing two-story education building (1990, O'Neill, Conrad & Oppelt, architects) on the site of the Gage house.

An even older structure on the next block (305) more recently served as a gift shop. It was the home of Dr. Benjamin E. Witte, a specialist in "stomach troubles" as well as one who "acquired distinction also as a city builder . . . He laid out the Witte Addition and the Witte Terrace, and has a record of having built 54 houses and constructed ten miles of improved streets."[18]

Three fine structures which can be documented remain extant on the 100 block of West Ashby. At the northeast corner of Main, the handsome two-story brick residence has known a succession of owners since B. G. Barnes, wholesale grocer and investor, was listed as its first resident in 1908. Six years later San Antonio gained "another prominent stockman as a permanent citizen" when Joseph C. Houston paid Barnes $20,000 for the property and received considerable notice in the local press.

Following so closely after the purchase of the Stribling home [117 East French] by Lafayette Ward, also a prominent stockman, the sale of this property to Mr. Houston brings out forcibly one of the best sources of San Antonio progress. A large number of substantial men who have been successful in the stock business in the territory adjacent to this city have come here, purchased homes, invested their money in enterprises here and become leaders among the city's progressive citizens.[19]

Shortly thereafter Houston sold the home to Captain Hal Howard, formerly of the Cross S. Ranch, who in 1919 received $20,000 for it from J. Frank Kline, president of the Creamery Dairy Company. Less than two years later, architect Carleton W. Adams acquired the property. After extensive remodeling it was his residence for perhaps a year. Several others resided there before Dr. Edgar F. Laird acquired the property. It remained in the Laird family for more than forty years.[20]

Two other beautiful new homes nearby were completed by the end of 1909. W. L. Martin moved into 115 West, where his family remained for years. If homebuilder W. D. Syers actually

Occupying an entire city block along Ashby Place is the Otto Koehler mansion (Carl von Seutter, architect), shown nearing completion in 1901.

resided at 111 West, he did so only for a brief period. A few years later, W. H. Vaughan moved into a similar home at 119 West and remained there until he sold it to a Judge Gaines of Bay City in 1921.[21]

Two early homes on the 100 block of East Ashby belonged to the Talcott brothers. That of Dr. James C., a veterinarian who married Colonel Belknap's daughter, was razed when Main Avenue was widened. Brother Daniel W. lived at 115 in a home built no later than 1887 and extensively remodeled in 1919. Purists will lament the changes described below, while the more pragmatic preservationist will be grateful that the structure still appears somewhat as it did after 1919.

A splendid example of civic as well as domestic pride is shown in . . . the house of Mr. and Mrs. J. W. Fuller at 115 East Ashby Place, before and after remodeling. Before the alterations were made it was merely one in hundreds of such cottages in the same stereotyped, old fashioned "ginger bread" style such as one sees all over the city, which must have been built by the same set of plans with variations. It was loaded down with meaningless ornamentation, gables, dormers and bays, and the interior was cut up into numerous small box-like rooms connected by a hall.

Now, one would never recognize in the simple, white colonial residence the "ginger bread" cottage of yesterday. The gables, porch and bays were all torn off. The new porch floor (in a red brick design) was dropped down near the ground; the main roof was brought forward ten feet and supported on four square columns. A feature was made of the front door with its colonial knocker, slender pilasters on either side and wooden fan with circular head and keystone above. Red paving brick steps lead up to it with a specially designed wrought iron railing on each brick buttress. New windows have been placed in the front, with the upper lights cut up and each group flanked with paneled blinds having ornamental bay tree cut-outs.

The interior underwent an even greater change, when the space occupied by four small rooms and hall was redivided into three large rooms and the living room, dining room and den; and these were thrown together by means of large glass doors and made still more attractive by the continuous oak flooring and new decorating throughout. A large brick fireplace with a simple colonial mantel shelf replaces the "still" little stock corner mantel. New semi-direct electric fixtures and dull brass hardware take the place of old designs of dubious origin. A tile floor was put down in the bathroom; a linen closet with drop fronts, and a medicine cabinet was built into the walls.[22]

Between the two Talcott houses, Louis A. Stumberg in 1922 built one of the earliest duplexes—then an "apartment house"—in San Antonio. Adams and Adams designed 109 East Ashby, a Georgian colonial colleagues declared "one of the most complete for its size in the city." The Stumberg family resided on the lower floor.[23]

One block to the north, some of the city's outstanding turn-of-the-century homes are in excellently restored structural conditions, including the Roy Hearne mansion at 324 (now 300) West and the Thomas H. Franklin home at 105 East.

J. Riely Gordon, who left San Antonio in 1902 to acquire a national reputation, drew plans for the Franklin house in 1891. Associated with his French Place neighbors in the firm of Denman, Franklin and McGown, perhaps the best-known attorneys in the city, Franklin had purchased the site from his partner, Leroy G. Denman. Architects Killis Almond, O'Neil Ford and Steve Tillotson assisted Dorothy McKinley and Mary Everett in preparation of the National Register application for this house, which Ford once described as "a good example of late 19th-century exuberance in architecture."[24] Tillotson wrote:

The two story house is wood frame construction resting on brick piers. Interior walls are wood frame with wood lath and plaster. Narrow oak board flooring is typical throughout. Millwork of typically Victorian profile is fashioned from pine and is darkly varnished. Interior doors are typically five panel with single lite transoms, and they are outfitted with mortise locks and five knuckle hinges.

Walls and ceilings are painted plaster, although several rooms were obviously covered in wallpaper. The exterior is a layered balance between Queen Anne vertical massing and the horizontality of the single coursing. The wrap around porches feature turned wood balustrades and columns, stems reversed, which convey a tapered effect. Broad expanses of shingle walls replace the expected spindlework to create a feeling of mass and solidity. Exterior walls sheltered by the porches are differentiated in treatment through the use of a rich profile waterfall siding. Porch bays are arched and chamfered, and truncated bay extensions are carried up to the roofline and expressed in steeply pitched gables with shingled and impaneled tympanums.

The variety of windows further enrich the composition: square openings, arched heads, coupled bays, in a variety of sizes. Prior to the turn of the century the house received several alterations. The first was the porte-cochere, which may have replaced an earlier porte-cochere of undetermined configuration. The present porte-cochere utilizes pitch faced stone and a large arch to further enrich the historic treatment. The over story is finished in wood shingles.

The stone craftmanship is identical to the work as seen on the carriage house (1891). The carriage house is square in plan, two stories tall, with a full attic. The configuration of the carriage house is archetypical of the Single Style, two intersecting perpendicular gable roofs with full gable ends.[25]

The Franklin house, sold to the F. M. Conlons in 1932, returned to the family in 1941 when daughter Catherine Franklin (Mrs. W. Lee) Hart and her husband purchased the home. Three years later they sold it to Saint Mary's Hall. In 1969 the Franklin House, along with the remainder of the Saint Mary's Hall campus, became the campus of San Antonio Academy.[26] Many local conservationists contributed to restoration of this "flagship" of the Monte Vista Historic District directed by architect Joe Stubblefield.

Another historic structure stands adjacent to the Franklin House on the academy campus, that of Eleanor A. Stribling. Built in the early 1890s by one whose inherited landholdings from her father, D. C. Alexander, were extensive in this area, this classic home has suffered a number of intrusive additions in recent years. It appeared in its original state in 1914, when well-known rancher Lafayette Ward purchased the home.

One of the distinguishing features of the Ward home is the old fashioned high ceilings and spacious rooms, which lend

"One of the showplaces of Texas" when built is the French Place home of E. B. Chandler (c. 1887, C. A. Coughlin (?), architect). Deeded after his death to become a home "for gentlewomen in needy circumstances," the home survives as the centerpiece of the Chandler Health Care Center.

themselves so admirably to the decoration of the artistic collection of antiques and curios they [the Wards] have picked up in their extensive travels.

Mrs. Ward continued: "When we purchased this home we decided to remodel and an interested friend said, 'Mrs. Ward, pull it down and rebuild,' but for some reason there was a charm and sentiment about demolishing this old home." . . . With judicious use of the space at hand and taking the advice of experts the home is today one of the beauty places of this city. The white room, or breakfast room, is a dream in perfection of coloring for the white tiled floor is in perfect harmony with the old blue and white curtains blended in blue of the identical shade, while around the plate rail are a set of breakfast plates in the same shade, and on the walls hangs an Onderdonk in the exact perfect shades of the Texas bluebonnet.[27]

Two other structures on the academy campus are of architectural interest. Harvey Page drew the plans in 1925 for the main building, Taylor Hall, on the campus of what was then Saint Mary's Hall. Mrs. John Bennett served as chairman of the committee for the Spanish Colonial structure, constructed of Nel-stone, a then new permanent building material made locally.[28] A more recent structure (1958), a dormitory designed by Robert Ayres, enables the academy to boast of the works of three of San Antonio's leading architects.

Beyond Main Avenue at 137 West French Place stands what "can truthfully be called one of the show places of Texas." Built as early as 1887, the E. B. Chandler home has had more publicity than any other structure in this historic district.

Attention is due to its distinctive design, Mr. Chandler's financial success, his wife's reputation as a hostess and their legacy of the property as a home for elderly gentlewomen.

Numerous printed accounts of this structure fail to reveal the architect's name. One can conjecture that it is the design of C. A. Coughlin, who served as architect of the Chandler Building (c. 1894) on Crockett Street and for the Chandler billiard room at a later date. Still later (c. 1905) Coughlin and his younger partner Atlee Ayres prepared plans for Chandler's barn, undated ink-on-linen drawings of which are to be found in the Ayres Collection in the Archives of the University of Texas School of Architecture.[29] Mattie Walthall Leman described the home in 1911:

One of the handsomest homes is that of Mr. and Mrs. E. B. Chandler on French Place. The spacious grounds (3-1/2 acres) are shaded in large trees of various kinds, with walks separating flower beds of bewildering beauty, open spaces of lawn giving the finishing note to the perfect piece of landscape gardening.

The house is built of grey brick with stone trimmings. The large drawing room and reception hall reflect the faultless taste of the owners, but it is in the dining room that the greatest interest is aroused, for in here the handwork of Mrs. Chandler is seen in a most unusual manner. Surrounding the room to a height of about four feet, the walls are wainscoted in the rich colored Texas Mesquite, every other panel being handcarved, in each a different design of fruits, flowers, or foliage. The remarkable feature of this work aside from its artistic beauty, is that it was done by Mrs. Chandler. A tall, graceful cluster of sunflowers is on one panel, a running spray of vines another; a cluster of oak leaves another, and so on around the room, alternating with smooth polished panels that form a pleasant contrast with the carved wood.

This mesquite is exactly of the same color as the cherry wood mantel that is so ornamented with elaborate carving done by Mrs. Chandler. The mantel itself is carved in a deep running border of berries and leaves, while a china closet is made above the mantel of heavy plate glass and cherry wood carved in oak leaves. Supporting the mantel are corbels of composition molded in grape clusters. The furniture is in perfect harmony with the woodwork.

Adjoining this room and adding much to its beauty and comfort is a screened-in palm room, where running vines around the side walls, swinging plants, palms and ferns make ideal scenery for the diners, and is a delightful summer living room in which the members of the household read, play bridge and entertain informal company in warm weather. This room opens on to a high rock balcony, around the ledge on which pot plants and ferns are also placed.[30]

After Chandler died in 1923, the property was bequeathed as The Chandler Memorial Home "for gentlewomen in needy circumstances, of good ed-

A survivor of French Place's landmark homes is that of cotton broker Roy W. Hearne (1910, Atlee B. Ayres, architect), shown shortly after completion. The Beaux Artes design includes a mix of the Alamo Revival subclass of the Mission Revival style in the scrollwork atop the third floor dormer parapet.

ucation and pleasant manners, at least 60 years of age, of sound mind and in good average health, [who] must present undoubted testimonials of high character and good disposition." Trustees were Gus J. Groos, C. Tarrant, S. L. Stumberg, Guy S. McFarland and A. S. Gage.[31] The Chandlers had made plans for the home before their death using Boston's Louise Cochran Home as a model. Many furnishings remained — silver, crystal, china, furniture and several Onderdonk paintings. Plans for a new wing, since razed to make way for the present nursing home, were likewise made by the couple.[32]

Hidden by the Chandler Apartments at the end of a long lane to the east was the home of William D. McCabe at 123 West French, on the grounds of the original Woodhull property. The living room served originally as the meeting room of the Laurel Heights Bowling Club, which thrived until advent of the San Antonio Country Club, to which the lanes were later transferred. Laurel Heights Bowling Club is clearly marked on the 1904 Sanborn insurance map of the city.

Across the street the five structures westward from Main Avenue, including the Gould-Onderdonk house, surprisingly remain intact. The W. D. Ayres Home (102 West) designed by Atlee Ayres in 1907, is now designated 2121 Main Avenue. This brick veneer colonial-style dwelling suf-

fered from fire damage and was remodeled in 1924 by Joseph E. Carroll, the resident, who had contractor John Westerhoff do the work. This structure retains much of its original appearance.[33] Ayres drew plans for another home next door (108 West) in 1911, which Bishop and Mrs. W. T. Capers occupied three years later. A spacious attic and basement, a servant's room and garage and two large sleeping porches added to the living space in this nine-room home.[34]

Next to the Capers family (110 West) lived Lon D. Cartwright, a West Texas cattle baron who sold the home to landman R. A. Porter in 1919.[35] The H. D. Kilgores lived at 118 West, followed by the J. S. Taylors for a decade. Attorney Thomas M. West acquired it about 1923.[36]

While no original structure survives on the 200 block, and only one on the 300 block, the home designed by Atlee Ayres for cotton broker Roy W. Hearne (now 300) in 1910 remains one of the grand residences in the Monte Vista Historic District. Local interest in the home was considerable, in part for its grandeur and perhaps equally so because Mrs. Hearne was a granddaughter of General Sam Houston. Extensive ink-on-linen drawings, one reproduced in the *Express* in 1911, are in the archives at the University of Texas School of Architecture.

The parapet scroll atop the David K. Furnish home at 501 West French Place (1903, Atlee B. Ayres, architect) adds a touch of Mission Revival's Alamo Revival motif. In the otherwise Beaux Artes design, shields typical of the Belle Epoch form portico capitals. The speck at the peak is a pigeon checking out the premises.

Here is a pen and ink sketch of the $50,000 dwelling which is being built at Belknap and French Place for Roy W. Hearne. The building will occupy one-half block and will face north. It will contain about fourteen rooms and be constructed of white stone up to part of the first floor. Above the stone will be a very light cream-colored brick. The roof will be of a very light tint of green earthen Spanish tile.

The front gallery floors will be finished with marble terrazzo floors. The dining room will be in mahogany, hall and breakfast room in birch, living room in early English oak. One of the attractive rooms will be the conservatory, which will have a tile floor and coved, ornamental ceiling with concealed electric lightng effect. The attic is to be finished for a large ballroom or billiard room.[37]

Hearne soon sold the home to Colonel C. B. Woods, in 1912. Oilman Sam Kone, formerly of Tampico, Mexico, purchased it in 1923 and lived there nearly fifty years before moving to the carriage house facing Belknap Place (306). The C. Robert Dauberts thoroughly restored the home in 1981.

Three impressive homes are in the 400 block of West French. Although that at 405 is not the original, Houston- and California-based Russell Brown, who designed three others in Monte Vista, planned it for Legare Bethea in 1928.[38] Stucco, hollow tile and concrete, plus the tile roof and floorings, suggest Lynwood and Hollywood homes more than those in Laurel Heights proper.

Research on 501 West by Jerry Totten suggests much speculation in city lots. Numerous divisions and exchanges took place between 1852, when the city began selling its land-grant rights, and 1892, when Leonora Gill and Andrew J. Thompson bought this lot and built their home (c. 1894). These sales illustrate local real estate development.

Judge Isaiah H. Paschal, first recorded owner in 1852, sold the land to James and William Vance two years later. They divided it. William sold to H. B. Adams and E. D. L. Wickes in 1878. A decade later Adams bought Wickes's interest and sold to R. H. Russell, who further divided it.

Two years later Russell sold the block to Charles H. Florian and Wilbert N. Beall, with it the 130-by-170-foot lot the Thompsons got in 1892. This went to the Furnish brothers, who had extensive ranching interests in 1899. Both brothers and their wives lived there for several years before their homes were built. D. K. built immediately to the west, but only John W.'s widow Rachel moved into their 515 Belknap home in 1903.

The Franklin C. Davis home at 509 West French Place (1907, Henry T. Phelps, architect) has a Neoclassical portico added to its standard Victorian-proportioned square design.

. RESIDENCE · OF · FLOYD · McGOWN ·

The architect's rendering for the home of attorney Floyd McGown (1907, Alfred Giles, architect) assured him of an idyllic setting for his family, with children playing on the lawn and Mrs. McGown about to be off in the carriage while he was absent advancing the family's welfare at his office downtown. The scene was changed nearly a century later. Though the McGown home at the corner of French Place and by-then busy San Pedro Avenue had changed little in form, it began meeting the needs of a new era as a complex of office suites.

In that year, D. K. Furnish sold 501 French to Augustus H. Jones and B. L. Naylor, who lived on San Pedro at Woodlawn. Jones and Naylor were men who "roped opportunity and wrestled a fortune from the cattle business, the kind of men who push their city into its widest form of usefulness." A singular collaboration was their investment in building the St. Anthony Hotel.

Elected mayor in August 1912, Jones died less than a year later in his suite at the St. Anthony, where he and his wife moved in 1911. The house was sold to George Hagelstein, who had come to the city as president and principal owner of the Los Angeles Heights Improvement Association.

C. B. Ellsworth purchased the home in 1921, then advertised it for sale in 1925 as a "palatial colonial mansion . . . . typical of the aristocratic South." Another lost the house to an insurance company during the Great Depression. The Carl Pools purchased it in 1941, after living there for five years.[39] Other older homes in the area reveal similarly peripatetic owners, yet few can match in tenure the Pool family, including daughter and son-in-law Mary and Jerry Totten.

Across the street at 418, reminiscent of Queen Anne styling, exterior wood trimming is laid diagonally over plaster. Dark interior woodwork has received a faux bois treatment, creating an illusion of beautiful grain. Two fireplaces are in the living room and six more elsewhere in the home. Twelve-foot ceilings, wide galleries and a dramatic staircase create a sense of spaciousness.[40]

This home appears somewhat different than it did in 1905. "Mr. O. E. Woestman is building a handsome residence in French Place, Laurel Heights and it will be beautifully decorated by Fred Hummert."[41] A decade later, the upper floor burned. Frank C. Davis Jr. vividly recalled this nighttime fire, which threatened other homes on the block. He was assigned the care of his younger sister, Mary, during the memorable experience. The subsequent owner, architect Carleton Adams, did not replace the cupola but was able to retain the brick structure on both floors. Adams sold the home to J. P. DeLesdernier.[42] Longtime owners Dr. and Mrs. E. D. Dumas installed central air conditioning in the early 1950s, one of the first such residential systems in the city. More updating has occurred since 1973, when it was purchased by architect Paul Kinnison Jr. and his wife, Trudy.[43]

During the first decade of the twentieth century, other fine homes appeared on French Place. After thirty years in ranching in Colorado and Texas, David K. Furnish came to San Antonio, purchased a lot at 501 West in 1903 and associated with B. F. Nicholson in real estate.[44] By 1923 he and his associates had sold 2,500,000 acres of land and participated in development of Beacon Hill.[45] Built in 1903–1904 in a style similar to his brother's house at 515 Belknap, both are attributed to Atlee Ayres, who did other designs for Nicholson and Furnish.[46]

Next door at 509 West, the 1907 Franklin Coley Davis house remained in the family until recent years.

A handsome two-story Colonial residence is now being built on West French Place for Frank C. Davis of this city. The house is built after the fashion of the old homes of Virginia, and Mr. Davis will himself occupy it. The residence is to cost $13,000 and is constructed after plans by Henry T. Phelps. The color scheme of the exterior is white and colonial yellow. The interior will be attractive wall tints and all of the interior woodwork will be stained.[47]

Within the year, Davis's brother-in-law and fellow attorney, Floyd McGown, announced plans for his Alfred Giles–designed home next door at 511 on the corner of San Pedro.[48] Upon its completion architect Giles declared, "No residence is more complete in all its appointments, being one of the latest and most modern in San Antonio."[49] After McGown died the home was purchased by W. F. Thompson of Pearsall, who in turn sold it to Mrs. George W. West in 1926 for $35,000.[50]

In May 1905, inventor Frank W. Weeks obtained a building permit for a "six room cottage, basement, and stable" at 510 West.[51] In less than a year it burned and was rebuilt, but it was sold to Mrs. Eleanor A. Stribling a few years later. By that time its appearance would be recognizable to today's visitor. "This Moorish villa hinting of old world beauty, elicits universal admiration. The sunken garden is filled with tropical plants and a wealth of vines overrun the walls. The richly carved pillars with their graceful outline give an oriental effect that is pleasing."[52] Mrs. Stribling's son, Ben, lived in the home after her death.

Facing page: A landmark at 510 West French Place is the Moorish villa built by Frank W. Weeks in 1905 and remodeled in 1925 under architect Harvey L. Page.

By 1925 the Luther B. Cleggs had acquired the home and called upon architect Harvey L. Page to do some remodeling. It is not certain whether the roof garden and an allegedly fifteenth-century fireplace were added at this time.[53] Frances and Bill Gifford completed an outstanding restoration.

At the corner of French Place but facing San Pedro at 1616, and later housing the engineering firm of Frank T. Drought, F. W. Weeks received a permit in May 1903 to build one of the city's most unusual homes. Similar in design to the Naylor House, later the restaurant Chez Ardid at the corner of Woodlawn and San Pedro, the home was acquired by George C. Vaughan several years later. His widow remained there until the World War II period. A 1909 description follows.

On a large lot fronting 150 feet on each of two streets, San Pedro and West French Place, is situated the picturesque residence of George C. Vaughan. This beautiful home, which is built of reinforced concrete, is of California architecture, a one-story structure with a basement. The house, however, is a hollow square with a patio or court in the center. This patio has a cement floor and at the present time is filled with ferns and plants. These plants may be cared for as if out of doors, as a hose may be used in watering.

Over the patio a roof, consisting of plate glass windows suspended by weights, is arranged. In this way any portion of the roof windows may be raised or lowered to give ventilation, light or shade to the rest of the rooms. Around this patio a gallery is built and from which entrance is given to each one of the twelve rooms the house contains.

Two large porches running some distance on both the south and east sides of the house give sufficient room for a large company at one time. The five front living rooms are finished in oak with plastered and decorated ceilings. The other rooms of the house are finished in pine. On each side of the house, and connecting with the sleeping departments, is a bath room finished with tile complete. The bath, however, on the south side of the house, is a large sunken one, coming up just even with the floor, and of a capacity for the reception of several bathers at the same time. In the basement is the heating apparatus, laundry, and cellar. The house is furnished throughout with mission furniture, while the dining room suite is considered the most handsome in the city.[54]

5. Belknap, Craig, Woodlawn and Mistletoe

Intersecting French Place in both directions on Belknap are some of Laurel Heights's noteworthy structures. Two are just south of the Monte Vista Historic District boundary. The most active architect in the entire neighborhood, Atlee B. Ayres, built his home at 201 Belknap in 1909. Regarded as "one of the best examples of early English architectural designing in San Antonio," the timber work inside and out retains its eye appeal.[1] It was built a decade before he became enamored of Hispanic architecture.

On the same block Temple Beth-El, built in 1926, was designed by the firm of Seutter and Simons, with Albert S. Gottlieb of New York City as consulting architect. Dielman Construction Company built the temple of brick, tile and reinforced concrete.[2]

Visiting architects, according to some of their local hosts, are more likely to be intrigued by the Queen Anne style structure at 505 Belknap than by any other residence in this historic district. Built in 1893 by Laurel Heights developer Jay E. Adams, design for this home had been attributed to J. Riely Gordon, although more recent searchers are convinced that it is the work of Gordon proteges McAdoo and Worley.

Eight fireplaces, a circular parlor, leaded windows, ballroom, handmade oak paneling, carriage house and octagonal fern house, plus griffins flanking the front entrance, are features seldom found in recent years. Limestone for construction came from nearby San Pedro Park, while shingles have traditionally been painted "barn red."[3]

Distinguished San Antonio families who lived at 505 include those of W. E. Moore, Dr.

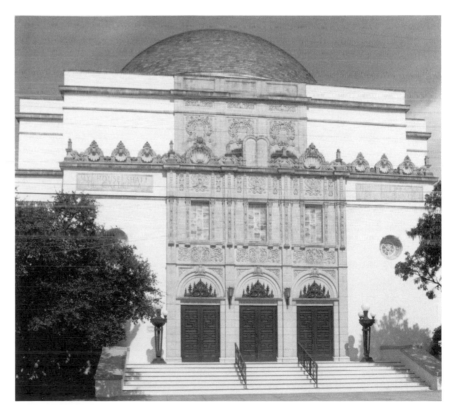

Temple Beth-El (1926, Seutter & Simmons, architects) on Belknap Place at West Ashby Place incorporates elements of Spanish Colonial Revival design with its whitewashed stucco walls, terra-cotta clay tiles and cornice of scallop shells.

This landmark Queen Anne–style home at 505 Belknap Place (1893, McAdoo & Worley, architects) was built by leading Laurel Heights developer Jay E. Adams.

Frederick Combe, J. O. Terrell and Frank R. Newton. It was the home of Mrs. Lola (David) Bell for some forty years.[4]

Immediately to the north stands the house (515) for which Mrs. Rachel Z. Furnish obtained a building permit in May 1903.[5] As mentioned earlier, her husband, John, apparently did not live to see the completion of his home, as did his brother David K., whose house at 501 West French is so similar.

While both homes are obviously the designs of a single architect, attribution can be based only upon other work by Atlee Ayres on behalf of David Furnish. This stylish Belknap Place home and its carriage house were owned for years by Edwin T. Rand, who came to San Antonio in 1909 "looking for a pleasant place in which to live and to enjoy the fruits of his labors in other fields."

Successful in railroading and lumber, the newcomer saw potential in the old Garza property bounded by four downtown streets. For it he paid $200,000 cash and contracted with Wolff and Marx to "erect and equip a building" if they would occupy it for fifteen years.[6] At the end of World War II, Dr. Robert L. Rhea acquired the home. Two succeeding generations of his family lived there until 1981, when it was purchased and renovated by Dr. and Mrs. (Rayne) Victor German.[7]

One of the most distinctive buildings in this neighborhood is Christ Episcopal Church. Parishioners worshipped in the former Laurel Heights Bowling Club, later the William McCabe home, following their organization, and later in a nearby temporary building during the construction period.

Christ Church has had several changes since its construction began in July 1913, under architect Atlee Ayres and contractor W. N. Hagy. Ayres, with son Robert, also planned a cloister in 1951 and a two-story Education Building in 1948. Work began in 1928 on the original Parish Hall, designed by John M. Marriott. Architect J. Fred Buenz designed conversion of the chapel to the north transept in 1958.[8] Plans for the A. S. Gage Carriage House, redesigned by Buenz for church use, were drawn by Ayres just after the turn of the century.[9]

A block to the north, Craig Place is named for the Reverend William Bayard Craig, of the Disciples of Christ (Christian) Church, who had come from Denver and purchased an eighteen-acre tract

The Beaux Artes Furnish home on Belknap Place (1903, Atlee B. Ayres, architect) with its shingle-style gables was later the home of Edwin T. Rand, whose landmark downtown Rand Building was restored in 1981.

The newly completed Gothic-style Christ Episcopal Church (1913, Atlee B. Ayres, architect) combines such features of English churches as buttressing, Gothic tracery and lack of a spire.

south of Woodlawn between Howard and Belknap. A decade after construction began on this street, however, there remained something of a rural atmosphere. In 1902, "Mr. L. J. Hart, residing at the Craig Place, has notified the police headquarters that cattle and horses are turned loose in that vicinity nightly and allowed to run at large and browse on the shrubbery and lawns."[10]

Oldest of the homes on Craig Place is that built by H. Elbert Hildebrand at 117 West in 1891; the design was drawn by the architectural firm of Giles and Guindon. Although it was a two-story frame dwelling at the outset, evidence suggests a later addition to the rear. A mural in the dining room attributed to neighbor Julian Onderdonk is among the numerous interesting details of this residence. Other local personalities occupied this home after Hildebrand, the original owner, moved to his more commodious home on McCullough at Woodlawn after the turn of the century.[11]

Colonel Jot Gunter, a power broker in state politics who came to San Antonio in 1902 after a successful career in cattle and real estate in North Texas, lived at this address until his death five years later. During this interim, Gunter, with his associate and across-the-street neighbor L. J. Hart, invested in Houston Street property. The two, along with George M. Maverick and others, promoted the Gunter Hotel, still not completed at the time of the colonel's death. Mrs. Roxanna Gunter, his widow, moved to 305 West Mistletoe and went on to build the Gunter office building.[12]

The family of attorney J. Marshall Eskridge occupied 117 West for four decades following World War I. Thereafter, for a time it was a gift shop before being purchased by the Reverend and Mrs. (Bobbie) Frank E. Jarrett in 1975.[13]

Next door at 107, a structure that now opens onto Main Avenue as well, Judge Winchester Kelso built a large two-story residence planned by

H. E. Hildebrand's home (1891, Giles & Guindon, architects), oldest on Craig Place, is now a bed-and-breakfast.

Atlee Ayres in 1906. This was the home of the distinguished jurist for nearly fifty years.[14]

E. B. Chandler advertised 120 West, built the same year as the Kelso home, as "brand new, elegant . . . . the finest thing of its kind" at $8,000. It consists of eight large rooms with halls, attic, large closets and butler's pantry; handsome hardwood finish downstairs, with beautiful mantels, sliding double doors, switches and paneled dining room . . . and there is a good two-story barn."[15]

Entrepreneur L. J. Hart, "capitalist and organizer of big enterprises," acquired this home in 1907 and resided there for some twenty years. He helped build up Houston Street through his association with Colonel Jot Gunter and the hotel.[16] General Walter E. Prosser resided in the home in later years until his death in 1981.

Next door at 134 West Craig is a home in which C. H. Mayfield lived as early as 1895, and Mrs. Jordan Irvin four years thereafter. Three decades later it was purchased as a winter home by an artist of international reputation, Lucien Abrams. The Abramses spent summers in Lyme, Connecticut. Abrams lived here only a few years. The house became vacant during the Depression.[17]

On the opposite side of the street, in early March 1893, "ground was broken by C. H. May-

field for a palatial home on the corner of Craig Place and Howard Street."[18]

Newspaper comment suggested residential property was much in demand. Moreover, as the grand Mayfield plans suggested, "the strong tendency toward the better class of suburban localities still prevails with increasing force and the prejudice heretofore existing against 'going out' from the center is fast yielding to the superior advantages which life in the suburbs affords." Electric street cars with "splendid facilities in transportation" made lower-priced suburban lots increasingly attractive, especially since they were on a higher elevation and receptive to the prevailing breeze.[19]

Judge DuVal West lived briefly on the southwest corner at 204 West Craig (c. 1904), and the family of Judge S. G. Tayloe moved there prior to World War I. His daughter, Lois Tayloe Ragland, continued to own the property.[20]

Also on the same block, another home has been identified with one family for even longer. Architect Henry T. Phelps designed the residence at 216 West Craig for John Taliaferro in 1904. The house descended to his daughter, Mrs. A. P. Barrett, and granddaughter, Mrs. (Virginia) Jack Harris Hein. As have others in the neighborhood, the facade of this structure has been altered, most notably as a duplex by architect Hein in 1940.[21] It was later restored as a single family dwelling.

House number changes on Craig, as well as elsewhere in the neighborhood, add to the diffi-

The Beaux Artes Winchester Kelso home on West Craig Place (1906, Atlee B. Ayres, architect) has Tudor gables and Craftsman roof proportions. It was near collapse in 1997, when new owners recovered many interior artifacts removed by a previous owner and began restoration.

An example of Mission architecture with an Alamo Revival motif is the home built for L. J. Hart (1906) at 120 West Craig Place, its third-floor quatrefoil window as reminiscent of a San Antonio mission motif as the top scrolling is of the Alamo's parapet. The exterior is of popcorn stucco, attained by throwing rather than troweling the plastering. Hart also installed a fence, having complained to police that cattle and horses on the loose at night were munching on lawns and shrubbery.

years. It then became the home of Oklahoma oilman Edward M. Galt and his family and after his death was acquired by General and Mrs. John M. Bennett Jr. The carriage house was restored as a separate abode by James McSwanson.

Changes in house numbers on the 300 block of West Craig likewise confuse identification of these turn-of-the-century structures. Frank M. Edwards lived at the corner of San Pedro, now 336 West, in 1897, but this home was long identified with the Gustav Gieseckes, parents of Mrs. Russell C. Hill, whose husband was a founder of Monte Vista, and her brother, longtime resident Martin Giesecke. A few years later (c. 1901) the A. H. Murchisons moved into the new home at 322 West and resided there for more than fifty years.[25]

culty of establishing construction dates of many homes. Even so, it is apparent that four structures, 225–241 West, date from 1905 or earlier. Indeed, in 1897 one A. C. Smith lived at Craig and Belknap (241), in later years the home of Miss Josephine Broadbent.[22]

Architects announced plans for many elegant residences in Laurel Heights from 1903 to 1906. That of recent arrival J. E. Jarratt, a prosperous lumberman who established an investment banking firm in 1912, attracted unusual attention.[23]

"Neo-Georgian Revival" is the term used in newspaper articles of the time to describe this structure at 238 West Craig in the San Antonio Historic Survey, but the announcement of plans for this brick home declared it to be "Colonial in every detail. The building is to cost about $15,000, and will be one of the most handsome of San Antonio homes." Atlee Ayres, the architect, declared that "the Colonial style seems to be the most popular at present."[24] This home was included in several "beautiful San Antonio" photographic features, stories and pamphlets. The Jarratts resided in the home for more than thirty

No event in the history of this block created more attention than in 1914, when Princeton graduate K. "Billy" Ewing inherited $5,000,000

The small Victorian home at 241 West Craig Place dates from the end of the nineteenth century.

Lumberman J. E. Jarratt built the Neoclassic home at 238 West Craig Place (1906, Atlee B. Ayres, architect).

from the estate of his father, Judge Nathaniel Ewing of Uniontown, Pennsylvania.

San Antonio now has another millionaire. He was made in a day. From a hard-working insurance agent he becomes the city's richest young man. . . . It would be a safe wager that not a half a dozen of his friends knew he was a rich man's son. . . . The friends of Billy Ewing are speculating whether he will return to San Antonio and make his home here or will he reside at his old home, and his father's home, in Pennsylvania.

Ewing did return to his home at 326 West Craig, which he had built shortly after his marriage in 1910, and lived there a decade before moving to Terrell Hills.[26]

Across the street, the homes at 321, 327 and 329 all appear on the 1904 Sanborn's insurance map. Real estate promoter L. J. Hart lived at 327 prior to his move to 120, Mrs. I. K. McKellar at 321 and C. M. Harlass at 329, which E. L. Swazey would occupy a few years later.[27]

Among the "newer" homes in this vicinity is that built on the corner of Craig at 605 Belknap by Hiram Partee, who began it in 1919.

The residence will be two-story and basement of tile with white cement stucco finish on outside walls. The roof is to be of red earthern tiles. A terrace will extend across the front of house. Floor to be of tile. The house will embody a reception hall, large living room, on south, running through front to rear. A sun parlor with a tile floor leads off the living room. Across the hall from the living room on northeast front is the dining room and adjoining this is the kitchen, butler's pantry and side entrance hall. The floor of the breakfast room is to be of tile.

The second floor will have four bedrooms and three baths, also an upstairs sitting room. A sleeping porch will be placed on the southeastern side. The house will be heated by hot air. All woodwork will be finished in white enamel and walls tinted. All floors are to be of oak. Atlee B. Ayres is the architect.[28]

On East Craig Place some fine homes, such as W. C. Silliman's at 101, have been razed. None dated prior to 1904.[29] Francis L. Hillyer came to San Antonio in that year and became associated with two other Laurel Heights residents as president of the Hillyer-Deutsch-Jarrett Co., lumber manufacturers. By 1907 he had built a magnificent home at 111 East. Architect was Harvey Page.[30]

To the east at 119, the W. B. Hamilton home (c. 1904), later occupied by Hillyer's partner, Albert Deutsch, has been beautifully restored for adaptive use by the Keystone School, a private institution for elementary and secondary students. Another pre–World War I restored structure on the Keystone campus (125) was the home of W. W. Lipscomb; August A. Herff served as architect.[31] Also on the Keystone campus, at 2415 McCullough, is the 1920 home of Mr. and Mrs. Gus J. Kray:

This one-story brick and hollow tile residence is a recent completion for that part of the city. It is finished in cream white stucco and has a variegated purple-green-blue slate roof. The terrace in front is covered with red tile with wrought iron railings at edge. A grape arbor covers the rear terracing. It has a large living room, dining room, pantry, kitchen, two bedrooms and two baths with tile floors. The other floors are of oak. There is a kitchen porch with woodwork covered in white enamel. It is heated with hot air. A. B. Ayres and Robert M. Ayres were the architects.[32]

Across from Keystone, at 132 East Craig (c. 1907), originally the home of Fred Hubbard, an extensive addition and remodeling in 1923 was the work of architect Richard Vander Stratten on behalf of E. P. Lipscomb.[33] The Lipscomb home in 1927 was the focus of a series of curious burglaries by a yardman who committed his crimes in the forenoon while residents were away. His specialty was silken garments, of which twenty-four pairs of silk stockings were found under the Lipscomb house.[34]

At 136 East Craig (c. 1904), across the street from his parents, W. B. Hamilton Jr. lived for nearly two decades. About 1910 Dr. J. E. Moore occupied the home at 110 East. Its future tenants included such well-known families as the H. R. Woffords. While staying at the Moore home in 1916, Mrs. Sarita Milmo Reeder died. A daughter

As landscaping work is being completed, Hiram Partee may be among those stopped to inspect his new Italian Renaissance home (1919, Atlee B. Ayres, architect) at 605 Belknap Place at the corner of West Craig Place.

of the famous Milmo banking house of Monterey and Nuevo Laredo, she was the sister of Princess Radziwill of Russia.[35]

North one block to spacious West Woodlawn Avenue, originally known as Layer Street, are several homes built before the turn of the century. Lee Adams informed son Paul that the one at 117 is the oldest home in Adams's Laurel Heights. In 1897 Dr. C. E. Tinkham, a dentist, resided there. Later it became part of the Learning Ventures School complex, as did 105, a more elaborate home of similar heritage. Francis Smith, listed as residing on Laurel Heights in 1897, is doubtless the Frank C. Smith listed at 105 in 1905. Sanborn's insurance map of 1904 places outbuildings in the same location they are today.

Smith sold the property in 1912 to R. H. Westen, who planned to raze the home and build a "modern and high-class apartment building" on the site.[36] Happily these plans did not materialize. Actually, Smith had put this property on the market three years earlier:

This ideal home, located on the corner of Main and Woodlawn Avenues, fronting both south and east with three lots 50 x 135 feet each, handsomely improved, with twelve beautiful shade trees and splendid lawn improvement. The house is a frame "Queen Anne" of ten rooms and bath. On the ground floor are four large rooms and a kitchen, and on the second floor are five bedrooms and bath. The house is well built throughout; foundations of brick resting upon solid rock. The house is plastered, not ceiled.

The rooms on the ground floor can be thrown into one, making a beautiful arrangement for receptions, etc. The rooms are large and the ceilings high; wide roomy verandas. Splendid closets, handsome mantels, etc. The barn is two stories, and has accommodations for four head of stock and two vehicles. Upstairs in the barn are servant's quarters. Adjoining the barn is the washhouse and woodhouse. Among the attractions of this place is a Marechal Neil rosebush covering the front of the veranda which has had as many as 500 roses on it at one time. It is a swell place and I am in position to give you a very attractive price on it.[37]

On the same side of the street, the home at 127 West Woodlawn (c. 1910) has been occupied by several related families. Dr. T. T. Jackson, the first King Antonio to preside over San Antonio's Fiesta Week and a respected surgeon, purchased the home in 1915. In subsequent years Mr. and Mrs. C. R. Goodrich, Mrs. Jackson's niece, lived there when their daughter Mary Dorothy (Mrs. George E. Pierce) made her debut. Then when former Congressman and Mrs. Maury Maverick, Mrs. Goodrich's sister, returned to San Antonio in 1947, it was their home until his death in 1954.

An assymetrical Victorian exuberance marks the distinctive late nineteenth-century home at 105 West Woodlawn Avenue, which in the 1990s became lawyers' offices.

Sometime San Antonio mayor and 20th Congressional District U.S. representative, with leadership roles in the Small War Plants Corporation and War Production Board, this consummate New Dealer had a greater national, even international, reputation than any resident of this neighborhood. His coinage of the term "gobbledygook" and his pithy quotes made him a media favorite. Terrell Dobbs Maverick, his widow, remarried world-renowned historian Walter Prescott Webb.[38]

To the west of the Maverick residence, at 133 West, one of the oldest apartment buildings in San Antonio, the Woodlawn, was completed in August 1917. This "handsome structure of Moorish architecture" was erected by Robert Duncan. James Atkin served as general contractor.[39]

Across the street at 124 West, constructed in 1908 for Louis Hartung, stands a residence in which he dwelled for more than fifty years.

A handsome type of the colonial style is the six-room residence of Louis Hartung, recently completed on Wood-

lawn Avenue, Laurel Heights, after plans by Atlee B. Ayres. A feature of the cottage is the large reception hall opening into the parlor, which in turn opens into the dining room. The house also contains an attractive conservatory. It cost approximately $8,000.[40]

On the northwest corner of Woodlawn and Howard, Norval J. Welsh bought five lots in 1902 for $3,300.[41] He lived in the nine-room home he built at 209 West (formerly 201), "one of the finest homes in that section of the city,"[42] until he sold it in 1909 for $12,000 with three and a half lots to Dr. James S. Davis, formerly of Waxahachie.[43] Most older homes on that side of the block gave way to Laurel Heights Methodist Church.

"This Millionaires' Church, But Four Months Old, Will Build $65,000 Edifice," ran the *Light* headline of April 3, 1910.

For this church is in store a brilliant future, situated as it is right in the heart of the wealthiest and most influential residential district of San Antonio, with a membership made up of 2225 members who are noted in the community for their business and social prominence. That the Laurel Heights

Methodist Church with its virile strength and the wealth and influence of its membership will not only become a power in the Methodism of San Antonio, but an influence of might in the municipality, is a foregone conclusion.[44]

Dedicated on Easter Sunday 1912, the Carthage stone and pressed brick sanctuary could seat 1,000. Atlee Ayres designed the building, its cost (with pipe organ) slightly above $80,000. On the building committee were Judge J. O. Terrell, Ed Rand, C. E. Hammond, John Warren, Mrs. C. E. Hammond, Mrs. G. Bedell Moore, Judge Winchester Kelso and Mrs. John W. Kokernot.[45]

Homes across the street from the church may represent the best preserved block of pre–World War I structures in the Monte Vista Historic District. On Woodlawn at the corner of Belknap (202), R. D. Inscho lived as early as 1897. Other early residents included William T. Way and John O. Ford (c. 1907–1914).[46] Sculptor Pompeo Coppini lived next door (206) in 1904.[47] Various families followed Coppini as residents until the property was acquired by Mrs. Alice J. Moore and underwent extensive renovation and additions in 1917. Contractors Mauth and Moody did the work, which involved turning the frame structure into a stucco duplex. Mrs. Moore had for several years lived in the brick duplex to the west (208).[48]

This symmetrical circa-1910 foursquare style house at 127 West Woodlawn Avenue, its plan of a type often purchased by mail, became the home of former Congressman and Mayor Maury Maverick and his wife after World War II.

Four homes at the western end of the block (281, 222, 234 and 240) are on Sanborn's 1904 fire insurance map. Two date even earlier. According to the 1897–98 city directory, Victor A. Raymond resided at 222 and V. P. Brown at 234. A year or so later Don A. Bliss moved into vacant 140. It is not clear whether the 1920 structure at 222 built for Mrs. Alice Moore replaced an older one or, more likely, was an extensive renovation job such as she did three years earlier at 206. Mrs. Moore built at least two more houses in the area, according to architect Harvey P. Smith's records of 1921, but they are not identifiable.[49]

Three extant homes on the north side of West Woodlawn (323, 331 and 339) appear on the 1904 insurance map. E. B. Lowry resided at 323, architect Harvey L. Page at 331 and Robert Reid Russell at 339. Before coming to San Antonio in 1899, Page studied architecture with J. L. Smithmeyer of Washington, architect of the Library of Congress. While Page specialized in clubs, apartment buildings and hotels, he designed several homes in the neighborhood and on Tobin Hill to the south. Page's home and sometime workshop originally had an arboretum with white columns extending toward the street. Otherwise it appears as it did originally. This residence later became the property (c. 1910) of George F. Lupton, general passenger agent of the Aransas Pass Railway and an individual credited with attracting immigrants into South Texas.[50]

Possibly no residence in San Antonio attracted as much attention in 1911 as that of Robert Reid Russell (339) when he enlarged his home:

Raising a house with all its furniture, every picture hanging on the walls, the china and glassware in the cabinets, nothing, in fact, touched, to a height of fourteen feet, and then building a first story under what is now the first story is what is being done in the fourteen room brick residence of Robert Reid Russell, corner of [339] West Woodlawn and San Pedro Avenue. It is the first time such work, at least on such a scale, has been done in San Antonio. . . . By the end of next week . . . the Russell house will be resting on stilts fourteen feet above the ground, with not a cracked wall, not a picture fallen, or a pin moved on the dressers. In fact, that is the stipulation in the contract.

In the neighborhood of eight jacks have been placed under the walls, and first floor. Bricks have been removed and dug in under to afford a foundation for the jacks. A comparatively small force of men is used and the jack-screws are worked entirely by manual labor. The house raises all together and at once by the work of the jack-screws.[51]

Beaux-Arts designs enhanced the tan brick and terra cotta Gothic style of Laurel Heights Methodist Church (1912, Atlee B. Ayres, architect). As with similar churches of the era, a tower was placed near the street intersection—West Woodlawn Avenue and Belknap Place—although in this case the dominant tower is set back along Woodlawn. The steeple was removed in 1927 when its slate shingles began to slide off.

East Woodlawn Avenue is a somewhat later development. The first single family homes appearing about 1906–1908, apartment buildings in the 1920s. The San Gabriel Apartments represented innovation in 1925:

Another high class apartment building is to be opened to the public today. The San Gabriel Apartments at 124, 126, and 128 East Woodlawn Avenue, just recently completed at a cost of approximately $100,000. The apartment house, two stories high, with a frontage of 180 feet and three entrances, furnishes San Antonio apartment seekers with a place well worth looking into.

It is Spanish style built of hollow tile and stucco, making it fireproof, while the shallow depth of the building gives each of the 12 apartments windows opening both north and south, two of the apartments having eastern exposure as well as two others having windows on the west side. The San

Gabriel Apartments are owned by Lewis W. Lipscomb, who can claim the distinction of being one of the youngest apartment house proprietors in San Antonio. Architects of the Kelwood Company drew up the plans on the building and the same company likewise had the general contract for the building.

There are a number of modern features that go with the apartments, [each] of them [with] four rooms which can be obtained either furnished or unfurnished. To begin with, each apartment has a complete kitchen and is equipped with Frigidaire refrigeration, from E. J. Hermann. Clow gas steam radiators are supplied in each room to warm the apartments, and there is a Pittsburg Water Heater in each apartment. A novel device in the kitchens known as the "kerenercator" provides for garbage disposal, which works somewhat on the principal of the laundry chute, there being a receptacle in each kitchen and tubes inside that carry the garbage away. Tile baths with showers and all modern bathroom equipment are connected with each apartment.[52]

One of the finer residences on this block, built in 1922 by A. G. Dugger, apparently for his own home although he never lived there, was sold to oilman Abe Goodman. Soundproof floors, damp-proof walls and gas steam radiators were features of this design by Harvey Smith and Robert Kelly:

Adding to the appearance in the vicinity of East Woodlawn Avenue, this handsome new home for Mr. and Mrs. A. G. Dugger has just been completed at 115 East Woodlawn Avenue. The student of building design can find a particular appeal in the plan of the home where the architects have eliminated all waste space, without sacrificing any of the spaciousness, beauty and comfort that distinguish the finest and largest residences.

The building is of semi-fireproof construction; reinforced concrete foundation with hollow tile walls stuccoed with stone trimming. On the first floor is a living room 28 by 15 feet at one end of which is a large mantel of original design and at the opposite end French doors open into a big concrete porch. The stairway entrance from the living room is a particular feature with its semi-circular arch and wrought iron scrolls on each side. The walls and ceiling of this room and also the dining room and breakfast nook are finished in silver gray by hand stripping in with varnish colors. The buffet kitchen is a model of convenience and beauty with its many built-in features, all finished in white enamel.

On the second floor are three large bedrooms, commodious trunk closet, linen case with a big glassed-in sleeping porch opening off the two bedrooms. The bath is a distinctive feature of the house, also having tiled floor and wainscoat. The plumbing fixtures include built-in tub, shower and an enameled gas heater sunk in the wall.[53]

Moving northward, one of the district's most distinctive Victorian cottages is at 108 East Mistletoe. Its heritage is confounding. Emily B. and John W. Rogers owned the lot as early as 1896, but the 1897 City Directory lists him at 118 East. They sold it to Annie M. Winn for $4,100 in April 1902, the price indicating a structure on it. In December 1902 Dr. William Hope Davis got a permit for a four-room addition.[54] Dan Withers's color research on the cottage at 108 is revealing:

With the exception of white is used on all trim work, only one other color has been applied to the wooden areas of this home. All lattice work, banisters, steps and shutters have consistently been painted green. The various shades of green used have been Mesquite, Acequia, Alameda and Senisa. Senisa is found only on the steps of the front porch, and is the earliest green found on the structure. These typical turn-of-the-century greens are usually drab and lifeless, but they achieve a distinctive and individual effect contrasted to the white trim work and the terra cotta brick of the house.[55]

Davis lived here for several years until he built a more elaborate structure in the new "Southern suburban style" at 134 East Mistletoe. J. Flood Walker departed from the conventional with a "mission style of architecture" in this 1905 design. At completion within the next year, Southern California architecture was in vogue locally:

The deep overhanging eaves casting long shadows and protecting the walls from the hot rays of the sun, together with simple lines and appropriate color scheme, go to make this style of dwelling attractive and one that will be found adaptable to this climate. The first story walls are to be of cement stucco, cream color. The second story will be singles in the brown shade, and the roof in moss tinted shingles. The entire scheme will be set off by a trim of white. The rustic brown stone columns supporting the second story overhang on the east and the plain red brick chimneys, of simple but massive design, are worthy features.[56]

Elsewhere on Mistletoe, Frank Matzow, in the 1900 census listed at 215 West in a since-razed house associated with the Judge Phil Shook family, bought the lot at 126 East in November 1904 and built there in 1905.[57] Sam Johnson got a permit for a "two-story cottage" at 127 East in September 1903. Twenty years later Judge W. W. Mc-Crory bought the property and planned to spend $7,000 for renovations; "It promises to be one of the show-places of this residence section."[58] Another structure, of cottage dimensions prior to World War I, was built for James H. Brack at 133 East in 1907. It matched, or surpassed, its neighbors in design and interior finish if not in size:

When a man speaks of building a five-room cottage, only a casual interest is manifested, but when a man informs you that he intends investing $10,000 in the erection and furnishing of a similar structure, he creates quite an impression. Therefore, the little five-room cottage of James H. Brack, formerly of Boston, but now of this city, attracts attention.

Located on Mistletoe Avenue, Laurel Heights, this little home actually represents an investment of the amount mentioned. The exterior is simple and unpretentious in design, but the interior decorations are the most elaborate. The house is finished throughout in hardwood, save the bathroom, which is in enamel and equipped with the most costly bath fixtures that money can buy.

Besides two bed chambers, dining room, basement and garret, containing a store room and servants' quarters, the house boasts an ample living hall, which is its most attractive feature. This is finished in the Mission design, but contains a fireplace modeled in the broad, low lines of the Flemish style. The mural decorations of this hall are probably the most costly in the city. Most delicate and refined taste is displayed in the furnishing. In spite of the fact that the house probably represents the investment of more money to the square inch than any other residence in this country. It is built after plans by J. Flood Walker.[59]

Later residents in this home included S. S. Searcy through the World War I years, insurance man Arthur C. Burnett until the mid-1930s, and F. A. Smith. Architect George Willis, praised for his designs of the Milam Building and the St. Anthony Hotel, acquired the property during World War II and embellished it extensively with additions and renovation. A feature of the home is a very large basement, where previous tenants allegedly enjoyed target practice.[60]

Other distinctive residences on East Mistletoe have been razed. Longtime residents particularly recall one "of mission style with decidedly Hindo-Arabian feeling" designed in 1907 for Dr. C. C. Higgins at the northwest corner of Main and Mistletoe. Several other homes were demolished for the construction of Laurel Heights Methodist Church on both Woodlawn and Mistletoe. Still others gave way to an apartment complex.

Among the original structures extant on West Mistletoe is that at 134-136. Atlee Ayres in 1909 designed this home for Charles Bertrand, whose widow continued to reside there until the World War I period.[61] On the same block, the Laurel Heights Grocery originally stood at 116, and later the Laurel Heights Post Office.

About 1907, the grocery moved to the northeast corner of Howard and Mistletoe, sharing that structure with the J. D. Fisher Drug Co. The latter in 1915 became known as Laurel Heights Pharmacy when it was acquired by Lester D. Gilmore. Even though there were other owners since, it became a neighborhood gathering place.

In early 1923, pharmacist Gilmore moved the business two blocks away to 2602 North Main. Phelps and Dewees drew the plans for the more spacious brick building, while Kroeger and Kroeger served as contractors. Steam heat and an air-cooling plant provided comfort in all seasons for Laurel Heights lingerers, who readily understood Gilmore's motto, "service about all things."[62] Meanwhile, the Laurel Heights Grocery relocated next door at 2604. The premises on the Howard corner remained vacant briefly, until occupied about 1925 by a Sommers Drug Store and Laurel Heights Beauty Shop.

Monte Vista Historical Association files include architectural drawings of homes never constructed, such as Dr. E. A. Holland's home at 128 West Mistletoe by architect A. Herrman in 1913.

A quite different structure there, designed by Reuter and Harrington, was completed for Dr. Holland in the following year. A basement in this home, commonplace elsewhere in the neighborhood, included a siphon to pump water following heavy rains. The W. N. Fleming family acquired the home in 1921, followed by the S. Finley Ewings in 1943. Mrs. Ewing lived in the home for more than thirty years.[63]

Civic-minded Dr. Milton J. Bliem became an original resident of the block, living at 117 West (razed) as early as 1897. At a time when public knowledge of sexual information came primarily from advertisements by charlatans and purveyors of patent medicine, Bliem gave an extraordinary lecture on "Personal Purity" that attracted two hundred men to the Y.M.C.A. in 1893:

The men present are not likely to forget the truths that were brought home with great force. The talk was personal and confidential. "Whatsoever a man soweth, that shall he also reap." That is one of the laws of nature. . . . Young men do things erringly which bring them to ruin. . . . You must not blush at such an important subject. Men develop the physical more than the spiritual, mental and social side. He gave some wholesome advice to married as well as single men . . . . for sixty-five minutes and was listened to with intense interest by the intelligent audience. Some things which were said sent a cold chill down the backs of those present.[64]

In a more modest home than Bliem's, Bernhard Mackenson lived at 131 (129?) West Mistletoe as early as 1897. A few years later it was the home of James C. Irwin, whose widow ran the Laurel Heights Grocery next door. In 1903 Mrs. Rosa Irwin got a permit "to erect [a] two-room addition on Mistletoe Avenue to cost $350."[65]

On the adjacent corner (203 West) the E. M. Rowleys constructed their home in about 1909. When the home was draped by Joske's in 1919, it was featured in an advertisement: "Home in one form or another is the great object of life."[66] Mrs. Rowley resided there for more than twenty years. The cottage next door (209) is on the 1904 map and was the home of Dr. C. A. Wilson, who was listed there in the 1900 census.

At 221 West is the home built by Ernest Altgelt Jr., who resided there according to the 1900 census. The original part of the Colonial structure features wide cypress boards and square nails. R. D. Inscho, who moved there from Woodlawn Avenue, lived in the home for a few years until it was sold to the Reverend W. D. Christian

Even ceiling fans, little used in winter, were decked with garlands as Laurel Heights Grocery celebrated Christmas in 1927.

in 1908.[67] Dr. W. E. Nesbit purchased the home in 1921, when it was entirely renovated and enlarged and acquired a new facade. Mrs. Nesbit lived in the home for more than fifty years.[68]

Another turn-of-the-century structure on West Mistletoe (235) is one to which Dr. Milton J. Bliem and his family moved about 1900 from 117 West. Thereafter, Bliem's reputation in civic, religious and charitable work increased. With more than twenty years experience as a YMCA officer and director, the Lafayette College Phi Beta Kappa graduate also played leadership roles in the school board, public library and Texas State Historical Association, as well as in medical circles.[69] The family lived there for nearly thirty years. Edward L. Porch Jr. purchased the home in 1929.[70]

The late-nineteenth-century residence at 239 West Mistletoe was the home of S. A. McIlhenny

as early as 1897 and, a decade later, of G. F. Jackson. After being vacant for some years, it became the home of R. W. Morrison following World War I. Morrison attracted considerable press coverage, as he was responsible for making the St. Anthony the first completely air-conditioned hotel in the nation. He also acquired oriental rugs from the Russian Embassy in Washington to give the St. Anthony its deserved reputation as a grand hotel.[71] Morrison later was president of the San Antonio Ice and Storage Company.

At 204 West Mistletoe stands the home constructed by Judge DuVal West in 1908. J. Flood Walker served as architect for the family which had lived successively on the 200 blocks of West Craig and West Woodlawn. With the exception of a few years of her early married life, Judge West's daughter, Ruth (Mrs. E. S. Emerson), lived in this

This circa-1900 shingle-style home at 318 West Mistletoe Avenue was apparently enlarged by 1910, as increasing property values made such additions worthwhile.

home until 1973. Her childhood recollections are recorded earlier in this volume.

Next door (210) the Sallie Walthall residence has disappeared, but the George J. Pancoast home (216 West), constructed beside it in 1907, stands. These families were interrelated. The Pancoast family resided in this home for more than sixty years. Others on the same side of the block, including that of social arbiter Simona Wofford Rubsamen, who grew up at 234, have given way to expansion of Laurel Heights Methodist Church.

On the north side of the 300 block of West Mistletoe only two early homes remain. Charles L. Sauer lived at 321 in 1897. The A. H. Currys moved to that address by 1905. By 1908, Dr. B. F. Stout and his family moved into 325 West, one of the earliest California-style bungalows built in this area (the rock facade is recent). It remains in an unusually good state of repair. An increasing number of similar homes were built in the neighborhood prior to World War I and into the 1920s.

The Stouts later moved into a large home (335), since razed, before they built the fine residence at 110 West Lynwood. Stout, a pathologist, was among local physicians for whom the public health of the city became a matter of professional concern.[72]

Homes on the south side of this block have fared somewhat better. At 306 West the D. W.

Lights built a home designed by Reuter and Harrington at an estimated cost of $40,000 in 1913. "The structure is modern in all respects and represents the latest designs of architecture. Steam heat and vacuum cleaners are installed in each room. The floors are hardwood and the bath rooms, three in number, have tile wainscoats and floors."[73] Rancher Light owned extensive lands in South Texas, some of them later sold to Dallas magnates Toddie Lee Wynne and Clint Murchison, formerly of San Antonio.[74]

The dramatically restored home at 318 West Mistletoe appears on the 1904 map. It apparently was of cottage dimensions and owned by W. H. Seacat. Don Morris in his restoration saw strong indications of two distinct building patterns. A 1907 advertisement offering a cottage of "four rooms, with basement and attic" bears out the observation.[75]

Mrs. D. C. Stebbins lived in the home in 1908, but when it was advertised for sale in 1910 descriptions approximate today's. Although the advertisement reports it just completed and never occupied, the probability remains that, like others in this area of rising prices, it became financially feasible to make major additions. "This house was built by day labor for a man who knows what good work is," suggests the quality of construction.[76] So does another description in that year:

A magnificent home in the very cream of Laurel Heights district . . . has nine rooms and large reception hall. . . open fireplace, built-in bookcase on each side, beamed ceiling; dining room is finished in white with paneled walls and built-in china closet; library and one bedroom, with large kitchen, pass pantry and large storage pantry on first floor. Three beautiful bedrooms, bath and outside sleeping porch on second floor. . . . Servant's room, garage, fuel room and abundance of storage in basement.[77]

Amelia D. Smith lived next door (322) as early as 1902, when she got a permit to erect a back gallery.[78] From dimensions and appearance, compared to its designation on the 1904 insurance map, this house has also undergone transformation. Of the two remaining houses on this West Mistletoe block less is known. C. T. Titus lived at 328 in 1924. Landman Theodore M. Plummer resided at 334 in 1914, but from the mid-1920s, and more than twenty years thereafter, it was the home of Miss Irene Pancoast.[79]

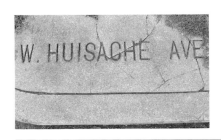

6. Magnolia, Huisache and Mulberry

Most of the homes on Magnolia Avenue, East and West, date from the decade prior to World War I, although perhaps ten of the extant structures are listed in the 1905–1906 City Directory. Many of the earliest residences gave way to apartment dwellings as early as the 1920s. Some of the fine homes on East Magnolia were turned into makeshift apartments in later years.

The spacious one-story and basement at 101 East Magnolia was built about 1910. Mr. and Mrs. Myron A. Pearce lived there in 1914. In 1929 it was the School of Childhood.[1] A. G. Dugger was already an established builder by 1914, when his family moved to their fine new home at 109 East. This was one of several he constructed on the north side of the block between 1909 and 1923.[2]

White two-storied columns are the obvious feature of the heavy frame house at 115 East Magnolia, one of several homes transported from one location in the historic district to another. This house was moved from East Mulberry to its present location in 1910. Longtime residents commonly identify it as the Sam Napel home, for that family resided there from the mid-1930s until Mrs. Napel's death in 1971.[3]

Another Dugger construction at 119 East Magnolia, built in 1917 as the home of Mr. and Mrs. William J. Moore for approximately $18,000, had two stories and a basement that featured brick, concrete, and stone material. One-time president of the Cattleman's Association and a veteran of the "long drive" to northern markets, in his youth the wealthy Moore had been a cowboy for Colonel John M. Bennett. Mrs. Moore continued to live in the home after her husband's death, less than a year after its completion.[4]

Possibly the structure at 141 East Magnolia, designed by Harvey P. Smith and Robert B. Kelly, represented the "ideal" in 1923:

An ideal modern residence of hollow tile and stucco has just been completed by A. G. Dugger at [141] East Magnolia and McCullough Avenue. Combining as it does, all of those qualities in design, construction, and convenience of every description most desired by home-lovers, this home stands out unique among San Antonio's newest and finest residences. Mr. Dugger has spared no expense nor effort to make this an ideal example of the modern medium-sized home as was possible. In exterior design it represents a slight departure from the conventional Italian renaissance style. This is accentuated in the color combination—a delicate pink, rough trowelled stucco of the lower story and a light ivory for the second story with pink quoins at the corners. Other ornamental trim is of cement stone. The reinforced concrete foundation rests on solid rock.

The walls of the reception hall, living room, dining room, and sun parlor are finished in pitted plaster and point stippled decorative colors to represent travertine stone blocks. The breakfast nook, above the wainscot, has a frieze decorated in bright colored designs.

The kitchen has all of the built-in features and conveniences that delight the eye of the housewife, including Asbestolith sanitary floor and drainboard surface, a swinging stool under sink cabinets and many other labor-saving devices. Among the most desirable of these is the Frigidaire in the rear entry which makes ice cream, desserts, and refrigerates the food storage compartment automatically eliminating the necessity of having ice delivered daily.[5]

Next door at 145 on the McCullough corner, architect Kelly and builder Dugger in 1923 again combined efforts in a well-constructed home for the Tom J. Newtons. Architecturally, most homes on the north side of the block are not unlike later ones on Elsmere or Hollywood, and are more likely of more permanent construction than their pre–World War I neighbors across the street.[6]

Each of the twelve apartments of the Spanish-style Magnolia Terrace (1928, Adams & Adams, architects) gets a southern exposure and a homelike feeling from the low-rise complex with spacious lawn.

Dating from 1905 or earlier, the eight-room "modern" residence at 112 East Magnolia was purchased from Sarah Burt for $4,000 in 1906. The Burts, however, remained there several years until Mrs. Claude R. (Janie) Bell acquired the home where she lived until 1951. It has since been the home of Sarah L. and the late James C. Talcott, whose Talcott and Belknap forebears built on Ashby and French places in the late 1880s.[7]

Next door at 116, in a structure of comparable vintage, the S. J. Ellison family resided in 1905. By 1921 it was the property of E. P. Arneson, who had architect Will Noonan draw plans for converting it into apartments in 1921. Apparently this did not take place as it continued to be a one-family dwelling until recent years.[8]

J. B. F. Showalter lived at 120 East Magnolia in 1908. The home for many years was associated with Dr. Edward W. McCamish, who died there in 1928. Both Dr. and Mrs. McCamish gave attention to the problems of tubercular children in the community. He was president of the Bexar County Medical Society and she of the Auxiliary.[9]

Five handsome residences (122–140 East) built by the Alamo Home Builders in 1912–1913 would "meet the increasing demand for the better type of dwelling in San Antonio." Featured in a newspaper photograph, they demonstrated "the clean-cut and striking appearance of a neighborhood of fenceless houses." Behles and Boelhauwe were architects for these structures, which did not sell as readily as the builders hoped.

In any event, the 1914 City Directory listed their occupants as three officers of Alamo Home Builders: R. A. Richey (132 East), C. M. Hocker (134 East) and Hugo Rhodius (136 East), with Mrs. Richard (Augusta) Pfeuffer at 138 and J. E. Jones at 140 in the others. "Positively the best buy on Laurel Heights under $10,000," the "splendidly built" home with its "mission lines" at 134 East could be purchased for $7,500 in 1913.[10]

Construction along West Magnolia began in the 300 block after 1905, when the streetcar line was extended north. Today West Magnolia to San Pedro presents a wholly different appearance than it did until the mid-1920s. Since then approximately half of the single family dwellings have been razed to make way for apartment buildings and the Second Church of Christ, Scientist (1924). Four apartment buildings appeared over a five-year period. The Georgian (128 West) in 1926–27 was owned by real estate man Loren W. Benton, who used contractor W. N. Hagy. Each apartment had living, dining and bedrooms.

Ideally located on the top of Laurel Heights, it embodies the finest in architectural qualities and scientific arrangement. The building is of face brick set upon a solid rock foundation. The architecture is pure Georgian in style. The building contains eight apartments, each containing unusually large closet space, Frigidaire, Clow Gasteam Radiator heat, tile baths, incinerator for garbage and completely arranged and equipped kitchen. The decorating and lighting effects complete the harmonious atmosphere which makes this apartment a home. These apartments may be rented either furnished or unfurnished.[11]

In less than a year a more elaborate apartment building appeared across the street. Magnolia Arms (127-133 West) featured twelve apartment units of five or six rooms, each with an outside exposure. The contractor was C. B. Wolfe for this structure of metal lath, concrete and stucco. Furnishings came from Stowers Furniture Company. R. L. Jernigan, cashier and treasurer of the Mutual Deposit and Loan Association, owned this investment property.[12]

A few months after completion of Magnolia Arms, Joe J. Nix opened Magnolia Terrace (219 West) on the next block. An investment of $150,000 provided San Antonio with one of the outstanding apartment buildings in the Southwest.

At the corner of Magnolia Avenue and Howard Street, the long Spanish-type building, finished with white cement

Second Church of Christ, Scientist (1924, Herbert S. Green, architect), at West Magnolia Avenue and Belknap Place, since the mid-1990s has been home to the Presbyterian Oakwood Community Fellowship.

stucco with cream-colored casstone trim, adds a note of dominating elegance to a neighborhood long noted for its high type of residences and apartment buildings. Wrought-iron grills, graded Spanish tile roof and wide red tiled front terrace extending almost the full length of the building, are features which further portray the Spanish note introduced by Adams and Adams, architects. . . . Each of the 12 apartments has a wide south exposure, and the fact that the building is 214 feet long and shallow in depth, assures a maximum of ventilation and good exposure to the prevailing southeast breeze. The apartments contain four and five rooms each and a separate building in the rear provides both garage and servants' quarters for each apartment.

In planning the apartment building, it was stated by Carleton Adams, it was intended that it should be sufficiently of the city, but it was decided to make the building wide or long, rather than high into the air in order that the improvement might be more homelike, and afford wide lawn and yard space. The 187-foot front terrace, with ample lawn furniture and electric torches, was provided to assist in carrying out the spacious, homelike character of the improvements . . . Automatic electric refrigeration is provided in each apartment, also gas-steam heat, fireplaces, ventflouvre ventilation for kitchens, garbage chutes, built-in ironing boards, communicating telephones, shower as well as tub baths, tiled wainscote in the baths, built-in tile fittings, rubber tiled halls and stairs, built-in mail boxes and other conveniences.[13]

On the adjacent property, Frost Carvel was architect/builder for the less luxurious Magnolia Courts (203 West), opened in the fall of 1930. R. L. Jernigan invested $80,000 in the sixteen-unit structure as the stock market crash began to affect the local real estate market.[14]

Among the distinctive nonresidential structures in this neighborhood, the Second Church of

Appearance of the 1904 Victorian farmhouse-style home at 324 West Magnolia Avenue is made more formal by use of a facade of river stones at the first-floor level.

Christ, Scientist followed designs by Herbert Stanley Green. Six hundred could be accommodated in the auditorium of this church, completed in 1924 for approximatly $100,000. Construction is of reinforced concrete, brick and artificial stone.[15]

Residential developments on West Magnolia near Main began just after the turn of the century. The structure on the northwest corner (103) was among the first. Vacant in 1905, the J. W. Roberson family resided there in 1908. Owner L. B. Hollowell offered this "strictly modern seven-room and bath two story" for sale in 1909. Three years later it was priced at $5,000.[16]

While other bungalow types of this era on the block

The Beaux Artes J. Bruce Martindale home (c. 1915, Atlee B. Ayres, architect) stood at 237 West Magnolia Avenue. Shown on the facing page are the living room and entry hall, with its classic Craftsman-style stairway and a fireplace with a frieze similar to a detail in Frank Lloyd Wright's first home in Oak Park, Illinois.

remain standing, their vintage is disguised by changes in appearance. On Magnolia's next two blocks westward, some of the finest pre–World War I Laurel Heights homes have been razed.

Fortunately, one of the earliest (324 West) remains. J. H. Kirkpatrick, San Antonio's foremost orator of the day, lived there in 1905. He sold the home in 1911 to Mrs. M. S. Taylor for $10,500. Daughter-in-law Mrs. Lane (Amanda) Taylor was a founding member of the San Antonio Conservation Society and remained in this home until her death in 1977. Kirkpatrick had diverse real estate operations, in which he would be succeeded by his likewise popular son, Oran.[17]

To the north, city directories show East Huisache Avenue with only five or six structures prior to World War I. The two earliest residents in 1905, apparently, were Joseph D. Shiner at 111 and M. T. Matthieson at 118. Other prewar residents included J. L. Felder (114 East) and Mrs. Florence Avery (124 East). Not long after the Armistice, and for several years, construction continued unabated on East Huisache.

Real estate man S. A. Freeborn built the house at 102 East in 1920. His widow continued to live there for more than fifty years.[18] Also in 1920, C.

B. Schoeppl drew the plans for the home of Judge C. K. McDowell at 124 East Huisache. Builder V. L. Rasmussen constructed the seven-room reinforced concrete and brick home and basement for $20,000. Its three-car garage provided an unusual conversation piece at so early a date.[19]

A Sunday *Light* in 1920 featured the Goeth residence at 125 East Huisache, longtime home of Mary Ann and Henry Guerra Jr. Architect Herbert S. Green's designs led an observer to report that "beauty and dignity characterizes [the] home of Dr. R. F. Goeth."[20] Across the street, George W. Mitchell built an $8,000 frame and stucco home at 128 East for Dr. C. D. Dixon in 1923.[21] The following year A. L. Thorman drew plans for C. E. McElroy's ten-room $7,000 frame home next door at 132 East.[22]

Specifications of Harvey Smith reveal that the 2,316-square-foot home at 138 East Huisache was constructed for $5.26 1/2 per square foot in 1924.[23] Built for thirty-five-year-old Walter W. McAllister, who became the legendary five-term mayor of San Antonio, one can be amused by a statement in the *Reference Work of Prominent Men of Southwest Texas*: "He has never mixed in politics nor sought public office." The home

Contrasting colors of brick give a graphic flair to 149 East Huisache Avenue, built in 1924 with a Neoclassic portico.

featured a concrete foundation, frame walls plastered inside and out, and a roof of cement tile.

Architect Beverly Spillman chose Dutch Colonial as the design for the house on the corner (148 East). Built in 1921 for shirt manufacturer Earl Johnson, it featured one of the neighborhood's early glassed-in sleeping porches. Its servants' quarters in the basement, however, could be found in a number of houses set on sloping terrain.[24]

Something new in the way of apartments, La Teresa with three-room efficiencies appeared in 1928–29 at 201 East Huische. A newcomer from Miami, Paul Sheffer, joined Walter Brown in this thirty-two-unit venture at a cost of $150,000. Architects Williams and Williams followed the Spanish design in the tile and concrete structure which featured a balcony overlooking the 30-by-108 foot patio. Shortly after its completion, John Scott of Detroit purchased the property.[25]

Bonnie Sue Jacobs traced the lineage of tenants of 235 East Huisache, built in 1928 for Mrs. William G. Tobin, in a "Trails and Tangents" column. Architect Kurt Beckmann's design attracted favorable comment for more than fifty years, but no more so than the Ayres design next door. The Ayres team designed 243 East Huisache in 1926 and its remodeling and additions in 1937. Built of the increasingly popular concrete, hollow tile and stucco, the story-and-a-half structure nestled into a landscape that earlier was the subject of a painting by neighbor Julian Onderdonk. For fifty years this "structure of infinite angles and levels" was

the home of the William C. Cleggs.[26] Here many of Mrs. Luther B. Clegg's heirloom pieces from French Place would delight another generation of that family.

Across the street (240 East) the California bungalow represented yet another design that continued to acquire increasing acceptance in San Antonio. C. B. Schoeppl drew plans for the home completed in 1924 for the William M. Fordtrans. Brick columns and a rustic effect met the eye on the large front porch, which opened directly into the living room. Space-saving efforts in construction of these bungalows called for small hallways and often, as here, a glassed-in sleeping porch.[27] Other simple frame family dwellings and an occasional duplex appeared along the three blocks to the east in the mid-1920s. The Coronado Apartments (302 East) were constructed a few years later, and the Carlton Apartments in 1928.

Immediately west of Main Avenue on Huisache is evidence that residential construction did not cease during World War I. Freeborn-Sherman Development Company built three Laurel Heights homes in 1917–18 and came up with a different advertising twist—"Cool Sleeping Porches and Steam Heat . . . But it fits all seasons. Now you need the sleeping porches, and in a few months the heat will be just as necessary for comfort." The home at 102 West Huisache featured hardwood floors and six large rooms. Increasingly, many of the new homes, as this one, boasted tile bathrooms. Another Freeborn and Sherman home at 108 West had in 1918 as its first resident Mrs. Cornelia VanderStucken. Members of the Vander-Stucken family lived here for more than sixty years.

Other contemporary structures included 114 West, which Freeborn resided in until he moved across to 102 East, and 116 West, in which his son lived for a short time. Another Freeborn-built home of this era, 123 West, remained the M. S. Barnett home for more than fifty years until it was purchased by Frank Barrett Hein in 1974. His father, architect Jack Harris Hein, drew plans for the remodeling in the following year.[28]

Perhaps no such institution has been a part of the lives of so many families in this historic district as has St. Anthony School, constructed in 1909. First conducted by the Sisters of Divine Providence, children of various Protestant persuasions also have long attended St. Anthony, increasingly so in recent years, and thus it has become identified with the entire neighborhood:

San Antonio's scholastic population is rapidly approaching the 18,000 mark. One of the illustrations of the increased demand of grammar schools is found in the new building now being erected by the Sisters of Divine Providence on Howard and Huisache streets, Laurel Heights, not so far from the Theological Seminary.

The structure is a handsome building costing $20,000, and is from the plans of F. B. Gaenslen, architect. It is modeled after the St. Joseph Academy building conducted by the same order in Dallas, is built of buff brick, two stories and a high basement, giving the effect of a three-story building. The dimensions are 66 x 80 feet, and there are eight classrooms, accommodating in the neighborhood of 500 pupils, boys and girls. Throughout, the school will have the latest, most modern equipment. It will be known as St.

A Neoclassical neighborhood landmark is St. Anthony School (1909, F. B. Gaenslen, architect) on West Huisache Avenue.

Anthony's School. The original St. Anthony's was in a frame residence two blocks down on Howard [311 West Woodlawn]. When the sisters opened the school in that part of Laurel Heights, the attendance was about fifty. Within the past year it reached 300, and the sisters were forced to build. The residence they occupied was entirely too small to accommodate the increasing attendance of day pupils.[29]

Elsewhere on the 200 block of West Huisache, a number of architectural styles add to the distinctiveness of the area. Architects Phelps and Dewees drew plans for the extensively remodeled home of W. L. Morrow (210 West) in 1927.[30] The Colonial-style stucco and trim pre–World War I structure at 227 West has been the home of the C. S. Greens, F. E. Smiths and James L. Pridgens.

The modified English Tudor home at 228 West Huisache boasts sixty-six windows, a coal chute to the basement and an original (1915) built-in vacuum system that still works. Although not the original owners, the L. L. Hess family moved there not long after its construction.

A handsome addition to San Antonio's homes was completed last week on Huisache Avenue for Charles Livingston. Ernest T. Behles was the architect. The house is semi-fireproof, built principally of interlocking tile and faced with dark red face Denton brick. There are eleven large rooms in addition to a conservatory, sun parlor, sewing room and servants' quarters. The dining room is especially attractive, the walls being finished in solid quartered oak. The tapestry and panel work there is beautiful. The living room is very large and imposing, being finished in birch-mahogany with a large stone mantel of Italian renaissance design.

All first floor rooms are connected with plate glass sliding doors. All porch floors are covered with tapestry tile while the kitchen and bathrooms have glazed tile wainscotings and floors. The floors throughout the living rooms and halls are of quarter-sawed polished oak. The house is equipped with a vacuum cleaning plant, hot air heating system and instantaneous automatic hot water heaters. The cost of building the house was $25,000. J. P. Harvey was the contractor.[31]

One of the most dramatic pre–World War I homes in this historic district is that of Mrs. Joseph S. Carr, 237 West Huisache. Certainly it is representative of a statement made in 1910 referring to homes along that block: "Probably no other style of architecture allows such an infinite amount of variation to suit the individual tastes of home builders and architects as does the mission plan. Houses built in this style are popular in San Antonio because they are in keeping with the climate, flora and traditions of this part of the

Patterned brick trim and attenuated Spanish-style windows at the entrance mark the apartment building at 323 East Huisache Avenue.

State."[32] Sometime residents at this address in the mid-1920s were two titans of the Texas oil industry, Clint W. Murchison and Thomas B. Slick.

Across the street, architect Ernest P. Behles drew designs for R. B. Cherry's new home at 238 West Huisache. Hot-air heating, vacuum system, "perfect" ventilation and the latest plumbing fixtures could be found in this "most complete" home. White stone on the exterior to the window sills and "variegated shades of tapestry brick" to the roofline provided an interesting contrast. Completed in 1913 at a cost of $15,000, the home was purchased in 1921 by C. W. Millard for $35,000.[33]

Mulberry Avenue extended eastward only to McCullough prior to World War I, when its westward extension reached some ten blocks beyond Main Avenue. In the years immediately following, the William E. Ochse home (103 East) attracted much attention. Its spacious side lawn abutting Main Avenue was greatly admired. The San Antonio Real Estate board chose it the Best All-Around Yard among 364 competitors in 1925.[34]

Across the street, the recently constructed Alfred M. Piper home (110 East) received the award for the best front yard the same year. K. G. Granberg was contractor for the Pipers' $18,000 home, completed in 1923.[35] A sometime resident of that block, Frank T. Maessen, a builder of diverse bungalow designs, had a year earlier completed the home at 120 East Mulberry. This mission-style bungalow was featured in E. A. Luck's *Greater San Antonio* (1923).

Another charming home, at 128 East Mulberry, was in the same family for more than sixty years. Mr. and Mrs. Walter T. Napier built it just after World War I. It was inherited by daughter Annie Napier Collins and then was the home of a granddaughter, Mrs. Charles George.[36] Across at 137 East, a prewar house on the block built in 1912 had eight rooms and a sleeping porch.[37]

One of the most publicized residences in 1921, the Logan L. Stephenson home at 201 East Mulberry, was designed by Harvey Smith and Robert Kelly. Landscaping brought the construction price to approximately $30,000:

This structure will be a truly unique addition to San Antonio's list of distinctive homes. The style will be a combination of the Italian and Old Spanish Colonial, and the details of design peculiar to those styles will be used throughout the interior in decorations and furnishings. The construction will be semi-fireproof with walls of hollow tile, stuccoed and reinforced concrete foundation.

All ornamental trim will be of buff-colored cement to harmonize with the buff-colored walls. The roof will be "Cordova" clay tile in variegated buff tones. The patio in the rear of the house will be an interesting feature with its fountain and pool, as also will be the flower garden with its enclosing walls and rustic gates. As illustrative of the studied care in design it is worthy to mention that all hinges for gates and exterior doors will be of handwrought iron after original Spanish patterns.

The house will consist of a living room, music room, dining room, kitchen, four bedrooms, a servant's room, two sleeping porches and a sewing room. There will also be four bathrooms with tile floors and walls. Many innovations in decorative treatment will be introduced in this house for the first time, locally. Instead of the usual stained effect for the doors, each door with its trim will be treated in an enameled two-toned effect in colors to harmonize with each particular room with its draperies. The living room with its ornamental plastered ceiling and the vaulted ceiling of the music room will afford interesting color treatment.[38]

Across the street, 212 East may be the only extant house advertised for sale on Olympian Way, the original street name for Mulberry east

Italian Renaissance is the style of the home built for oilman F. L. Thomson (1921, Atlee B. Ayres, architect) at 302 West Mulberry Avenue.

of McCullough. Sale price of the house in 1912, $3,200, included "100 feet of barns and sheds."[39]

Most razed 1920s homes in the 300 block, like 316 East (1922) and 320 East (1924), were frame bungalows, though George T. Jambers's razed 1922 "adoption of the Italian design" (326) had interlocking tile and stucco walls.[40] Several shorter streets crossed East Mulberry; construction on them attracted less attention. Francis Post Cannon's 120 Queen's Crescent English cottage (1927) became the home of David Yoachum in 1973.[41] The S. W. Scott (111) and F. A. Lapham (114) homes antedate it by a year or two.

Some nine homes were built on Princess Pass by the mid-1920s (116, 126, 130, 131, 132, 133, 135, 137 and 138), and Mrs. Maude C. Burney's four-plex apartment at 136 in 1925.[42] Eleven Kings Court homes north from Huisache to the city rock quarry (now Trinity University's campus) were also completed by the mid-1920s. Construction on Ledge Lane came after 1930.

Seven homes on Mulberry, lacking East or West clarification, are listed in the 1897–98 City Directory. By 1905, four are listed on East and

five on West Mulberry, but number changes make it impossible to verify the exact residence on the 100 block adjacent to Main Avenue. At no longer extant 225 West Mulberry in 1914, the Lewis Limited School stood alone on that block.

No school in San Antonio enjoys a better reputation for its health, location and thoroughness than the Lewis Limited School, a small, select school in Laurel Heights, one of the most beautiful, delightful and aristocratic suburbs of that city.

Founded in 1903 by Miss Mattie Lewis, its faculty of twelve offered art, music, expression, literature and foreign language classes to twelve boarding and sixty day students. At Lewis Limited "girls and young ladies need not suffer the heat and other distractions" of a downtown location.[43]

Most homes in West Mulberry's 200 block are of 1920s vintage. In 1927 Frank Maessen chose mission style for his home (207 West), designed and built by Frost Carvel Co. and home of architect Joe Stubblefield fifty years later.[44] In 1929 Emmet Burgess built the next door (215 West) masonry home for the J. R. Calhouns, occupied by the same family for more than fifty years.[45]

Next to the Calhouns, Richard Vander Stratten planned the Edward Sibleys' $10,000 brick-veneer two-story home (219 West) in 1927. They made extensive additions over a forty-year residence.[46]

Across the street, Max A. Krueger built 220 West in 1923 and sold it to the Charles W. Fitchners, the first residents. It remained in the family for more than sixty years. To the west, "A Trio of Attractive Homes Recently Built on Mulberry" was featured in local papers. Original owners included Ira Havins (222 West) Atlee B. Ayres Jr. (224 West) and Jack W. Neal (228 West). Atlee B. Ayres Sr. designed all three in 1918:

Mulberry Street is acquiring a number of handsome homes these days. The new home of Ira Havins . . . . is built of tile and finished in cream, white and cement stucco with dark red metal roof. The front floor has a large living room on the east side with a solarium in rear featuring large glass doors . . . . Jack W. Neal's residence stands at Mulberry Street and Belknap Place. An Italian motif is carried out in the architecture, the outside walls being of white limestone and the roof in dark red earthen tile. On the lower floor there are five rooms and four in the second story. The entrance to the house is through a large reception hall which adjoins a large living room and which is divided by columns. . . . Large verandas are located on the east and south sides. . . .

The residence of Atlee B. Ayres, Jr. . . . contains six rooms and has outside walls of hollow tile and is finished on the outside with white cement stucco. The roof is of dark metal shingle and painted green. A large living room is in the center of the house and on the east side are two bedrooms with bath between. . . . A sun parlor is in the rear of the living room. Double glass doors connect the living and dining rooms and the sun parlor.[47]

Architect Carleton W. Adams drew plans for his own home at 231 West Mulberry in 1922. With less square footage than some adjacent homes, it featured a small enclosed garden.[48]

Handsome as were these homes, Atlee Ayres drew plans for an even more sumptuous residence at 302 W. Mulberry in 1921.

With the completion of the residence of Dr. F. L. Thomson, president of the Grayburg Oil Company, at Belknap and West Mulberry avenues, Laurel Heights is given another beautiful and distinctive home. The new Thomson residence is an adaptation of the Italian style of architecture. It was built at a cost of approximately $100,000. The house consists of two stories and basement, constructed of light cream brick and trimmed in white ornamental stone. Roof is of red terra cotta tile. A wide terrace of black and white tile extends across the front of the home connecting with a loggia. On the east side is a corresponding terrace connecting with a pergola which serves as a porte cochere. In the rear of the sun parlor and opening from the dining room is another terrace.

On the first floor is a large entrance hall, living room with ventilation on four sides, dining room, breakfast room, kitchen, library and sun parlor. The second floor consists of three bedrooms, gymnasium, sitting room and two baths. The gymnasium is one of the features of the new home. Dr. Thomson, who believes in keeping "fit," has equipped it with numerous exercising devices, including rowing machine, punching bag and trapeze. The gymnasium also has shower facilities.

The new home has hardwood floors throughout and woodwork of tinted enamel. Ceilings in the living room, dining room and reception hall are finished in ornamental plaster. The house is heated by a steam vapor system, radiators being concealed in the walls. The kitchen of the Thomson home is declared by the architect to be one of the most complete in the city. It has tile floor and wainscoting and several cabinets with marble tops. The kitchen also has many built-in features, including a compartment for ironing boards and a broom closet. Sockets for connection with electrical devices are conveniently located.[49]

7. Agarita, Summit, McCullough and Main

Summit Place, contrary to its present-day identification as a single street, included Agarita and Kings Highway in its original development. While prospective purchasers did not fulfill speculators' hopes at the outset, this became perhaps the most prestigious San Antonio neighborhood by the 1920s. No family is more associated with this area than that of Judge J. O. Terrell. Three of his children (Marshall, Dick and Mattie) built homes on Agarita, within two blocks of that of their parents at the head of Main Avenue.

Ten homes of distinction stood on Agarita prior to World War I. L. H. Browne bought three lots on the northeast corner of Main and Agarita in 1911, sold half the property to Henry C. King the same year and began his antebellum-style residence at 101 East Agarita. The similar home of Methodist Bishop E. D. Mouzon at 116 East costing $12,000 in 1911 was built by W. N. Hagy.[1]

Motorists on McCullough frequently admire, and wonder as to its history, the Atlee Ayres–designed home at 145 East Agarita, allegedly one of "the two first absolutely fireproof dwellings" in San Antonio. Built in 1909 for Mrs. Carrie A. Bonner, mother of renowned artist Mary Bonner, the painter lived there in her youth:

Somewhat different will be the fireproof residence for Mrs. C. A. Bonner, to be built in Laurel Heights. The first floor will contain a large reception hall, drawing room, dining room, den, pantry and kitchen. The second floor space will be divided into five bedrooms. The bath and toilet will have tile floors and wainscoting. All the woodwork in the principal rooms on the first floor is to be finished in dark Flemish stain. The floors will be of oak laid in special design. Half of the space under the house will be excavated and used as plunder room, laundry, and heating apparatus. A stairway from the second floor leads to a roof garden. A large,

deep loggia with a tile floor is to be in front of the reception hall and to connect with the dining room and drawing room. All the outside walls of the building will be built of brick and finished with a smooth coat of plaster. All inside partitions will be fireproof; also all the floors and roof.[2]

Three homes on this block are of the post–World War I decade. A. J. Vick's widow moved from French Place to 129 East Agarita by 1924, joining her daughter and son-in-law, the Oran F. Swifts. Mrs. Swift, for more than forty years, lived in this home built by Ed Steves and Sons. It was restored by Dr. and Mrs. (Lyn) David R. Senn.

Next door at 135 East, architect James L. White drew plans for Moise L. Apel's $11,000

Artist and printmaker Mary Bonner, in Paris for much of the 1920s, spent part of her youth on East Agarita Avenue.

residence in 1927.[3] Across the street at 126 East, Mrs. Q. C. (Mattie Terrell) Couch's $13,000 hollow tile and stucco home, taking advantage of the sloping lot, appeared lower than its two-stories. Builder C. H. Blount built the home in 1926.[4]

A few homes on West Agarita date earlier than any east of Main. Although additional information is not available, the 1905–1906 City Directory lists the following residents: 112, H. Tyroff; 125, H. J. Rick; and 129, S. E. Hoard. Mrs. Kate S. Hamilton lived in the c. 1912 residence at 134 West. Architects Harvey P. Smith and Robert Kelly drew plans for Herman Lichte at 134 West for extensive alterations in 1920.[5]

At Howard and Agarita (131 West), the Adams and Adams–designed brick home of Mrs. L. H. Browne got attention in 1915. Its living room was "almost like a glassed in sun parlor, having windows that completely filled two sides of the room."[6] A handsome wedding present for Mr. and Mrs. Temple Calhoun in 1923, the Schoeppl-built home at 122 West Agarita was a gift from her parents, Mr. and Mrs. Robert N. Martindale.[7]

Dwellings built in the decade before and after World War I appeared on Agarita in the second block west of Main Avenue. Back from their wedding trip in February 1909, Dick O. Terrell took his bride, the former Flossie Denman, to their new residence at 213 West Agarita.[8] Brother Marshall W. Terrell's home, built in 1914 at 223 West, for which Atlee Ayres was architect, reflected the new trend of "open to the outdoors" residential style increasingly favored locally.[9] Architects Reuter and Harrington, in the same year, drew plans for the Seth S. Searcy home at 231 West.[1]

Reuter was architect for the even more pretentious 1917 home of Morris Stern at 228 West, a modified Italian Renaissance structure built by H. N. Jones Construction for $35,000.

Arched porches and spacious terraces of concrete and tile surround the house. The walls are of interlocking tile, with Oriental stucco finish on exterior, and stone trimmings. The roof is of red Spanish clay tile. The reception hall has a wainscot seven feet high and the entire room is finished in quarter-sawed oak, stained dark. The mantel in this room is of carved Caen stone. The living room, the dimensions of which are seventeen by thirty-one feet, will have a beam ceiling and

---

Facing page: A Palladian entry with Romanesque proportions highlights the Carrie Bonner home (1909, Atlee B. Ayres, architect) at East Agarita and McCullough avenues.

The courtyard of the apartments at 203 East Agarita Avenue, built about 1940, adds a Mediterranean note to the neighborhood.

wainscot, finished in white enamel. Walls are of figured fabric. This room will also have a large mantel, eight feet in width enclosed, with lattice walls worked out in appropriate design. A feature of this room is the fountain of Rockwood tile.

The dining room is carried out in white and old ivory. The walls are wainscoted and paneled and a plaster cornice of classical design finished the room. The library is to have a wainscot seven feet high, mahogany finish with fabric on the walls. The entire second floor is carried out in white enamel and is to have quarter sawed oak floors.

The landscape treatment will be one of the special features, with its Italian sunken garden, fountains, summer house, and tennis court. The planting of trees, flower gardens and layout of walks are all carried out along systematic lines to produce the delightful vistas and generally artistic effect so often found in romantic Italy.[11]

Nearly a decade later (1926), construction began on another Italian Renaissance residence next door at 222 West for E. N. Requa. James L. White provided the architectural plans, which featured tile floors and cast stone interiors. With a stone tile exterior "finished with two-tone Oriental stucco" and a roof of variegated mission tile, "a home of this class" cost $40,000. Six rooms on each of two floors were "larger than conventional present-day chambers." Plastered two-tone interiors, floors of polished white oak or tile and "stippled Tiffany blend on woodwork" added to

The Neoclassical frame home built by J. O. Terrell in about 1910 at 101 West Summit Avenue was later moved across the street to become 118 East Summit.

the home's beauty and also to its expense, escalating with "mechanical refrigeration, gas steam radiators, cedar closets and built-in telephones."[12]

A year later Frost Carvel planned the C. E. Tolhurst home at 206 West Agarita. Del Mar Corporation built this brick-veneer structure "of Italian type" for $20,000.[13]

Near the northwest corner of Belknap (309 West), for his own home, builder Robert L. Burney had Emmett T. Jackson design a traditional colonial residence in 1922. Colonial design extended to the interior and to the landscaping, which included "a rose garden with trellises and gravel walks" in the rear. The beautiful interior woodwork came as a gift from various local lumber companies.[14] A year earlier, architects Phelps and Dewees drew plans for Z. E. Bonner's home at 315 West Agarita.[15] At the corner of San Pedro (341 West), G. L. Gwin got a $7,800 building permit for his nine-room home in 1924.[16]

Standing at the head of Main Avenue, the stately Summit Avenue home of J. O. Terrell commanded "a magnificent view of country and city." According to granddaughter Mrs. William C. (Agnes Terrell) Clegg, Judge Terrell often quipped that while Judge Denman demanded that the city jog around his property when it extended Main Avenue northward, Terrell forced the city to halt altogether in its construction of the thoroughfare when it reached his home on Summit.

Built before 1910 at 101 West, it was moved across the street a decade later and became 118 East with a somewhat altered appearance. It was briefly the San Antonio Kindergarten–Primary Training School, then home of oilman Clint W. Murchison and still later the townhouse of Falfurrias's leading family, the Edward C. Lasaters. Mrs. Lasater allegedly cared little for ranch life and enjoyed cultural and social affairs during extended stays in San Antonio.[17]

Captain Ira C. Ogden's home across the street (117 East Summit) received press attention during its construction in 1915. Ernest Behles designed the $12,000 tapestry-brick home of nine rooms and two sleeping porches. J. M. Watson got it four years later for $18,500.[18]

Next door at 129 East, Atlee Ayres designed the frequently photographed two-story stucco home of Dr. Garrett P. Robertson. Described as

Architect Atlee B. Ayres said the inspiration for the Byzantine design of the doorway arch at 129 East Summit Avenue came from European travels.

TOP: THE UT INSTITUTE OF TEXAN CULTURES AT SAN ANTONIO, COURTESY OF ANN RUSSELL; BELOW: W. EUGENE GEORGE "the Italianate farmhouse type," this 1922 structure featured numerous architectural details. The "artistic entrance," Ayres noted, was the only one of its kind in San Antonio. He said he acquired the idea for the Byzantine design on the arch over the door from his European travels.[19]

Probably the oldest house on Summit, and indeed of the entire area north of Mulberry, is that at the southwest corner of McCullough (142 East). The Frank J. Doyle family lived there from about 1906 and may not have been the first residents. Summit at that time marked the northern boundary of the San Antonio city limits. For a time Doyle kept a small dairy herd, which he pastured across from his home between Summit and Kings Highway. Dr. G. N. Keeling, who previously lived two doors to the west, purchased the home and in 1929 had architects J. Clyde and Percy W. Williams draw plans for additions and remodeling.[20]

In the late 1920s Robert McGarraugh built the attractive bungalow at 138 East Summit for the A. C. Leslies. Architecturally, this home appeared similar to those McGarraugh constructed on Lullwood. At about the same time, McGarraugh began development of oak-studded Gray Gables across McCullough, leading to the eastward extension of Summit. Only two homes in Gray Gables were built within the time frame of this volume, one being that of his brother-in-law, Murray F. Crossette, at 333 East.[21]

Across the street (334 East), in 1929 architect John Marriott drew plans for the home of English design for the Morris Adelmans. This structure, "of face brick, cast stone trim and stucco with half-timbers in second story and gables," also featured one of the early story-and-a-half living rooms in the area.[22]

Arlington Arms, at the southeast corner of Summit and Main, stands in contrast to other structures on the street. The third such "arms" constructed by R. N. White and Joe J. Nix brought the following comment in 1925: "Arms are replacing apartments in San Antonio for the simple reason that the name attracts tenants. Why do they call them Arms? In the North 'Arms' suggest high class buildings occupied by the more fashionable, while apartments suggest the tenement house class of buildings." Eight suites were in this structure, designed by Phelps and Dewees.[23]

In stark contrast to the classical styles of neighboring homes are the sleek lines of the Moderne home at 330 East Summit Avenue, built in about 1939 for Ned Dupuy.

Driving north on Main Avenue, at the terminus one never fails to delight in the native stone structure at 101 West Summit, the second home at this location. John M. Marriott drew the architectural plans for this "modified colonial home" for Mr. and Mrs. V. H. McNutt. A well-known geologist throughout the American West, McNutt and his wife were best known locally as the proprietors of the legendary Gallagher Ranch some twenty-five miles from town. Extensive landscaping and the slate roof have always added to the dramatic effect of the property.[24]

Two other magnificent homes had already been built on the north side of the block. At 119 West the Paul O'Briens constructed a stately brick in the early 1920s. Paul and Peter O'Brien, in real estate, built a number of fine homes into which they moved briefly. That at 119 West became the home of Logan L. Stephenson in the mid-1920s, at which time the O'Briens moved to the purchaser's home at 201 East Mulberry.[25] At Howard and Summit (125 West), another outstanding home had been constructed for the Guy S. Combs in 1913. This two-story gray pressed-brick, designed by Adams and Adams, featured a finished attic and basement. This home was the scene of many musicals before Mrs. Combs's untimely death in 1919.[26]

Across the street, at 124 West, in 1923 Dr. and Mrs. R. A. Barber chose Beverly W. Spillman as their architect. The two-story tile and stucco structure cost approximately $11,500.[27]

Some of the outstanding homes in the Monte Vista Historic District are on the 200 block of

Mingled shades of red and brown brick, cast stone trim and a tile roof mark the 230 West Summit Avenue Tudor-style home built for Henry H. Bryant (1925, Adams & Adams, architects).

West Summit. These include the James M. Cavender home at 202 West. Herbert S. Green designed the two-story stucco, "the use of which local contractors say is becoming popular," in 1920. Built by Ed Oeffinger for the president of Frost Brothers, Joseph M. Frost, it was "among the new San Antonio residences that incorporate the latest in architectural design and advanced construction."[28] The two-story hollow tile garage was added by subsequent owner Robert A. Kampmann in 1924. Richard Vander Stratten drew plans for this $5,000 addition.[29] Later owners were Mr. and Mrs. (Polly Jackson) George Spencer.

An earlier "substantial" structure (205 West) on the opposite corner was completed in 1913 after plans drawn by architect August A. Herff. The George C. Walker home contained twelve rooms, a conservatory and extensive galleries on both floors. Its "beautiful vine-clad garage and pergola" was featured in a 1919 photographic essay on outstanding garages, which were rapidly replacing carriage houses in San Antonio at that time.[30]

A still earlier residence in "English suburban" at 211 West Summit, the H. C. Lane home "in white stucco with moss trimmings" was a departure for architect J. Flood Walker. "An immense fireplace of (blue delft) tile, eight feet wide, and flanked by heavy bookcases of natural mesquite, deeply carved by a member of the Lane family" was the focal point of interest downstairs, with massive wood treatment in the entrance hall, finished in Flemish style, and "life size pictures of little Dutch children" in the nursery upstairs.[31]

"This beautiful Summit Avenue home in the high class restricted district," ran the ad for 233 West in 1917, could be had for $13,000. There were nine spacious rooms and ninety-six feet of galleries as sleeping porches. When the house was for sale again in 1929 the price was $25,000.[32] At the corner (241 West), real estate man Hamper Ross's new home cost approximately $22,000 in 1926. John Westerhoff was general contractor for this two-story stucco home.[33]

In addition to the Frost-Cavender home at 202 West Summit, three other distinctive residences stand on the south of this block. One, built in 1920 at 240, is among Monte Vista's "finest."

Another resident in Italian Renaissance design which will be added has been designed for Dr. and Mrs. Oscar Hunt Judkins. It will be built on the southeast corner of Summit Avenue and Belknap Place. It will be of hollow tile and stucco with a fireflashed Spanish tile roof. Every detail of the exterior from the wrought iron rails and stone columns to the chimney tops have been inspired by old Italian masters.

The interior will consist of a large living room with a Caen stone mantel of paneled walls, a sun porch adjoining finished in lattice work, a breakfast room, stair hall and a paneled dining room. The kitchen provides for a built-in ice box and a cabinet with bitrolite top and all walls will be of cement, enameled white. The service stair is on the side with the lavatory and basement stairs. The second floor will have four bedrooms with two-tile bath rooms, with large closets one being 8' x 10', a cedar closet and linen closet. All floors except sun porch, breakfast rooms and bath rooms, which have tile, are of oak. The house will have a large basement and will be heated by hot air.

The garage will be of the same design and construction as the home, and provide room for two cars, gardener's room, two servants rooms, a bath and laundry. The service court will be of concrete, and in the rear of the house has been planned a beautiful formal garden with sun dial, seats and box-bordered paths. The cost will be approximately $40,000. Ralph H. Cameron is the architect.[34]

When the home of the Thomas Weir Labatts at 212 West Summit neared completion in 1923, its photo caption in the *Express* read:

Handsome two-story rock house being built on Summit Avenue for Mr. and Mrs. T. W. Labatt. The exterior of the house is finished in cut stone with slate roof. Large reception hall. Entering from the reception hall is a sun parlor, living room, dining room, breakfast room, large service room, and kitchen. On the second story will be four bedrooms, two bathrooms, dressing rooms and large sleeping porch. The house will be heated with hot air and all finished up with the latest modern improvements at a cost of $40,000. Herbert Stanley Green, Arch., A.I.A.[35]

Two years later, Adams and Adams provided an English design for the Henry H. Bryant home at 230 West. Walls of "tapestry brick in mingled shades of red and brown, with cast stone trim and tile roof" described the exterior. Four bedrooms, two baths and a sleeping porch on the second floor offered spacious living. Servants' quarters and a laundry room in the two-car stucco garage had become commonplace in Monte Vista. W. C. Thrailkill built this imposing structure.[36]

The spacious hollow tile and stucco bungalow at 308 West Summit received considerable attention for its "originality" in 1920 when it was built and since then for its beautiful east lawn. Constructed for James T. Coleman and purchased less than two years later by D. Leon Harp, it has remained in the same family for more than sixty years. The Harps received the "most beautiful yard" award in 1932. It later became the home of their daughter, Mrs. Eva M. Lancaster.[37]

Neighbor J. F. Hair (at what is now 311 West) drew attention with a sunken garden. Architect Harvey Smith's files on the Hair plans offer interesting information on 1922 construction costs for a 2,604-square-foot home ($4.03 per square foot) requiring four months to build. Smith noted that "old lumber and some mill work (was) used on construction—also old plumbing fixtures."[38]

Craftsman style and Spanish eclectic mix to form this distinctive bungalow, built in about 1920 at 308 West Summit Avenue.

Building Permit	$ 6.00
Total Payroll (Carps & Comm.)	2,510.00
Piece Work, etc. (Labor)	41.05
Excavation Labor (Labor)	35.35
Masonry Labor	200.00
Miscellaneous	29.72
T. J. Cecil (Tile Mantel Hearths)	176.60
D. P. McCullough (Painting & Dec.)	840.00
C. B. Christmas (Metal Lath)	134.59
Turner Roofing Co. (Rock, Sand)	155.14
Jud & Orman (Plumbing)	405.00
Alamo Iron Works (Iron & Steel)	26.87
Sam Dean (Sheet Metal Work)	285.85
William Song (Medicine Case)	27.20
Ernest Stapper (Flue Lining)	27.35
Roy Thompson (Walks, Driveway)	480.00
John Healy (Stucco Work)	531.00
Ed. Steves & Sons (Lumber)	938.36
Steves Sash & Door Co.	860.85
Praeger Hdw. Co. (Rough & Fin. Hdw.)	99.11
S.A. Portland Cement Co. (Cement)	114.80
Acme Brick Co. (Face Brick)	46.66
Travis Electric Co. (Wiring)	101.00
Schroeder Elec. Co. (Fix.)	215.00
Lehne Bros. (Floor Finishing)	153.75
W. W. McAllister & Co. (Ins.)	79.07
H. Pianta (Cement Stone)	60.00
[Subtotal]	8,540.42
Credit Item	1.00
[Subtotal]	8,859.42
Old Lumber, Plumbing, etc.	1,000.00
[Subtotal]	9,539.42
Arch'ts & Const. Mgrs. fee (10%)	953.94
TOTAL	$10,493.36[39]

A portion of this three-story Neoclassical building, dedicated in 1903 as St. Anthony Seminary, remains as the chapel of St. Anthony Catholic High School. Still owning its original tract purchased in 1890—bounded by McCullough Avenue, East Kings Highway, Shook Avenue and East Summit Avenue—the Catholic Church remains the largest single landholder in the Monte Vista district. At the block's southwest corner is the 1938 Our Lady of Grace Catholic Church (below).

Residents of Old Alamo Heights immediately recognize 314 West Summit as a near replica of the Ernest Scrivener house on Morton Street—more recently the Albert McNeel home—and indeed it is. Insuranceman Ed Fitch admired the home and called upon the services of Scrivener, a well-known builder, who began the Summit construction in February 1922. Just as the Scrivener residence served as a model, the Fitch home is a paradigm for later structures in the Monte Vista area. Classic lines prevail in the design of this home, in which four generations of the Fitch-Churchill families have lived.[40]

Another 1922 vintage residence (321 West) designed by C. B. Schoeppl presented "a balanced design of colonial home architecture." A spacious living room extended across the entire front, allegedly to display owner E. N. Requa's numerous hunting trophies. "Simplicity of form, straight lines and a delicate use of decorations give an air of dignity to this home."[41]

Summit, once the northern city limits, at the turn of the century had no cross streets from McCullough to San Pedro. Few dwellings remain on these thoroughfares, which once boasted fine residential property. Of the vestigial remains, some, such as the Fitch Insurance Agency at 2615 McCullough, have been transformed for commercial purposes. Cattleman Fisher Atkins built this house in 1909. The Fitches purchased it from his estate in 1952. An even older structure, 2419 McCullough, is associated with the H. E. Hildebrands. Alfred Giles and Guindon drew the plans for this stately home in 1891, when it had a panoramic view of downtown and the countryside.[42]

The most venerable institution in the Monte Vista Historic District is St. Anthony Catholic High School, previously St. Anthony Seminary. Actually, plans had been announced a decade ear-

Behind La Fonda's facade can still be seen outlines of the Main Avenue home of Winchester Kelso, Jr. (1920, Schoeppl & Hardie, architects). The restaurant, which moved to the site in 1932, has since served Mexican food dinners to Generals Eisenhower and MacArthur, Presidents Franklin Roosevelt and Lyndon Johnson and movie stars including John Wayne, Gary Cooper, Yul Brunner, Veronica Lake and Roy Rogers.

lier (in 1893) for construction of a "great Catholic college" to train young men for the priesthood "who are to labor in the religious fields of Mexico." Such an institution was prohibited by law in Mexico. Apostolic Delegate Right Reverend Diomede Falconio came from Rome in 1903 and laid the cornerstone in a ceremony about which "it is not too much to say that today will witness the great religious and civic demonstration in the history of San Antonio and the Southwest."

In a day when less attention was directed at separation of church and state, U. S. troops from Fort Sam Houston and city and county officials joined thousands in an April 1903 "grand procession, which with flying banners, brilliant regalia and martial music, will escort the Apostolic Delegate through the principal streets of the city to the site of the new seminary on Laurel Heights."[43] Of the original structure only the chapel remains. Daniel Withers detailed its interesting ceiling design:

The intricate pressed metal work on its ceiling has not been repainted since it was installed. Because the chapel's high ceiling was never exposed to a great deal of light, there has been very little discoloration of the paint. The ceiling has fifty-two pressed metal sectional rosettes, sometimes called circular panels, [which] are divided into eight "spokes" and are Gothic in design.[44]

A new Provincial House with long galleries, costing $15,000 in 1910, reputedly was "better supplied with bathrooms than any other building in the city." Nowhere else in town would one likely find a "sun bath room, which covers half the gravel roof, [and] is covered only by sections of glass, resembling a hot house. A ladder leads to this [addition] on the graveled roof, where the priests and fathers may walk in the evening hours when it is cool."[45] Subsequent additions included a major renovation in 1949 for which Phelps, Dewees and Simmons served as architects.[46]

José H. Cassiano, among the earliest residents on Main Avenue, first sought the cooling breezes of Laurel Heights for convalescence. He and Mrs. Cassiano built a home on the southwest corner of Main and Craig, where he lived at the time of his death in 1913. Named for a grandfather who fought for Texas independence under General Sam Houston, Cassiano owned several ranches and served as both county and city tax collector. It is not clear what happened to the original dwelling, but the "new residence of Mrs. Pauline Cassiano" at the same address, 2321 Main Avenue, appeared in a 1919 photograph much as it does today.[47]

On the corner to the north, Judge Winchester Kelso built his home in 1906, but it had a West Craig address. Later, in 1920, Winchester Kelso

Jr. built his at 2415 Main Avenue, next door to his father. Schoeppl and Hardie drew the plans. Patrons of La Fonda Restaurant can identify its description: "Concrete will be used for foundations, and the large front porch will have a cement surface. There will be a beautiful sun-parlor on the east side of the house, and a lovely screened sleeping gallery on the south." Less than two years later Dr. George N. Ricks purchased it for $9,100.[48]

Zoning had not become a factor, so in 1923 L. D. Gilmore built his new Laurel Heights Pharmacy on what became by 1926 such a flourishing commercial corner that a newspaper photo spread was captioned "Community Stores Aid Busy Housewives and Increase Home Property."

Only Laurel Heights Parmacy remains a landmark. Phelps and Dewees drew the plans, but nothing of the original facade can be seen due to renovation in recent years at 2604 Main Avenue.[49]

Two dwellings built in 1909 on this block are extant. "Superb" interior decorations in the eight-room home with a gallery off "every sleeping room" added to the attractiveness of 2616 Main Avenue, priced at $9,000 in 1909. When B. S. Clements sold his home to W. D. Hicks a decade later, the sale price had escalated to $11,250.[50]

Next door, at the corner of Magnolia, "handsome and attractive" 2620 Main was built in 1909 for Captain Walter T. C. Napier. Ten years later it sold to Dr. T. W. Robertson for $10,000.[51]

At 2807 Main is another area home probably built by S. A. Freeborn in 1921, the year he sold it to F. W. Lemburg. That year contractor Freeborn also built the New England salt box at 2911 Main Avenue for Edward Dwyer Jr.[52]

Two dwellings at 2811 and 2815 Main antedate the northward extension of the avenue. Elizabeth Horner and her brother, Louis H., provided later owner Farrell C. Tyson (2811 Main) with this information on the two nineteenth-century structures. The Tyson home is

built of rough lumber with the bark still on in some places. Blacksmith nails are used to put the building together. This house and the house next door (at the corner of Mulberry and Main) had been a school at one time. The school, Magnolia Hall, was located at the approximate corner of what is now Magnolia and Howard. This was supposedly a finishing school for girls.

In 1900 the building was split into sections and moved to their present locations at which time the Horner family moved into 2811. At a later date Main Avenue was extended out north and went in front of the two houses. This accounted for the small yards. They [the Horners] also told me that the house next door [2815] was exactly like mine in appearance until it was remodeled to look as it does today.[53]

"The Avenue of the Cattle Barons"
8. Kings Highway

Kings Highway—the Avenue of the Cattle Barons some called it—early on became the ultimate in palatial living. Thirty-five splendid homes face this broad avenue between San Pedro and McCullough. Ten of these are of pre–World War I vintage. Seven have been built since 1930. There were those who quipped that Kings Highway, more than a cattle barons' abode, was the Avenue of Bishops: Catholic (Archbishop Robert E. Lucey), Baptist (Dr. Perry Webb of the First Baptist Church) and Republican (Joe S. Sheldon, longtime chairman of the Bexar County Republican Party). Kings Highway became the city's most prestigious address after World War I, but 1917 advertisements still referred to it as part of Summit Place:

San Antonio's most delightful and uniformly built residential district. It is a community of palatial homes of many of the first citizens of San Antonio—a locality where broad avenues planted on either side with tropical plants and foliage, have invited the building of stately mansions which have given a high value to the property and serve as a guarantee that a still greater advance will be made in view of the high character of further improvements contemplated. Summit Place has the advantage of a high elevation above the center of the city, giving it a panoramic view of the beautiful hill scenery to the northwest and also an attractive view of the metropolis of Texas in the valley to the south.[1]

Architect Ralph H. Cameron drew the plans for oil and gas pioneer Fred A. Hornaday's spacious brick home at 101 East Kings Highway in 1929. Jim Chittim won the general construction contract at a figure of $41,455, while A. H. Shafter did the wiring for $890. Plumbing and heating expenses added to these costs. It remained the Hornaday home for more than a decade and was the residence of the O. Scott Pettys for more than thirty years. Petty, who headed his own geophysi-

cal engineering company, was also a leader in the Texas oil and gas industry. His longtime interest in large-scale ranching, moreover, would likewise qualify him as a cattle baron.[2]

Traditional Tudor design with solid brick walls at 102 East was selected by H. A. Reuter for Judge Robert Lee Ball in 1913. Renovations, familiar elsewhere in this historic district, included the conversion of the stables into a garage and the hayloft above into servants' quarters. During the tenure of the Houston C. Munsons, there were enlargements on the upper floor, and, later, bibliophiles Mary and Dr. Richard H. Eckhardt turned a terrace into a library.[3] Architect Reuter, just prior to designing Judge Ball's home, could see the completion of another of his handiworks next door at 114 East Kings Highway. This house was listed on the San Antonio Historic Survey (1972) as being in the Renaissance Revival style.[4]

Herbert L. Kokernot was described as "ruler of a kingdom embracing 260,000 acres in Brewster, Jeff Davis, and Pecos Counties." He boasted one of the most palatial townhouses of the cattle barons, designed in 1912 by H. A. Reuter. Kokernot lived at 114 East Kings Highway until 1920, when he sold his fourteen-room "mansion [which] has long been considered one of San Antonio's most beautiful residences" to attorney-oilman Harry H. Rogers of Tulsa for $100,000.

"Here's another home that oil has bought," according to the *Express*—this in a decade during which a number of Oklahoma oilmen found tax refuge in San Antonio. Both Kokernot and Rogers figured prominently in the business and civic life of San Antonio. Banking and religious activity occupied Kokernot's interests, even though "first

A doorway recessed behind a broken-pediment Palladian entryway is the focal point of the 1929 home built for oilman Fred A. Hornaday at 101 East Kings Highway (1929, Ralph H. Cameron, architect).

and last, H. L. Kokernot is a cattleman." Rogers's diverse investments involved cotton mills, a railway, and the Maverick-Clark Litho Company.[5] During World War II this magnificent home became known as the Bishop's Palace after it was occupied by Catholic Right Reverend Robert E. Lucey. Not until the late 1960s did it again become a private family home.

The Kokernot home served as the public's paradigm of grand living on Kings Highway at no time more than in 1917, when Elizabeth Kokernot reigned as Queen of the Order of the Alamo.

Honoring their daughter [Elizabeth Thekie, Queen of the Court of the Butterflies], Mr. and Mrs. Herbert Kokernot threw open their palatial residence in Summit Place last evening at a large reception and garden party following the ceremonies. The spacious lawn of the Kokernot home was converted into a veritable fairyland with myriads of vari-colored electric lights glistening in the trees. Over the entrance of the arched pillars was suspended a large amber-colored butterfly studded with lights of the same hue, and giving the first impression of the butterfly theme.

The music room in its exquisite color tone of blue and white was converted into the throne room. The white walls with panels of blue satin tapestry were softened with the rich blue velvet draperies over the lace curtains of the room. Twenty bracket lights around the sidewalks made brilliant the room which was further adorned in vases of Ophelia roses shading from pink to yellow. In her royal robe of golden sequins with her long velvet court train elaborately designed and trimmed in beaded butterflies, and her court jewels, of diamond and emerald, crown, collar, bracelets and scepter, Queen Elizabeth received the homage of her guests.[6]

Across the street at 119 East, brother John W. Kokernot's home, designed by Atlee Ayres, was completed during the winter of 1910–1911. John was also a leading cattleman, with ranches in the Alpine area, where he remained active even after he built his "miniature palace" in San Antonio.

The residence of John W. Kokernot on Kings Highway, Summit Place, just north of Laurel Heights, is one of the most expensive in the city. It is a two-story brick with basement and finished attic, with slate roof. The general style is colonial and Atlee B. Ayres, the architect, has taken advantage of the commanding site, with its view over the entire city, and erected truly a house beautiful.

There are five bedrooms and a sitting-room parlor, reception hall, living room, dining room, and conservatory. The lower floor is finished in oak with the exception of the parlor, which is finished in white enamel. All the floors are oak inlaid. The principal rooms have beam ceiling and panel wainscoting. One of the features of the house is the broad, gracious stairway, in the hall with the large circular glass windows on the stair landing. The two bathrooms have tile floors and tile wainscoting and are finished with porcelain fixtures.

The system of heating is hot water and is one of the most complete in this city. As an indicator of up-to-dateness in every respect, in this twentieth century home a vacuum system of cleaning has been installed, something by which the housekeeper is beginning to demand in San Antonio, and it is safe to say the great majority of the new homes in the future will have these labor-saving systems. The Kokernot residence has large, spacious galleries around the house on the outside, the floors of the galleries being covered with terrazo. The third story space is very large and can easily be arranged for a ballroom. One of the most complete garages has ample capacity for storing two cars and three carriages, and has also stalls for horses, room for laundry, a wood room, etc.[7]

Another renowned rancher resided at 125 East Kings Highway. David St. Clair Combs as a youth served during the Civil War in Terry's Texas Rangers and fought for the Confederacy in the Battle of Shiloh. Combs's residence, its plans by Carleton Adams, featured Southern colonial designs throughout: doors, transoms, side lights, stairs and fireplaces. Extensive use of white enamel paint gave expression to the colonial design. Constructed of brick over hollow tile, numerous columns add to the stately appearance. Moreover, "the cement terrace in front of the house is one of the

Built by West Texas cattle baron Herbert L. Kokernot, 114 East King's Highway (1912, H. A. Reuter, architect) was known as the Bishop's Palace in midcentury for being the official residence of Catholic Archbishop Robert E. Lucey.

few in San Antonio that properly harmonizes." Hardly a year after its completion, Mrs. Combs died. A daughter, Mrs. J. H. McGehee, kept the family residence intact for nearly fifty years.[8]

One of the most appealing homes in the Monte Vista Historic District is that owned for many years by Ike S. Kampmann Jr. at 131 East Kings Highway. Some of the attraction to this "masterpiece in stone" lies in its antecedent, the house of his grandfather, Herman D. Kampmann:

When the old Kampmann residence was torn down to make room for the present magnificent Scottish Rite Cathedral on Avenue E, the lintel over the front door was preserved and with the other stone taken from the old Kampmann home was carried to Kings Highway where it now graces the entrance to the new home of Ike S. Kampmann.

The old Kampmann home was erected in 1880. While it was under construction, a strolling Italian stone cutter came into San Antonio and applied for and secured the contract to do the carving on the entrance. The result was an extraordinarily beautiful and intricate piece of carving. With his work completed, the stranger shouldered his pack and departed and today his name is unknown but his labors have lived as another example of the artist unrewarded.[9]

Architect Henry T. Phelps designed this home, but attorney Ike S. Kampmann Sr. acted as his own contractor in 1921–22. Bay windows in the stone room—visible from the east—as well as the gazebo on the back, are a century old, as they, too, were transported from the downtown Kampmann homestead. Other materials from the old

The Beaux Artes home of cattleman John W. Kokernot, who built across Kings Highway from his brother Herbert, was built with a grand arched entrance and, indoors, a vacuum system for cleaning (1911, Atlee B. Ayres, architect).

home incorporated into the Kings Highway structure are much of the stone, floors and cabinets.[10]

Other construction in the immediate vicinity included the hollow tile and stucco home of Thomas E. Lyons (111 East), which C. B. Schoeppl designed and built in 1923.[11] For many years this was the parsonage of the First Baptist Church and its minister, Dr. Perry Webb. Two years after the Lyons home was built, the Kelwood Company, architects and builders, completed the Pleas J. McNeel home at 126 East Kings Highway. As Lola Kokernot, Mrs. McNeel had grown up in this block.

The house and garage had been planned to fit the contours of the lot without cutting the fine oak trees. It is of pure Spanish colonial design, the exterior done in Spanish stucco over hollow tile, with ornamental stone, wrought iron and a mission tile roof of varied colors. The interior has plastered walls and ceilings with oak and tile floors and stone mantels. The front entrance is an exact copy of a Spanish castle entrance. On the first floor will be the living room and dining rooms, main hall, service halls, butler's pantry, kitchen, maid's room and bath, with a porte cochere, loggia and private terrace. A stone wall encloses the lot on the south and east forming a charming patio. The second floor arrangement

includes four bedrooms, two sleeping porches and three bathrooms. The house will be heated with a hot air plant in the basement. Completed, it will cost approximately $15,000.[12]

The oldest home on Kings Highway (105 West), one of the few constructed when the Summit Place development first came into being, is that originally owned by Christopher H. Surkamp, general manager of the San Antonio Waterworks Company. Atlee Ayres designed this "most substantial and modern" home in 1907. White enamel interiors, so popular in this period, appeared in the bedrooms, parlor, and reception hall, which also had a dark red tinted finish. Seats flanked a large fireplace and the entry featured a "massive stairway." Heavy beams in the dining room finished in Flemish made this the "handsomest" of the eight rooms in this $15,000 dwelling.[13]

Most large homes in this area reflected such vestigial remains of the Victorian period as heavy furnishings and a closed-in feeling. Not so the residence Atlee Ayres designed for Robert N. Martindale at 108 West Kings Highway in 1914. This house would later be the home of Judge

Robert L. Bobbitt. Recently built bungalows carried out the new theme of "letting in the great outdoors," but Martindale's spacious home achieved this design more than other imposing residential structures. More recent owners, the Harry B. Jewetts, emphasized the architect's original idea of open space.[14]

Another distinctive residence next door (118 West) was completed the previous year. Later observers could see the Frank Lloyd Wright influence in the longtime home of Colonel and Mrs. (Zelime) Henry J. Amen, built originally for lumberman John J. Kuntz. "Specimen of Frank Lloyd Wright architecture. Drawn in offices of Atlee B. Ayres, architect," one photograph caption read.[15]

Spacious throughout, the flow of rooms on the first floor extended to the eastside gallery. Oak floors and mahogany wood finish added to the elegance of the interior. When Kuntz sold this twelve-room house to Frank A. Winerich in 1919 for $42,500, it was "the highest price ever paid for residential property in San Antonio." Turner Roofing Company reroofed the home in 1929 "with Dresden tile of the B. Miffin Hook Co., a texture tile of various soft red tones."[16]

The home at 123 West Kings Highway of onetime thirty-year resident Mrs. Charles A. (Ella) Holshouser, a founder of the Monte Vista Historical Association, is associated with that of the house next door. Rancher Thomas E. Burns built next to his mother, Mrs. Hugh Burns (115 West), in 1925. Adams and Adams provided the architectural plans and V. L. Rasmussen was general contractor on the son's two-story brick home at 123, which cost approximately $17,000.[17]

Mrs. Burns's "fireproof" home attracted more attention in 1914. When it caught fire in recent years, some attributed the minimal damage to its construction:

The erection of fireproof residences has been commenced in San Antonio. The latest of such character is the handsome home of Mrs. Hugh Burns on Kings Highway, Summit Place,

Spanish Colonial Revival ornamentation above the entrance highlights the facade of the home built for Pleas J. McNeel at 126 East Kings Highway (1925, Kelwood Company, architects).

which was completed recently. It was built at a cost of $30,000 and . . . designed by Reuter and Harrington, architects and engineers.

The Burns home is constructed on reinforced concrete and hollow tile throughout. It has a concrete frame and there is not an unnecessary stick of wood about the place. Of course, the concrete flooring is covered with wood, and wood has been used for the doors and window frames, but the architects say that the house could not burn. It is built according to standard specifications for fireproof construction.

The roof is of green glazed tile. Outside, the residence is finished in brick and stone. It has eleven rooms and is equipped with all modern conveniences, has a hot water heating system and is even supplied with a vacuum-cleaner plant.[18]

Architect Harvey Page followed classic Mediterranean lines in the palatial structure at 215 West Kings Highway, which commercial real estate man William F. Schutz's family called home for fifty years. C. Robert Daubert's restoration, in which he added the garden wall in 1976, updated this dramatic mansion. Interior designer Valda Cox subsequently acquired the property. Her distinctive touch was a successful blending of antique, oriental and contemporary furnishings. One can understand that a dwelling of such dimensions drew extraordinary attention in 1924:

The foundation of this building is reinforced concrete; the walls are of brick with white atlas stucco finish, with here and there a touch of art stone and wrought iron. The roof is of fire-flashed clay tile with copper cornice. The brick garage in

The Robert N. Martindale home at 108 West Kings Highway (1913, Atlee B. Ayres, architect), basically Tudor, features a Prairie style porte-cochere.

the rear has space for five cars and servant's quarters with three rooms and bath. With a frontage of 68 feet and a depth of 43, the house is most symmetrical in design, the spacious terrace with stone balustrade across the entire front giving it a gracious charm. This terrace is paved with mosaic tile, with an attractive fountain in art stone as its central feature.

The walls of the entrance hall are of Caen stone, with quaint groined ceilings and arches, and from it the broad stair of Italian oak and wrought iron ascends to the second floor. To the left of the hall, three steps lead downward to the stately living room with its recessed fireplace defining the character of the room.

The dining room on the right is the same level as the main hall. Fifteen by 24, its Venetian wainscot of oak rises to the height of the doors, with Venetian interlaced moulding ceiling in plaster. Attractive French windows open onto the terrace; while the French doors at the east end of the room point the way down three marble steps to the sunroom. The kitchen, store room, cloak room, and carriage entrance are on the north side of the house, and on the second floor are three large bedrooms, two baths, tiled according to the special design; den, sitting room, sewing and linen room.

All hardware on the second floor is of handwrought silver. The kitchen has a floor of mosaic tile, and many of the attractive built-in conveniences that make the modern home so desirable. Among these is the built-in refrigerator, which may be iced from the back gallery. The heating plant is located in the waterproof basement; and a laundry chute leads from the second floor to the basement. Generous closet space, mirror doors, all the thousand little niceties that would be expected in a house of this character emphasizes its charm.[19]

Alfred J. Ridder, "capitalist, landowner and pioneer cattleman," had Ralph H. Cameron design his two-story stucco home at 221 West in 1922. It featured a "concrete foundation, tile roof, oak

floors" and also plastering throughout. Other residents included Dr. Hesiquio Gonzalez and John F. Canty.[20]

Dr. and Mrs. Frederick J. Combe moved to 235 West Kings Highway from the original Jay Adams house on Belknap Place across from Christ Church. Combe, a Spanish-American War surgeon, sold the Kings Highway home to the Joseph H. Frosts following World War II. In 1958 ownership passed to the Joe Centenos, whose son and daughter also lived in the neighborhood. This became the home of an extended and closely knit family of four generations, at no time so characteristically as in August of that year, when longtime friends, neighbors and employees received invitations to participate in the celebration of the "Sesenta Aniversario de nuestra queridos padres, José Centeno y Jesusa Lopez de Centeno." By coincidence, this home was built in 1922, the same year in which the Centenos were married.[21]

The longtime home of William Bradford Bugg, at 224 West Kings Highway, was built in 1923 by real estate man R. A. Richey, maternal grandfather of former City Councilman Van Henry Archer, and sold to William B. Lupe in the mid-1920s. It remained in the Lupe family approximately fifty years. Carleton Adams did plans for this twelve-room residence "designed in Italian architecture and finished in creamy pink stucco with fire-flashed tile roof." Through the years, luxurious shrubbery has added to its attraction.[22]

Next door at 230 West Kings Highway one finds a colonial creation designed by architect Robert H. H. Hugman, best known for his efforts to beautify the river downtown. Builder Amye Bozarth, whose speculative ventures in fine homes could be found in other southern cities, sold this 1929 two-story structure of stone, tile and concrete to oilman T. Noah Smith. Few other residential properties of such dimensions sold for $45,000 locally after the stock market crash.[23]

Among the mid-1920s structures on Kings Highway, 234 West represented another project

"Specimen of Frank Lloyd Wright architecture" read the caption on a photo of the new Prairie-style home at 118 West Kings Highway (1913, Atlee B. Ayres, architect). George R. Willis, former head draftsman for Wright in Oak Park, Illinois, came to San Antonio for his health and was a draftsman for Atlee Ayres from 1911 to 1916.

of builder R. A. Richey. He sold it to hotelman Joe L. Nix, its first resident. Neighbors, however, associate this house with a family that occupied it for more than forty years. General Thomas H. Slavens purchased this home just prior to World War II, and it went to his son and daughter-in-law, Mr. and Mrs. (Jane) Stanley G. Slavens.[24] Of similar vintage is the large residence next door (238 West), its first occupant being Mrs. Alice T. Houston. Several families resided here through the years until the late 1960s, when it became the home of Congressman Henry B. Gonzalez.

C. B. Schoeppl and Company designed and built 302 West Kings Highway for Mrs. J. D. Houston in 1922. A tapestry brick finish and a clay tile roof with copper cornice gutters added to the appearance of this two-story home, which had a concrete basement. After attorney Josh H. Groce acquired the home, architect Bartlett Cocke drew plans for extensive remodeling in 1940.[25]

"Modernized Italian, which is so adaptable to this climate," was the design that Carleton Adams provided oilman Claude L. Witherspoon for his home at 305 West Kings Highway. Constructed of "concrete, hollow tile, and brick, [and] finished with cement stucco and artificial stone trimming," the home's tile floors downstairs and variegated tones of Spanish tile on the roof added to the

motif. During the 1960s this was the home of Federal Judge John H. Wood, whose later assassination shocked the country.[26]

Another Schoeppl-designed and built home (315 West), under construction at the same time as that of Mrs. Houston in 1922, featured a twenty-five-square-foot living room in which Edward N. Requa could display trophies from his hunts. Requa's previous home on West Summit likewise accommodated his hobby. "Simplicity of form, straight lines, and a delicate use of decorations gave an air of dignity to this home." Realtor Requa sold several of his homes in the neighborhood after a brief residence. Though there have been other tenants, for the past thirty years neighbors have known it as the Goggan-Kuntz home.[27]

At 322 West Kings Highway, J. E. Roos appears to have been first owner of this stately home, constructed about 1913. A decade later real estate investor Arthur H. Morton purchased it, and in 1926 he asked architect Richard Vander Stratten to plan "for remodeling and making a one-half story addition to his residence." E. W. Frischmuth was contractor.[28] It was the Kenneth A. Biedeger home for more than twenty years.

Classic colonial is the design architect John M. Marriott drew for Jesse Y. Womack's ten-room brick home at 330 West Kings Highway. Though

A spacious front terrace marks the home built for William Schutz at 215 West Kings Highway (1924, Harvey L. Page, architect).

the Womacks lived there only two years after its 1928 construction, the Henry C. Striblings' tenure ran some three decades, and that of Mr. and Mrs. (Margo) George A. Olson about fifteen years. John Westerhoff did the general contracting and W. E. Simpson and Co. the engineering. A slate roof added distinction to this stately home.[29]

John Westerhoff had also been the general contractor for the structure across the street at 331 West Kings Highway. The Joe S. Sheldon home of hollow tile and stucco followed the traditional Spanish style as drawn by architects Atlee and Robert Ayres. Turner Roofing Company proudly used this home in an advertisement. "The Sheldon home is of B. Miffin Hood Rough Texture, Riviera Vari-Colored Tile in soft tones. It has a pleasing gable roll finish and is an outstandingly beautiful and different roof."[30]

W. C. Thrailkill, "builder of fine homes," lived up to his reputation in construction of the Southern Colonial residence at 334 West Kings Highway in 1924. L. Harrington and Co. did architectural and engineering work on the $37,000 home for Charles S. Guilhem, president of Texas Cold Storage Company. Subsequent occupants included Tom Benson and the Oblate Fathers.[31]

Doubtless much of Summit Place's success had to do with property restrictions. Prospective homeowners, as Ike S. Kampmann did in his contract with the Summit Place Company, agreed to the following:

Provided, However, that, Whereas, Summit Place has been dedicated as an exclusive residential district, Now Therefore, for the purpose of so maintaining the same, the property herein described is conveyed under the following conditions and restrictions, which conditions and restrictions shall apply to and be binding on the grantee, herein, his heirs, devisees, executors, administrators and assigns, Namely:

That said premises shall be used for residence purposes only, and no part thereof shall be used for business purposes. That no apartment house, double house, flat, lodging house, hotel, nor any building for business purposes, or any structure whatever other than a first class private residence with the customary out-buildings, including private stables, garage and servants house, shall be erected, placed or permitted on such premises, or any part thereof.

That such residence shall cost and be fairly worth not less than Twenty Thousand Dollars ($20,000) and no part thereof, except the steps descending from the gallery or building, shall be located nearer than forty (40) feet from the curb line on the front of said premises, nor nearer than thirty feet (30) from the curb line of McCullough Avenue, and shall face the front line of said premises, to wit: on King's Highway. That no out-buildings or private stables shall be erected, placed or permitted on said premises at a distance of more than thirty (30) feet from the rear line of said premises.

That no fence or coping shall be erected on any lot outside of the proposed sidewalks, as shown by the recorded plat of said addition, and provided further, that the four-foot strip designated on the map of said addition as a sidewalk is dedicated to the public for such purposes, and the Summit Place Company reserves the right to build a sidewalk along said strip, as provided in said map.

That said property shall not at anytime be leased, sold, demised or conveyed to, or otherwise become the property of, any person other than one of Caucasian race. That all and each of the restrictions and conditions herein contained, shall in all respects terminate and end and be of no further effect...on or after January 1st. A.D., 1930.[32]

Building restrictions were extended in 1926 for thirty-five additional years. Also, in the future "only homes costing $30,000 or more may be built."[33]

"Architectural Diversity"
9. Gramercy, Elsmere and Belknap

While Kings Highway may be the most memorable of Monte Vista avenues, many people are especially attracted to Gramercy Place, with its large trees and architectural diversity. A majority of its homes date from the 1920s. Even though the stock market crash in the autumn of 1929 was followed by an economic depression, real estate sales agents noted a lively interest in Monte Vista homes the following spring.

Among those pursuing their residential plans, Mrs. Frost (Eloise Thomson) Woodhull and Dallas architect Henry B. Thompson, assisted by local associate Fred G. Gaubatz, drew plans for her home at 101 East Gramercy in 1930. The two-story brick of English design had nine rooms. Investment at that time, including the site, was estimated at $30,000. Contractor was D. F. Steele. Mrs. Woodhull, who formerly lived at 2317 North Main Avenue, resided for several years at the Gramercy address. For the next three decades, until 1970, it was the home of Mr. and Mrs. Walter Giesecke, and then that of the Dennis Neills.[1]

Monte Vista residents and their architects paid considerable attention to entryways. Newspapers sometimes featured articles with titles like the "Doorways of San Antonio." One noted entrance was that on the 1927 Richard Vander Stratten-designed $20,000 home for Theodore M. Plummer at 100 East Gramercy. John Westerhoff, the contractor, gained a widespread reputation for his stucco or brick over hollow tile structures. He also used reinforced concrete in many foundations, such as this brick with clay tile shingle roof.[2]

During the summer of 1928, "15 or 16 houses now under construction or just completed" in Monte Vista involved a building program of nearly $500,000. In July, "Allen F. Barnes, Jack Locke, and L. A. Casey . . . [had] just moved into their newly completed homes on [East] Gramercy Place."[3] E. B. Flowers occupied his the following month. The Barnes home, designed and built by Frost Carvel Co., remains a beauty spot at 107 East, the home of Angela and Al Notzon.

Situated in the midst of a grove of nine live oak trees, the home of Allen Barnes at 107 East Gramercy Avenue is a beauty spot of the Monte Vista section. The house is two stories, of Elizabethan type. Construction is of brick and stucco with hewed beams on the upper half. The roof is covered with green copperclad shingles. The home has nine rooms and three full tile baths. An attractive feature of the structure is the sun parlor. The floor of the parlor is of green and white tile, with walls of travertine stone. The ceiling is arched with green lattice work over which is growing vines. Star lighting system is used, carrying out the outdoor theme throughout. The garage and servant's quarters building is of the same construction as the house.[4]

The L. A. Casey home (106 East Gramercy), "another beautiful English-type structure," cost about $25,000 in 1928. Frank M. Edwards did the contract work for real estate man Casey.[5] Cattleman E. B. Flowers's home at 135 East also cost in the $25,000 range. Adams and Adams, architects, planned this nine-room brick home with a three-car garage, increasingly found in the neighborhood.[6] Richard Vander Stratten drew plans for the $25,000 Jack R. Locke residence at 138 East Gramercy, which received general praise.

Simplicity in architectural style accentuates the attractiveness of the Jack R. Locke home at East Gramercy Place. As can be seen in the picture above there are few "fancy lines" in the exterior of the building. A beautiful entrance of cut stone sets this general style off to the best advantage. The house is two stories high with stucco finish, with the Italian style of architecture followed.[7]

Rustic cobble brickwork adds graphic impact to the white stucco Tudor facade of 107 East Gramercy Place (1928, Frost Carvel Co., architects).

Elsewhere on the block, John M. Marriott designed and John Westerhoff built the D. L. Keiser home at 114 East Gramercy in 1925, but perhaps within a year it became the property of banker John L. Matthews. Architects John Richard Walker Jr. and Philip Carrington designed an extensive renovation in 1952. Landscape architect Terry M. Lewis redesigned the garden in 1981 for Colonel and Mrs. (Ann) Leonard H. Sims Jr.[8]

During 1924, Will N. Noonan planned Mrs. Beulah Brice's home at 115 East Gramercy, and lumberman Roy Campbell built his $20,000 at 121 East.[9] The 1920 Charles Katz home at 122 East is among the oldest Gramercy homes. Subsequent owners included Pleas McNeel and the Harry K. Hartleys.[10] Dr. and Mrs. J. W. Nixon's 1924 colonial home at 129 East Gramercy has always enjoyed an attractive setting. Designed by architect Beverly W. Spillman with G. W. Mitchell as contractor, it was the family home for six decades.[11]

Schoeppl and Company in 1923 designed and built the home at 130 East Gramercy. Hollow tile and stucco represent the major materials in this structure, built for the Randolph Carters.

The exterior is simple in treatment. The simplicity of the whole is broken by a few well placed ornaments and an ornamental entrance. Entrance is into a reception hall from where the living room is reached through large French doors.

In the living room is a mantel in keeping with the general scheme and French doors again lead into the dining room. There also is a large pantry and a comfortably arranged kitchen, as well as a breakfast room. The stairway is so placed in order to do away with the usual rear service stair. Upstairs are found two large bedrooms and a guest room, two bathrooms, a sleeping porch and a trunk room. There are exceptionally large closets in this house.[12]

After the stock market crash, Will N. Noonan designed the 1930 Spanish type at 135 East, with extensive terracing and landscaping. L. D. Middleton was contractor for this $40,000 house for its first owner, L. L. Stephenson.[13] Nearing McCullough are two large homes constructed in 1922, Charles T. Fincham's at 141 East and Jay E. Adams's on the corner (151 East). Carleton Adams designed his family home with a stone masonry wall.[14] Intermittent residents included the T. W. Menefees and J. O. Chapmans.

One of Monte Vista's stateliest homes, at 109 West Gramercy, was built for Bexar Petroleum Company President Clarence M. Hocker. Completed by contractor John Westerhoff in early 1929 and designed by Robert B. Kelly, the ten-room English-style home is of brick veneer and reinforced concrete and stone with a slate roof. The Donald Alexanders later built a garden wall and extensive additions. Mrs. Alexander lived here for some thirty years.[15]

Builder L. A. Casey lived in Monte Vista and did ventures in the area. One, 112 West Gramercy, was "carefully built and planned for a real home." Ten closets, an unusual number in 1928, storage and a playroom in the third-floor attic, a waterproof basement and "on the rear roof . . . a health-giving open-air sunbath" suggested an early sale, but the stock market crash came before it had an occupant, Mrs. A. P. Carroll.[16]

Of the four elegant homes in the Monte Vista Historic District by architect Russell Brown of Houston and Los Angeles, three have varying degrees of Spanish influence in their design. The one he did in 1928 for his niece and her husband, Louise and Rexford Cosby, is more traditionally American, brick with a New England influence. When owners Molly and Jim Branton planned to repaint the white brick at 125 West, removing the old paint revealed the original beautifully toned red brick. One of Brown's architectural assistants, named Ancira, did much of the detail work.[17]

Others of this vintage include the Logan L. Stephensons' at 135 West, their third in Monte Vista; they moved in early in 1930. Kelwood Company completed 117 West for the W. W. Woodworths in 1924.[18] Cattleman George Noah Evans in December 1925 was "just completing a $80,000 residence in [124 West] Gramercy Place, and during the past week purchased an additional 50-foot lot adjoining his homesite, making a total of 150 foot frontage."[19]

The 200 block of West Gramercy represents a singular development in 1926–1927, with lot sites at $54.50 per front foot. Gateways at Howard and Belknap even today delineate this project.

One of the most pretentious developments of its type ever undertaken was started this week on Gramercy Place by the Sam C. Bennett Company when they initiated improvements and construction that will cost more than $300,000. The property is on Gramercy between Belknap and Howard and comprises two blocks of choice frontage. The tract is to be laid out in 14 home sites with massive ornamental gates leading into the court from Belknap and Howard.

This is the first time in the history of San Antonio that a piece of property is to be developed along modern scientific lines by a group of specialists. Laying as it does in the heart of the more exclusive residential section of the city, it is planned to make it one of the real show places of San Antonio. Working with Gerald Melliff, lumberman, the Bennett Company has employed Harvey P. Smith, San Antonio architect, to plan the entire development. The W. E. Simpson Company has been employed as consulting engineers for all foundations and reinforced concrete work in the development of the "addition." The landscaping will be carried out under the supervision of a competent landscape artist.[20]

Twelve houses, actually, were built on the block, the first at the Belknap corner (226 and 227) open to the public on August 15, 1926. At the outset it was determined that architect Smith would follow colonial designs, which he did in these two, offered at $27,500 each. Specifications in his papers indicate building costs of 226 were $17,500—3,312 square feet at $5.28 1/4. At what became the Herman Gieseoke home on the north corner at 227, "entering the living room from the flagged gallery the downstairs has a den and a solarium as well as kitchen, pantries, and service porch. The upstairs has four bedrooms, two baths and a large center hall."[21]

Costs were the same as at 226, but this smaller home at 2,932 square feet resulted in $5.95 1/2 per square foot.[22] Smith's plans for 226, to be the Sylvan Lang home, won second place (to Robert M. Ayres's own home on Laurel Heights Place) in the 1926 residential design awards of the West Texas Chapter, American Institute of Architects.[23]

Smith did not design all homes on this block as planned, nor were all of colonial design. Edmond M. Notzon of San Antonio Building Materials offered the John Westerhoff–built 209 West Gramercy

Patterned brick work distinguishes the Tudor home built for oilman Clarence Hocker at 109 West Gramercy Place (1929, Robert B. Kelly, architect).

Gateways built in 1926 continue to define each end of the 200 block of West Gramercy Place.

for sale in October 1927, but this "beautiful stucco" was Notzon's home for a few years.[24]

Notzon apparently had earlier built and lived briefly across the street, in 210 West. John Westerhoff was the contractor. The Frank Pancoasts moved in before the end of 1927 and resided there for more than forty years. At 219 West Gramercy, Glenn C. Wilson employed a "French type of architecture" for the Charles Roos Jr. home in 1929. Mitchell Construction Company was contractor for this two-story brick veneer.[25]

At 204 West Gramercy, the Herman Richter mission-style home likewise did not follow the original colonial concept for this block. This $30,000 structure for the general manager of Richter's Bakery used tile, concrete and stucco.[26]

Homes on the 300 block of West Gramercy tended to be less pretentious, but the "modern stucco" residence of Reo Motor Company manager W. P. Bates at 302 West represented "an investment of more than $16,000" in 1927.[27] Another commodious home was completed at the opposite end of the block at 343 West for Mrs. R. A. Grant in late 1921.[28] Alfred P. Ward, who managed his family's estate, acquired this home within a short time. More modest homes included those of Charles F. Dwyer at 323 West, which dates from 1921, when it was featured in a *Light* photographic spread, and that of artist Herbert Barnard at 310 West, purchased in 1925 by M. L. Kirby.[29] Perhaps a dozen other homes on this block were constructed by 1924.

Elsmere Place was a product of the 1922–25 building boom, when construction of most of its fine homes took place. Some of the city's best

contractors and architects were represented, but the "lady of the house," Mrs. Martin Wright, designed one of the most publicized projects in 1923, 104 East Elsmere. "New Wright Home Has Almost Every Electrical Feature" ran the *Light* headline of December 30, 1923, appropriately enough since it was occupied by one of the city's leading electrical contractors. It had a swimming pool, allegedly the first in Monte Vista, and was later home of the family of Dr. Charles J. Thuss.

Imagine a home with almost every convenience known in the modern home. Visualize its electrical contrivances which include practically everything in this line known to the modern dwelling, and its steam-heated garage in the basement, the large swimming pool in the back yard, a roof garden, some of the most elaborate fixtures available and a fireplace that takes up almost one entire side of an unusually spacious living room. Such a home as this is being occupied by Martin Wright, his wife and daughter. It is considerably better than this, however, for its grandeur can hardly be described in few words. It was built by the San Antonio Development Company at 104 Elsmere Place in Monte Vista.

Using ideas from the Spanish-Italian style of architecture, Mrs. Wright designed and planned the house . . . With hollow tile, stucco, concrete and cement, the San Antonio Development Company, with Mrs. Wright supervising, has completed the construction of a wonderfully arranged building. Its interior as well as exterior decorating features are pleasing as they give that atmosphere of welcome, which places the guest at ease immediately upon entering this exquisite home . . . The outstanding feature of this home, with all apologies to Mrs. Wright's expert planning, is the electrical equipment . . . However, most of the electrical appliances and contrivances were installed at the order of Mrs. Wright. Hand-wrought floor lamps, chandeliers, boudoir lamps, shades and other attractive creations may be found in practically every room.

On the roof garden different colored lights have been arranged around the sides of the dance floor. Lights have also

Yet another distinctive doorway provides the focal point of 142 East Elsmere Place (1923, Adams & Adams, architects), built, like many of the finest Monte Vista homes, by general contractor John Westerhoff.

been placed in the floor of the swimming pool which doubtless will give a most attractive effect . . . A master switch installed in one of the bedrooms controls the entire lighting system of the house. Another switch controls the lighting of the grounds . . . The basement of the house is a real feature in itself. It has servants' quarters, a garage which is steam heated and which will accommodate four cars, a wash room, a furnace room and a large den. The den, which is Mr. Wright's private room, is decorated with various hides of wild game killed by the owner.

The living room of the house probably is the most attractive. Entering from a small ante-room directly inside of the front door, one's gaze is first centered on a massive stone fireplace—one of those that monopolizes the interest of the occupants of the home during cold weather. It is unusually attractive. It takes up the largest part of one side of the large living room. Built with rough stone, its antique appearance lends charm to the entire main floor of the house. It is the distinctive feature of the main floor although the furnishings are elaborate and the decorating is wonderful. Bedrooms, a long and well-arranged sleeping porch, kitchen, dining room, and solarium are on the main floor in addition to the large living room. A Spanish patio court in the rear and on the east side of the house around which a high white stucco wall has been built, is the feature of the grounds.[30]

Elsmere Place East was a busy scene in the mid-1920s.[31] Kelwood Company was doing the 115 East $35,000 home of builder Augustus G. Dugger, who had a longtime association with Kelwood Company architect Robert Kelly, the choice in 1924 for this spacious tile and stucco home with a four-room basement. Additions included a wall-enclosed garden and swimming pool.[32]

C. B. Schoeppl & Co. completed another distinctive home at 124 East Elsmere for Dr. and Mrs. J. L. Felder in 1923. It became the home of Wallace Rogers, one of Monte Vista's two founders, and later of the Charles H. Jacksons.

The house is of stucco with a Spanish tile roof, the structure being of brick. Entrance is had into a roomy reception hall, from where the living room is entered. Off the living room is the dining room and accessible from both is a spacious sun parlor. This plan embodies an excellent up-to-date kitchen arrangement with an unusually large butler pantry and a large breakfast room opening from the dining room and kitchen. There is a side entrance and service hall leading to every room in the first floor. On the second floor are three family bedrooms, a guest room, two sleeping porches and three baths, with more than usual amount of closet and storage space, while the attic is also arranged with a stairway for storage. Altogether, this home is one of the best in plan and design of any home in recent construction.[33]

Of colonial design in brick veneer, oilman Henry A. Pagenkopf's slate roof residence at 138 East Elsmere added beauty to the street in 1928. John M. Marriott, assisted by Roy W. Leibsle, did the ten-room structure along with one of Monte Vista's finest builders, John Westerhoff.[34]

Another superior Westerhoff home, designed by Adams and Adams in 1923 at 142 East Elsmere, was for developer Wallace Rogers. Within a year, however, broker Morris R. Volck moved in. Mrs. Volck was just back from a year abroad where she was presented at the Court of St. James.[35] Of "Spanish with a variation of Italian" design, it was of stucco on brick with clay tile roof.[36]

Across the street, Dr. A. F. Cook's two-story house of hollow tile and stucco (145 East) had Phelps and Dewees as architect and general contractor B. R. Heath in 1925.[37] Construction executive A. J. McKenzie's large home at the corner of McCul-lough (151 East) conformed to a similar pattern in 1922.[38] The expensive bungalow at 148 East followed a wholly different motif in 1923:

Old English motif enters into this new home. Another new home in the $20,000 class has been added to the attractive and exclusive Monte Vista. It is an English cottage that has recently been completed for R. B. Cherry at McCullough and Elsmere Avenues. The architecture indicates the tendency of home builders to select a historic style of planning and shows that old English is quite as adaptable to San Antonio as the Spanish and Italian which have been more commonly used. This home is built of dark fire flash brick with English tile roof. Adams and Adams are the architects.[39]

West Elsmere appeared to be the domain of the Kelwood Company, architect/builder of more homes than any other one firm, but several reflected the efforts of Robert McGarraugh. Others might be represented by a single dwelling. "Spanish colonial, always a favorite with homemakers in San Antonio," is found in three mid-1920s West Elsmere Kelwood structures. The John Anthony home at 103, with high ceilings in the living area, was stucco over hollow tile.[40] At 231, another spacious bungalow, which became occupied by the Leo Ehstroms, followed similar lines.[41]

The most expensive of the three, 241 became the home of attorney Fred W. Frost. "Typically

Spanish in its impressive exterior, . . . the interior is also carried out in the same appropriate manner." Vaulted ceilings, garden walls, wrought iron archways, a patio and fountain, Moorish stenciling on the parlor doorway and a patio with a fountain emphasized the Spanish theme. Distinguished by a roof of unglazed Mission tile built on different levels, the house featured parapets and gables not commonly found hereabouts.[42]

Harvey C. Wood of Chicago in 1921 began two "modern California bungalows" at 311 and 315 West.[43] Wood and architect Robert Kelly became principals in the Kelwood Corporation. One of its most successful ventures was, in 1926, 230 West, later purchased by the Charles D. F. Ladds:

More like a fashionable reception than an inspection of houses and their furnishings, opening of the House Beautiful Exhibit sponsored by the San Antonio *Express* and *Evening News* . . . became a social event when whole groups of friends found themselves in the same room admiring the furniture, draperies, and rugs. . . . At one time on Sunday afternoon 142 limousines, sedans, and expensive touring cars were parked on Elsmere Avenue near Home No. 1 [230 West]. . . . This home built by the Kelwood Company and furnished throughout by the Stowers Furniture Company was the center of attraction for visitors estimated at over $12,900. The home on Elsmere is valued at $29,000. It is English in style, typical of many of the old cottages to be found in rural districts of England, still with the modern conveniences and arrangement of light and ventilation.[44]

Robert McGarraugh entered the Elsmere market in 1928 and 1929 with several homes on West Elsmere—210, 217, 219, and 220. For 210 he selected "Italianate"; local architects had yet to use the term "Mediterranean." Along with the expansive English rock structure next door (220), it opened to the public in October 1928. At a later showing, visitors found the Thornton Shop's "draperies, furnishings, ornaments and pictures" and paintings of Miss Katherine McIntyre, "whose work was shown this year at the Paris Exposition." Prior residents included J. D. Rockafellow, the E. P. McMahons and, for more than three decades after 1948, the Alvin C. Hopes.[45]

The two-story English stone at 217 East, of "everlasting beauty that embodies the comforts, plus every thoughtfulness, by the master builder of homes," had a "combination solarium, music room, and living room, reached from the main entrance hall." Comfort and convenience marked the floor plan downstairs, while upstairs bedrooms had the feature most desired before air condition-

Italian Renaissance and Georgian styles were combined in 1301 Belknap Place (1920, Ralph H. Cameron, architect).

ing—southeast exposure. A den, connected by a hall to the master bedroom, "is large enough to accommodate a table for billiards or cards." Mrs. Kathryn Johnson purchased the home in 1929 for $22,000 cash, prior to the stock market crash.[46]

"Inspired by the Spanish type of design," the 1923 Mr. and Mrs. Glen H. Alvey home at 342 West Elsmere had innovative use of floor space:

The Alvey home reveals the departure from the commonplace. Featured in the design is the entrance porch with its decorated window and wrought iron grille work. Entrance is made into the living room from the porch. In the center of one wall of this room is a beautiful mantel. . . The plan calls for an attractive breakfast nook. There are two large bedrooms with ample closet space, a trunk closet and a room bath. There is only one small passage hall between the two bedrooms, thus utilizing all available space within the main walls of the house. There is also a glassed-in sleeping porch. C. B. Schoeppl & Company are the architects.[47]

Although few homes faced Belknap Place, three fine ones appeared on the Agarita, Summit, and Elsmere corners. E. A. Herff and Company designed and superintended construction of the 1923 Bruno F. Dittmar home at 1201 Belknap.

B. F. Dittmar's newly constructed home at the corner of Belknap Place and Agarita Avenue probably is one of the most beautiful homes in the northern part of San Antonio. It is of an Italian type of architecture and is constructed with brick and stucco. The home has eight rooms in addition to an attractive breakfast room, a large sleeping porch, three bath-

rooms equipped with showers and specially arranged dressing rooms. The baths represent the latest in modern plumbing ideas.

The kitchen is finished in white enamel. It has a McCray refrigerator which is built in between the dining room and kitchen. It can be iced from the exterior of the house. The inside walls of the home are plastered and decorated in café aux lait color. The garage has adequate space for two cars and servant's quarters. It also has a large basement containing space for laundry, heating and storage rooms. The grounds have been laid out by an expert landscape architect.[48]

A block north, at 1301, William S. Seng announced plans for his home in the late summer of 1920. Architect Ralph H. Cameron did an "adaptation of the Georgian style, with a little of the Italian influence." Red brick, white trimmings, a variegated green tile roof and a white stone entrance made for distinction, as did a terraced lawn "with red brick pavements, harmonizing with the color of the house." Dr. Witten B. Russ bought it for $40,000 in 1924. It remained the Russ home for forty years.[49] Dr. and Mrs. Larry Cohen made extensive and appropriate renovations.

The steep roof and half timbers of the expansive cottage at 1601 Belknap are of English-style design. Built in 1924 for the Kelwood Company's H. C. Wood, the Porter Lorings purchased it in 1926. "The white plaster walls are in effective contrast to the dark tone of the blinds and window casings, with which the shingle roof is in pleasing harmony."[50]

"High Class and Substantial"

10. Lynwood and Hollywood

In keeping with her history, San Antonio home builders have adapted Moorish and Spanish Colonial architecture, the Italian types predominating with, of course, the usual amount of English, American, Colonial, French and Dutch Colonial intermingling. Tiled roofs against white walls are often seen and mission arches are popular over doorways and for windows.[1]

This statement succinctly described the homes along Lynwood and Hollywood. No other developing San Antonio areas in the mid-1920s, moreover, were being compared to the famous Country Club District of Kansas City, which served as a model for Rogers and Hill in Monte Vista.[2] Prospects of residing among "high class and substantial homes" attracted Harry J. Benson and others to these two "boulevards."[3] Of the two, only Lynwood could properly be described as boulevard width. Restrictions on Lynwood were similar to those on Kings Highway—100-foot lots minimum, no businesses, Caucasians only—although minimum building costs were somewhat lower at $15,000.[4]

Homes on Lynwood generally exceeded the minimum, as in the $20,000 English-style residence of Mannie Goldsmith at 106 East. Frost Carvel Company, in 1926, served as architect/builder of this two-story brick house with ten rooms.[5]

Still one of Monte Vista's most intriguing residential designs, Mr. and Mrs. Everett Love's 112 East Lynwood, remained in the planning state for nearly two years before construction began.[6] Molly and Jim Branton's restoration in 1986–87 required a similar period of time.

Construction has been started [1922] on the home of Mr. and Mrs. Everett Love in Monte Vista. It is located on a large site on Lynwood Boulevard, having a frontage of 175 feet. The design . . . is Italian, and was prepared by Adams & Adams,

Adams, architects. "Villa Amore" is the name that will be given the new home.

The exterior will be built of concrete and hollow tile and will be finished in pink-toned cement, with cast stone trimmings, and with contrasting grilles, gutters and entrance hood of wrought iron. The broad roof will be of variegated color tile and the terraces and steps will be of red quarry tile. Evergreen shrubs and flowers will be banked against the walls and a wide garden lawn will extend across the east front of the property. The main level of the floor is six feet above the lot, which is also terraced above the street.

The entrance doors open into a hall and the opening to the right are those of the reception room and dining room. There is a spacious living room, a den and loggia or sun room, it being into this sun room that the five arched windows enter. There is also a large breakfast room, kitchen, a separate dining alcove for the help, pantries, three bedrooms, bathrooms, dressing rooms, stair hall all on the main floor. Below are service rooms and above is a large glassed-in room or sleeping porch with connecting bath and closet space.

The terrace and several of the rooms will have tile floors, including the loggia, which will also have a grained vaulted ceiling. The living room will have an Italian beamed and wood paneled ceiling, and the dining room walnut panel walls to the ceiling. The owner's bedroom and the other rooms will have plastered cornices and similar details. The main rooms will have cast stone mantels of proper Italian period design. All of the main rooms will be finished with hardwood floors, except where tile is used. There will be a hot water system of the most modern selection. A vacuum cleaner and private refrigerating system will be installed. The garage also will be of similar stucco finish with tile and stone trimmings, and will have space for three cars as well as servants' rooms and bath. James Aiken is the contractor.[7]

Simultaneous construction in 1928 of two homes across the street by Houston- and California-based Russell Brown added to Lynwood's distinctiveness. Cattleman Herbert L. Kokernot was leaving his Kings Highway mansion for a smaller home, but the 102-foot-by-71-foot 115 East Lynwood hardly suggested an austerity move.

Spanish-style Solomonic corkscrew columns with massive finials and scrolling treat the entrance to 115 East Lynwood Avenue (1928, Russell Brown, architect) as furniture.

Russell Brown designed this outstanding home, constructed at a cost of some $75,000, in the Italian style. Hot air, gas heat, and a basement, as well as servants' quarters, could be found. Modern features of the day were hardly the prime attraction, however, for visitors still admire the dramatic effect of its grand staircase ascending from the spacious entry hall. Subsequent owners included Mayor and Mrs. J. Edwin Kuykendall and, more recently, Mr. and Mrs. Gus N. Van Steenberg, she (Virginia) being the first president of the Monte Vista Historical Association.[8]

That there was simultaneous construction next door designed by the same architect should not be surprising, as it was the home of the Kokernot daughter. Mistress of 127 East Lynwood was Mrs. Gunter Hardie, the former Elizabeth Kokernot, Queen of the Order of the Alamo in 1917. While this residence contained many features found in that of her parents, construction costs were considerably less—$50,000. Although of different design—the Hardie home being Spanish style and featuring interior work reminiscent of

the sixteenth century—the two commanding structures complemented one another.[9]

Elsewhere on East Lynwood, the Kelwood Company designed 130 in 1927 for Dr. J. L. Felder. Lumber and materials for this two-story came from the Hillyer-Deutsch-Jarratt Company. "The home will be of Stone-Tile and will cost about $30,000."[10] Other homes on this block, such as those of the Randolph Carter (146 East, 1948) and Charles Toudouze (150 East, 1968) families, are of more recent vintage.

"Whatever your taste in homes might be, you will be astonished at the innate beauty and true conformity to type as expressed in this recently completed example of the quaint old English architecture." So ran a large advertisement in the *Express* on February 8, 1925, when the public might view "this typical English manor house of exceptional beauty" at 110 West Lynwood. Pathologist Dr. Beecher F. Stout purchased the home for his family, who lived there for nearly four decades. After that it was the home of Mr. and Mrs. (Rosalie Richter) Clifton Bolner, descendants of nineteenth-century San Antonio families.

A typical English home has been built at 110 West Lynwood Boulevard, in Monte Vista, by Kelwood Company and is open for inspection. This house is constructed of stone, brick, stucco, and half timber. It has been treated to make the house appear old and weathered. The random brick walls, set at all angles, with stone interjected, make the house look more like homes in Old England. The roof is covered with random-laid shingles, carrying out the style. All valleys are laid with curved shingles instead of tin, giving a thatched appearance. The English design is also carried out in the interior. Hand-hewn beams and ceilings are in the hall.

A spacious living room with an Old English stone fireplace adds attractiveness to the interior. A library is to the right of the hall. The kitchen includes several built-in features, such as a stove hood and automatic refrigerator. The basement contains servant rooms, bathroom and laundry. Servants' stairs also connect the kitchen with the second floor. There are three bedrooms, a glassed-in sleeping porch and baths on the second floor. One of the features of the house is that every room can be reached through halls.[11]

Another distinctive home at 111 West Lynwood, built later than the confines of this volume, should be recorded. Architectural plans by Ayres and Ayres (1939) for Mr. and Mrs. Fred Strauss as well as the addition to the servants' quarters (1953) for Mr. and Mrs. Jeff Roe are in the archives of the University of Texas School of Architecture.[12]

San Antonio's abundant sunlight added patterns to the Spanish Colonial Revival facade of the newly completed David J. Straus home at 315 West Lynwood Avenue (1923, Ayres & Ayres, architects).

A 1925 "modernized Spanish renaissance" Carleton Adams "$75,000 or more" brick and stucco home for Mrs. Mary A. Stowers at 131 West Lynwood enjoyed a 300-foot frontage:

The walls of the residence are of concrete and brick, and will be finished with buff cement stucco, trimmed with cream colored stone. The roof will be of variegated shades of Spanish tile. Contrasting against the light toned walls will be red quarry tile floors, wrought iron grilles, and railings, as well as evergreen shrubs and flowers. Between the residence and pool will be a sunken rose garden. There will also be an informal garden and terrace in the angle sheltered by the building . . . The front entrance leads into a reception hall with circular marble stairs. The living room and sun room are on the right of the hall, and at a lower level. The dining room, kitchen, and service rooms are on the left. The breakfast room is opposite the entrance . . . The second story includes a large room for dancing and entertaining; as well as four bedrooms, baths, dressing rooms, etc. A unique feature is a large all-tile bath, instead of the usual enamel or porcelain tub.[13]

Two later designs by Fred Gaubatz are the homes of Mr. and Mrs. (Edna) Van Henry Archer Jr. (1935) at 218 West Lynwood and the Harris K. Oppenheimers (1938) at 230 West. At 201 West is the Austin cut-stone home (1951) of Imelda and the late Lawrence Deason by the Frost Carvel Company.[14] Merchant Abe Kaufman's J. C. Windner-built home (215 West, 1926) was in a photo spread on the city's "Beautiful Homes."[15]

Residential construction on Lynwood began in 1920 after Ralph H. Cameron designed the $60,000 structure at 241 West for Mr. and Mrs. Lee B. James, formerly of Kansas City. It was later the home of Edythe and Tom Toudouze, who was a past president of the Monte Vista Association. John Westerhoff served as contractor.

The house will be constructed of hollow tile and stucco, the stucco being given a pinkish tint resembling the better known Italian villas, and will be crowned with a fire flashed, red tile roof. The entrance loggias on either side of a wide terrace are practically square, and each side of the loggias have an arch with columns fashioned after that of the entrance to the Villa Medici on the outskirts of Rome.

The entrance loggia leads into the reception hall, at the end of which there is a doorway into the sidehall. This hall also contains a stairway harking back to the colonial period and a doorway into the living room, which extends across the south side of the house with three French doors opening onto the terrace.

The living room is finished with a plastered wall and a vaulted ceiling of ornamental design which will lend distinction to the room. In the center of the room on the north side is a fireplace, and on the east side is an entrance into the dining room, which is finished in paneled walls and plaster cove ceilings. Adjoining the dining room is the breakfast room, which will be used also as a serving room on occasions. The kitchen is a model of convenience with its range and hood concealed and china closets and sink combined. . .

On the west side is a porte cochere which connects with the side hall, and from the hall there are entrances to the lavatory and to the basement as well as to the reception hall, kitchen and breakfast room . . . In the basement will be located a den finished in pine stained fumed oak with an artistic mantel of tile with a copper hood with hand-made studs. Adjoining the den is a small gymnasium with shower

A vaulted ornamental plastered ceiling supported by walls finished in cast stone marks the just finished reception hall of the David Straus home on Monte Vista's West Lynwood Avenue.

bath. There is also in the basement a large furnace room and coal bin and coal will be dumped into the bin from the north side. All floors of the first story will be of quartered-white oak with an oak floor in the kitchen. On all porches will be red rectangular quarry tile laid up in herringbone fashion. . . .

Between house and garage at the rear of the house will be a large paved court where cars may be washed and moved around and where coal trucks can easily maneuver and will also serve as a laundry yard. The garage will be of the same character as the house with pony stall, laundry, and garage for two cars on first floor and two servants' rooms and bath on the second floor.[16]

Dr. and Mrs. Thomas J. Walthall were among the early residents on Lynwood. Pleased with their Adams and Adams–designed home at 242 West, Walthall wrote a testimonial in a Rogers-Hill advertisement: "I believe Monte Vista will grow more beautiful and more inviting every year." Described as "a handsome two-story brick, one of the stateliest homes on the hill," it remained in the Walthall family. Construction costs were $65,000 in 1923.[17]

Another home on the grand scale, designed by Ayres and Ayres for D. J. Straus in 1923, was the stucco over hollow tile at 315 West Lynwood:

The first floor will contain a reception hall, which is in the center of the house and on the east side will be a living room and palm room. On the west side of the dining room, pantry, kitchen and service porch and storerooms. The second floor will contain the owner's bedroom, which will be placed over the living room with its private bath and shower. Guests' room with the private bath will be placed over the entrance hall with an additional bedroom adjoining. The servant's room and bath is placed over the kitchen. Two sleeping porches will be provided. There is a tile-floored terrace across the front of the residence and a loggia terrace on the east side which connects with the living room.

The reception hall is to be finished with a black and white marble floor and walls to be finished in cast stone with a vaulted ornamental plastered ceiling. The living room will...have paneled walls and ornamental plastered ceiling. On the north side of the living room is placed the palm room. It is entered through a large arch. The palm room will be semi-circular and will have a fountain at one end. The ceiling is to be arched and the walls treated with lattice work and the floors will be of tile in attractive color designs. The dining room is to be paneled and will have ornamental plaster cornices and ceilings. There is to be a rear entrance to the house, which will connect to the main stairway. This entrance will be one of the most attractive features. All bathrooms are to be finished with tile wainscoting and tile floors will be equipped with special design fixtures. . . . The house is to be heated with vapor steam system of heating, which will also supply the heat for the garage. The garage . . . will contain spaces for three cars and three servants' rooms with baths.[18]

Still another of the great houses on Lynwood was of Carleton Adams design. The terraced landscaping with 300-foot frontage was a promising site for the Charles Baumberger home at 325 West in 1929:

Both living room and music room are wings of a story and a half. There also is a wing to house the service portion of the residence, including garage. Walls are constructed of concrete, brick and cast stone, finished in white concrete. Terraces and steps are in brilliant Spanish tile, and the roof is variegated tile. When the walls are banked with evergreens and flowers, the variety of color will be a distinct asset to the house. Ceilings in the first floor are of cove or vaulted construction. Upstairs there are four bedrooms and four baths, an enclosed sleeping porch, closets, store rooms, and other service departments.

The rooms are finished in toned and textured paints. The home service portion of the house is also completely finished. The kitchen has a high tile of wainscot in green with a cap band displaying bright red spots. Equipment includes two electric refrigerators, electric dishwasher, silver and kitchen pantry sinks, built-in cabinets, tile range hood and exhaust fan.[19]

Paralleling Lynwood one block to the north, Hollywood did not boast such grand houses. Even so, it appeals to those driving along the street. "Hollywood Boulevard was designed by both nature and man to fulfill your dreams of a perfect location for your home,"[20] ran one of the many advertisements in the spring of 1922. But two years passed before sales and building tempo would gladden the hearts of developers. In October of 1924, twelve of seventeen homes under construction in Monte Vista were on Hollywood.[21]

At 103 East Hollywood, a two-story frame structure of colonial design built in 1925 apparently briefly had Dr. R. R. Lewis as a tenant. The Milford C. Yates family resided there from 1925 to 1961, when Mr. and Mrs. (Dorothea) Paul R. Busch purchased the home.[22]

San Antonio Baseball President Harry J. Benson was one of the first residents on Hollywood, purchasing 110 East in 1922. Rogers and Hill counted him among the growing number of residents willing to make public testimonials in behalf of the neighborhood. "A glance at the number of high-class and substantial homes," Benson declared in his tribute to the area, "will convince you that Monte Vista . . . is today [1924] the most desirable residence addition to San Antonio."[23]

A distinctive home dated later (1936) than others in this volume is the Albert F. Sayers family's at 118 East Hollywood. Seven technical drawings of this structure are in the Atlee B. and Robert M. Ayres collection at the University of Texas School of Architecture.[24]

San Antonio Broom Company President Otto L. Fortman and his family moved into the $18,000 Dutch colonial at 138 East Hollywood in 1925, designed and built by Will N. Noonan. Effective walnut trim throughout is highlighted by intricate handwork on the banister.[25]

Among the numerous homes under construction in 1924 was that of one of Monte Vista's founders. "The contract will be let shortly for the construction of Russell C. Hill's $15,000 home [123 East] on Hollywood, a one-story dwelling of an English type."[26] O. W. Stapleton's $8,000 home across the street (126 East) was built at the same time.[27] Next door to the Stapleton residence, "unusual originality" marked the design at 122 East:

The home at 122 East Hollywood, purchased last week [1924] by George Loven, possesses unusual originality and gracefulness of line. The house is designed after the Italian style of architecture. It has walls of cream-colored shingles which turn into a soft greenish gray. The porch is tiled in a soft rich red which adds its share of color and interest to the exterior of the house. The porte cochere and driveway to the east of the house and the stucco gateway which leads to the side garden at the west, do much to add to the Italian atmosphere of the place. The interior, which includes eight rooms, is well planned, and boasts of the most modern of sleeping porches and a breakfast room. The house was purchased for a consideration of $15,000.[28]

In 1947 Henry Dielmann drew the plans for the solid rock structure at 154 East. One of the more distinguishable homes in Monte Vista, at 314 East Hollywood, is a modern brick, wood and glass design by architect Joe Carroll Williams.

Conquest

NOW, more than four centuries after the Spanish discovery of America, the architects of America have discovered Spain and have captured the "charm that was Spain's."

Spanish architecture has flourished. Unique and artistic examples of the "Spanish Influence" contrast the deep shadow of their Moorish arches against San Antonio's brilliant sunshine with a forceful beauty which is more exotic than the originals of Spain's enchanting architecture.

There are three charming cottages on Hollywood Boulevard, in Monte Vista Addition, nearing completion which are an ingenious portrayal of the best in architecture from the shores of the Mediterranean.

Built by

Carvel & Company

"Builders of Beautiful HOMES"

301-2 Frost Nat'l Bank Bldg.   Crockett 8137

By the mid-1920s, Monte Vista builders were rhapsodizing that their homes were "more exotic than the originals of Spain's enchanting architecture."

Built for Jim Brooks in 1960, this gem tucked away behind the Landa Library became the home of Brigadier General and Mrs. (Kay P.) Dorr E. Newton Jr. in 1969.[29]

Moving on to West Hollywood—only Monte Vista residents seem to know that one must look for the east-west signs between Summit and Lullwood, where an extended Main Avenue would have bisected these streets—at 109 West one finds the well-designed classical Spanish stucco built for Joseph Rosenfeld in 1924. Eight drawings of this structure can be found in the architects' (Ayres and Ayres) collection at the University of Texas School of Architecture.[30]

Another 1924 structure is that of Irvin Stone at 112 West Hollywood. This two-story tile residence cost $18,000.[31] In the same year, Adams and Adams designed the J. S. Sweeney frame house at 115 West. Throughout 1926 and 1927, the Sweeney home was on the market—asking price $21,000: "High class, really homey with eight large rooms exceptionally well arranged, light and airy, very artistic."[32] At 109 West the eight-room veneer J. Frank King residence was under construction in September 1930.[33] This structure is changed radically in appearance today.

Across the way at 116 West Hollywood, John M. Marriott designed the Albert Prucha residence in 1928. J. W. Yarbrough was the contractor for this two-story, seven-room frame and stucco structure. A tile roof and gas steam radiators were among its features.[34] Next door at 120

This shaded home at 233 West Hollywood Avenue (1926, Frost Carvel, architect) was built "in the true style of old Spain."

West, the C. B. Schoeppl Company prepared plans in 1922 for the Paul Scholz home. A feature article on "Chimneys of Unusual Design," based upon an interview with architect Harvey P. Smith, included a photograph of the Scholz chimney.[35]

The two-story stucco at 126 West Hollywood was built "upon a solid reinforced concrete foundation" by engineer J. M. Johnson in 1927. Extensive use of tiles and an "Aztec mantel" was found in this $30,000 home. The Clow Gasteam Radiator added to the beauty of its rooms "instead of harming the appearance as some of the older systems of heating" had done.[36]

Frost Carvel began to promote Hollywood as a "Street in Spain" by 1926. Six of his designs featured tile roofs and rough plaster finishes.[37] One of these, 132 West Hollywood, was second prize winner in a national contest sponsored by *Woman's Home Companion*. The Alfred V. Campbells' $20,000 residence, "Villa Carmona," featured a Batchelder handmade tile mantel ordered from Los Angeles. Carvel built the structure along the lines suggested in *Woman's Home Companion*, which included three photographs of the house in its May 1927 issue.[38]

Similar architectural styles appeared on the next block, including that of Herbert Spencer's residence at 201 West Hollywood "under construction" in July 1928.[39] Frost Carvel homes at 223, 229, and 233 West Hollywood also contained one or another variation of the Spanish theme in 1926. That of 223 West featured a "delightful patio with playing fountain—living room that achieves a medieval atmosphere with vaulted ceilings . . . wrought iron grilles . . . quaint old world charm." Carvel offered this seven-room house for $14,500 in 1926.[40] One could also acquire 229 West for the same price:

This attractive place, expertly designed with adequate living room, dining room, dome-ceilinged breakfast nook, kitchen, 3 bedrooms and commodious bath—yet preserving the cozy atmosphere of a cottage—represents the best in Spanish architecture. . . . Thick stucco walls, steel-reinforced concrete foundation, hardwood floors, tiled roof . . . solid oak doors. . . . assure this a home to stand for the ages.[41]

Another Carvel home, at 233 West, likewise priced at $14,500 in 1926, contained two bedrooms and a study. "It's built in the true style of old Spain, with typically Spanish tiled roof, thick white stucco walls, Moorish arches, stone terrace, wrought iron railings."[42] Across the street, the 1925 home of Isidor Schoenberg at 226 West followed lines similar to others on the block:

This beautiful seven-room home is built in the Italian-Spanish style of construction. It is of white stucco with red tile roof and red tile portico. A feature of this home is the quaint iron gate that goes through the arch with a flagstone walk through the flower garden to the fountain and pool in the rear. The interior is quite distinctive with the massive tile fireplace in the living room, its large sunroom and artistic breakfast room with a small flower conservatory and handsome walls of hand-blocked imported paper.[43]

Several of the earliest homes on this block featured a more traditional design, as did that at 202 West Hollywood in 1922. Plans for this distinctive modified colonial, home of Mr. and Mrs. John Bowen, came from C. B. Schoeppl Company, the builder-architect.[44] A "modernized colonial stucco" built in 1922 at 206 West Hollywood had developer Wallace Rogers as its first resident. This two-story residence contained four upstairs bedrooms and a tile bath. Downstairs, French doors opening onto a sun parlor, a fireplace, hardwood floors and a lavatory provided other amenities.[45] Trail driver James M. Dobie, uncle of the legendary J. Frank Dobie, lived there before his death in the late 1920s.

Another Rogers-Hill traditional at 210 West Hollywood, of clapboard, became the home of William T. Beard in 1924.[46] Construction of a $10,500 colonial design, by architect Ellis Albaugh, began in December 1922 at 214 West for Milford C. Yates.[47] Another 1922 colonial, the two-story built for Dr. William T. Beard at 230 West by Rogers-Hill, was sold two years later for $13,000 to George H. Chadwick, a newcomer from Rochester, New York.[48] Another colonial of later (1938) design by Ralph H. Cameron was built at 211 West Hollywood for Mrs. Arthur Baird.[49]

Architect Beverly Spillman drew the plans for the James S. Curtis one story frame residence at 218 West completed in 1923.[50] Owner Jeremiah Rhodes offered his seven-room English cottage at 238 West for sale in June 1925. "Seven closets, lavatory on first floor, bath on second, gas and electricity in every room."[51]

Few homes attracted more attention than the New England colonial designed by Harvey Smith in 1924 for the Julius Barclays at 301 West Hollywood. Costs of $12,802.75 for the 2,905-square-foot home were about $4.40 per square foot. Bock Construction Company did the building:

This structure is perfectly balanced with no suggestion of the symmetrical, and throughout will maintain the unmistakable character that is inseparable from colonial construction. The entrance hall is accessible from either the front entrance or the porte cochere; and gives directly upon the large living room, which in turn, opens into the dining room and the sun parlor. To the rear of the hall are the kitchen, butler's pantry and rear

entry. And from this hall an attractive open staircase leads to the second floor, which comprises three sleeping rooms and baths, and a large glassed sleeping porch. The garage, at the rear, also affords servant's quarters and laundry room.

Harvey P. Smith, the architect, has taken one of the oldest types of good American architecture, and incorporated in it every modern idea that the builders of today have approved. Ample closets, linen cases, tiled baths, the refrigerator iced from outside the house, the package delivery door in the cooler closet, the kitchen ventilation system and a multitude of electrical conveniences stamp it as a modern of the moderns. Beautiful colonial fireplaces supplement the steam heating plant; and the entire house, laid on a reinforced concrete foundation, is to be plastered on metal lath.[52]

Another house of distinction, the two-story built for Mr. and Mrs. Fidel Chamberlain, was completed at 302 West Hollywood in 1922. It appears to be of modified colonial design, but its construction of hollow tile and stucco suggests the Spanish style found elsewhere on Hollywood.[53] Construction next door at 310 West, of similar design but with a frame structure, began in 1921 for the William Fordtrans. Within two years, Mr. and Mrs. Joseph R. Straus purchased this home:

It is a two-story frame structure set on a brick base and with brick porch trimmings. There is an open porch on the side directly under a large summer room. On the first floor are the reception hall, large living room, dining room, breakfast room, kitchen and closets. On the second floor are three large bedrooms, the summer room, closets, and sewing room. There is a fireplace upstairs and downstairs. There are also built-in hat racks, shoe racks, cedar closets and ironing boards. One of the unique features of the new home is the sliding doors on the second floor which are a big saving in wall space. Large brick flower beds are being built on each side of the portico and immediately over the entrance. Colonial mantels are built in the living room. All floors are of oak. The house will cost $12,500. C. B. Schoeppl Company are the architects.[54]

Frost Carvel had built twenty-eight homes by 1927 in Monte Vista, eighteen of which were located on Hollywood. Described as a "Beautiful Spanish Villa," the $20,000 residence at 311 West was situated on a 100-foot lot:

Ideally arranged for comfort and convenience. The living room is two stories high with cathedral type ceiling, balcony, and a fireplace with a Batchelder tile mantel and hearth. Large dining room, breakfast room done in oil, butler's pantry and an unusually attractive kitchen. There are four bedrooms with southeast exposures and two tile baths, one with separate shower. A circular stairway leads from the entrance hall to the balcony and upstairs. This home is plastered throughout and artistically decorated. It has a heating system, cedar closet, loggia, roof garden, double garage and servant's quarters with bath. Over $1,500 worth of draperies and $600 Frigidaire are included.[55]

In the diverse tradition of Monte Vista architecture, an American Colonial Revival home was built at 301 West Hollywood Avenue for the Julius Barclays (1924, Harvey P. Smith, architect).

Carvel's two-story stucco at 319 West Hollywood featured two roof gardens. This 1925 structure of rough trowel finish was painted "a pearly white shading into misty gray." The D. Stanley Collands purchased the home.[56] Next door at 323 West, "with its lovely rose walls, its green roof in striking contrast, its old ivory woodwork and the black wrought iron at doorways and windows" exemplified the Carvel style. "Inside, the same originality is apparent in the new landscape tapestry paper, paneling the walls of the living quarters—each panel a different scene!"[57]

On the north side of the block, a newspaper photograph of three 1925 Carvel residences was captioned "Mediterranean," a rather uncommon term locally at that early date. Judge E. A. Hall purchased the traditional brick at 326 Hollywood.[58] J. A. Matthews acquired 334 West. Dan Withers described the Matthews home in his study of residential colors in San Antonio:

It is a charming house accented with Baroque-like rope columns at the front entrance and east portico. The use of the arch is extensive throughout the house. The exterior stucco was originally painted white, and later Caliche. The oldest color used on the trim work is Yanaguana green, with a later application of Quadrangle green. A non-historic green now covers the latter two coats. The columns have always been painted Hot Wells with a glazing of Nueces Brown.[59]

Thousands of San Antonians visited the Carvel-built Spanish residence at 336 West Hollywood upon its completion late in 1924, attracted by publicity for the National Better Home Lighting Contest, designed to improve the lighting of American homes. Hundreds of San Antonio school children joined others across the nation in this essay contest on proper lighting. Carvel and his partner, Robert Bethea, designed and built this $15,000 home, but the Electric Club of San Antonio wired "this house for lighting according to the plan approved by the highest authorities in America on the subject." E. W. Crenshaw Jr. became the first owner of this home.[60]

Another "of the most striking examples of Spanish-type architecture in San Antonio" was at 337 West Hollywood. Here, Carvel chose "a green Spanish tile roof with the walls finished in white stucco and cream stone trim." The conservatory opened onto a terrace. A roof garden was an added attraction to this 1925 home, purchased by the Joseph Haegelins.[61]

Three southeast bedrooms, an enticement for most San Antonians seeking the prevailing summer breeze, may have drawn Dr. and Mrs. Austin O. Hull to 339 West Hollywood. Carvel included a roof garden and used tapestried landscape papers to panel the living quarters of this 1925 residence. "Black wrought iron balconies and railings contrast brilliantly with the soft pearly gray whiteness of the stucco [to] give an impressive foreign look to this lovely home."[62] Across the street at 342 West, simultaneous construction of another Carvel-inspired dwelling proceeded on the corner of San Pedro. This two-story white stucco became the home of Eldred T. Rogers.[63]

One cannot be certain of a Carvel involvement in 343 West Hollywood, but he did not draw its plans. According to architect Harvey Smith's specifications, this 2,446-square-foot home for lumberman Gerald E. Melliff began on August 15, 1924. The building cost was $13,747.95, and the square footage figure came to $5.575.[64]

"Rock, Brick and Stucco Bungalows"
11. Rosewood and Lullwood

Rock, brick and stucco bungalows, some of them spacious and two-story, could be found among the first structures built in 1923 north of Hollywood. An uncommon purchase plan, as well as the reputation of builder W. A. Baity, suggested that these were not speculative homes of the type one finds in present-day suburban developments.

The Rogers-Hill company will erect a home on one of these sites to suit the desire of any buyer. All he has to do is present the Rogers-Hill company with plans and specifications and the home will be erected accordingly. When completed, if the buyer does not like the house he does not have to take it and if he has put up earnest money it is refunded. If the buyer does take the house, he is required to make a twenty-five per cent cash payment on the property and to pay the balance in monthly installments.[1]

Most Rosewood and Lullwood homes, such as those built in 1929 on sixty-foot lots at 109 and 113 East Rosewood by developer Edward J. Mitchell, date from later in the decade.[2] Advertised concurrently, 105 East Rosewood offered similar amenities. Builder Ed Mitchell chose a modified English style with slate roof for this rock, tile and plaster six-room home. Beam ceilings in living and dining rooms added to the motif.[3] Still another of the scheduled twenty-four Mitchell-constructed homes on Rosewood—108 East—attracted 1,400 visitors to its first public showing in March 1929. This six-room frame, concrete and stucco home sold within a month to W. Leslie Evans.[4] Shown as an "escort house" with 105 East, the Mitchell-built 113 East Rosewood boasted a "guaranteed interlocking tile" roof.[5]

Mitchell's "sterling service" construction did not produce all homes in this vicinity. A few ante-

dated Mitchell's Rosewood projects. Contractor Amos Schweitzer provided Mrs. Maude B. Hall with an attractive residence at 104 East in 1927. Hillyer-Deutsch Jarratt Company furnished the materials for this $11,000 dwelling.[6] Nearby, the Irwin I. Uhrs moved into 112 East Rosewood in 1925 and remained there nearly fifty years.[7]

Two of East Rosewood's earliest homes, 129 and 133, are more spacious and of different design than most that came later. Both represent Rogers-Hill's efforts in 1923 to present "something new, something different from anything else in San Antonio." Their builder, Baity, undertook "to put into moderate priced homes much of the artistic charm and many of the conveniences possessed by very costly residences."[8] J. B. Wilson purchased 129 East. At 133 East, Mr. and Mrs. Kenneth C. Perry chose a dwelling in which "the awnings, shutters and entire trim of the house are in soft brown tones, harmonizing with the creamy sidewalls and the vari-toned shingles."[9]

Few residents of the Monte Vista Historic District have lived in the same home as long as did the Kurt D. Beckmanns. Beckmann, then a young architect in the firm of Giles and Beckmann, designed his own home at 146 East Rosewood in 1923. The one-story brick home with a concrete foundation cost approximately $7,000.[10]

Homes, duplexes and apartment houses in the 200 and 300 blocks of East Rosewood between McCullough and Shook are a later development. Laurel Heights had few multifamily dwellings prior to the mid-1920s. By the time development of Monte Vista was well under way young couples had become attracted to this lifestyle.

The duplex at 236 East Rosewood Avenue (1929, Harvey P. Smith, architect), designed to appear as a single-family dwelling, has in fact been converted to a one-family home.

One of the most attractive duplexes found in this area is at 236 East Rosewood. Harvey Smith designed it to appear as a single family dwelling, which indeed it has become in recent years. It was built in 1929 for Douglas A. Skinner and his sisters. Amos Schweitzer served as contractor for this twelve-room, two-story duplex at a building cost of $18,573. With a square footage cost of approximately $4.70 for the 3,954 square feet, materials in the walls included face brick, stucco and half timber.[11] In recent years it became the home of Cynthia and Norman McNair, active participants in the Monte Vista Association.

Board member Dan Laird and his wife, Kay, converted another duplex on that block into a single-family dwelling. Their home at 266 East, built in 1928 for Amory D. Cross by American Building Company, is of Spanish design.[12] Still another duplex at 258 East, built for J. A. Johnson, has twelve rooms and is of rock veneer.[13]

Among single-family dwellings, architect Emmett T. Jackson drew the plans (c. 1929) for the Jack Flaherty rock home at 273 East Rosewood. John Westerhoff was the builder.[14] Another 1929 structure, the brick veneer at 230 East, was built for the W. L. Martin family.[15] The fourplex of rock veneer at 255 East is likewise a 1929 construction by Anton Eiserloh, an Alamo Heights

builder. Mrs. Norma Adams purchased it from Eiserloh in March 1930.[16] The two-story home of "modified English design" at 262 East Rosewood was built in 1928 for Guy Borden, vice president of National Carbonic Company:

This home will occupy a high location overlooking the Olmos Basin and adjacent territory. Full advantage of the high elevation and beautiful view was taken by the Kelwood Company, architects, in the designing of the structure which, it is declared, will be a highly attractive and efficient home. The exterior will be of a light colored stucco and half-timber, with wrought iron used as trim. American Building Company is the contractor for the project. Outstanding features of this home, a 10-room structure, include a living room which will extend across the entire front, a screened porch which will serve the living room and the dining room, and an open paved terrace which will extend across the front of the house and along the east side of the living room.[17]

Only a few structures appeared on the next block by the turn of the decade. John A. Johnson built a duplex in 1930 at 301 East Rosewood.[18] The Andrew J. McKenzie home at 302 East is of similar vintage.[19] One of the first and most distinctive structures on the block was built at 314 East in 1927 by the Busby Building Corporation for Junior Chamber of Commerce President Youngs C. Crook, whose family resided there nearly fifty years:

The exterior of the building is of many kinds of stone and brick. In order to secure the very best effects in a mingle of rough stone and face brick, some of the stone was secured in the "hill country" north of San Antonio, while the darker brown mineral stone was secured beyond Elmendorf, south of San Antonio. A study of the harmony of colors as shown in this home, and the beautiful effects obtained, reveal the painstaking care with which the home was designed and constructed. It is a home of seven rooms and tile bath, and among the outstanding features in the interior arrangement is the reception hall, with its arched entrance leading to the living room and the curved ceiling in the living room with recess cove mould. The interior of the home is plaster finished throughout, with the newest textures and color blends.[20]

Rosewood east of Shook Avenue represents a distinctly different type of residential development. It will be treated subsequently as part of the more restrictive and exclusive cluster of homes in the residential section known as Oakmont.

By the mid-1920s, construction on the 100 blocks of East and West Rosewood was well under way. Hundreds of San Antonians had been visiting model homes since late 1923. Rogers-Hill Sales Manager Paul Adams claimed the number of visitors on Sunday, October 28, broke all records.

It is interesting to note "new" features that attracted so many viewers to these homes:

The Model Homes, located on Rosewood Boulevard, between Howard and McCullough Avenue, were built by W. A. Baity, veteran San Antonio home-builder. Mr. Baity's chief idea in constructing the Monte Vista Homes was to include in dwellings of moderate prices the conveniences and attractions found, as a rule, in very costly residences. Some built-in features are cedar lined closets, shoe boxes, hat boxes, mirrored doors, chifforobes, breakfast nooks, bookcases and kitchen cabinets. In the bungalows there are oak floors in every room. Particular attention has been paid to the interiors. In each home a striking color scheme has been developed in which draperies, paper and electrical fixtures harmonize. These interiors have been so skillfully arranged that practically no space has been wasted. Visitors have been especially enthusiastic about this feature.[21]

Other improvements not found in many developments were "cement driveways, cement-floored garages, servants' quarters and storage rooms." Pictures advertising 134 West Rosewood noted that prices for these model homes "range from $6,950 upward" in October 1923. Curiously, the minimum figure was $7,450 a month later. Individual home sites could be purchased—and some were—from $1,250 up.[22] Dwellings at 106, 122 and 126 West Rosewood are among the early ones. Down payments in the $1,500 range enabled one to move into a "charming home."[23] Architect and Mrs. Humberto Saldaña made contemporary additions in the rear of 106 West that did not detract from the vintage 1920s facade.

A semi-enclosed, arched entrance adds a sense of spaciousness to smaller Spanish-style homes like this at 223 West Rosewood Avenue (1925, Kelwood Company, architects).

It is an English squash joint brick home of eight rooms, with two bedrooms, two tile baths, living room and dining room. Breakfast nook, kitchen, service porch, club room. It has a southeast exposure and is highly elevated. A two-car garage and servant's quarters add to the convenience of this home. The interior is textoned, hardwood floors throughout, with cove ceilings. It is of everlasting construction, being built on a steel beamed foundation.[24]

Contractor J. M. Balch completed 123 West late in 1925 for Mr. and Mrs. N. M. Welsch.[25] The Roy H. Gamble home was completed at 127 West in 1929.[26] The frame structure at 135 West, completed in 1924, had Dr. and Mrs. Albert N. Champion as its first residents. The L. T. Mattingleys lived for a short time in the 1924 house at 130 West before the Hans R. F. Hellands acquired the property. Around 1925, 131 West became the home of the Guy S. Hensley family.[27]

Most homes in the 200 block of West Rosewood date from 1924 to 1930 and are likely to be in stucco of Spanish design. The "imposing two-story" at 200 West was built in 1929 by Ed J. Mitchell for cattleman Buck West.[28] Another attractive home across the street at 203 West, completed in 1930, became the home of A. J. Mendive. F. A. Nunally was general contractor for this Spanish-style stucco built for "nearly $10,000."[29]

Urban H. Wagner, superintendent of the Kelwood Company which constructed a number of homes on Rosewood as well as elsewhere in Monte Vista, moved into the spacious one-story at 206 West in about 1924. This seven-room brick featured high ceilings. J. Benjamin Robertson became the first resident of another Kelwood structure in 1923 at 214 West. This stucco with rock trim has a very steep pitched roof with a floored attic.[30]

Architects Adams and Adams were not without representation hereabouts as their superintendent Gerard M. Baker moved into his home at 210 West Rosewood in 1925. George W. Mitchell, whose firm became one of the leading contractors in the city, provided a floating concrete foundation. Two other mid-1920s dwellings on this block included that of Luther H. Duncan at 224 West and Maurice Cohen at 233 West.[31]

Contractor Alfred Eberle built the six-room brick veneer dwelling at 218 Rosewood for Harry Leopold in 1929. Apparently, Albert Arstein became its first resident.[32] A 1927 structure at 229 West became the new home of Miss Bydie and Miss Reba Whitesides.[33] Architect Richard Vander

The Spanish-style bungalow at 302 West Rosewood Avenue was built for Jake M. Kerman (1925, Frost Carvel Co., architects).

Stratten drew plans in 1930 for Stanley Mewding's home at 241 West. John C. Windner received the general contract of $12,000.[34] Across the street at 230 West Rosewood, a 1927 advertisement listed the attractive features of this dwelling:

A two-story stucco home of unusual quality and value, on a beautiful 62 1/2 x 129 corner lot. Has large living room with fireplace and winding stairway, dining room, kitchen with every convenience, breakfast room. Upstairs are three bedrooms, cozy sitting room with fireplace, two tile baths with shower; floors of finest hardwood; heating system, garage and servant's quarters.[35]

One distinctive structure on the 200 block of West Rosewood (233) received considerable attention in January 1926. This Spanish-style dwelling, designed and built by the Kelwood Company, was chosen for the citywide "Home Beautiful" exhibit. Asking price was $11,250.[36] The following year, 1927, construction proceeded on 324 West for Mrs. W. F. (Amelia) Rose.[37] Carvel and Company also built two adjacent homes in 1927— 302 West for Jake M. Kerman and the English-style brick at 306, for Thomas E. Powell.[38]

Lullwood, both East and West, is essentially a production of Robert McGarraugh, an established builder before he moved into northernmost Monte Vista. He called his development west of McCullough "Greenwood Village" and at the outset kept his office in a home at 201 West Lullwood.

A McGarraugh publication featuring photographs of many of his homes is interesting in itself, but also for advertisements revealing the names of those who furnished construction materials. Quality materials could be expected from such firms as Martin Wright Electric Company, Prassel Sash and Door, Geo. H. More Jr. (casement windows), Martin Bauml (plumbing), Louis Bauml (plastering and stucco), McAbee Tile and Marble, Walton & Arneson (consulting engineers), Fred Hummert (wall paper and paint), Emmett T. Sweeney (landscape architect), Turner Roofing & Supply and the Kelley-Maverick Co. (lumber).

In the foreword to this publication McGarraugh wrote: "In presenting to a discriminating public this book of homes, all of which have been designed and built recently by this organization, we feel that we have added in some measure to the architectural beauty of San Antonio. . . . Our business is to build fine homes of permanent construction; we are interested in no other kind."[39]

Stone and stucco characterized a number of McGarraugh homes, including the stone one at 112 East Lullwood in 1928. "Homes built by McGarraugh have individuality of their own" ran the advertisement for 112 East; "harmony of design in finish, inside and out will instantly appeal to you."[40] Photographs of 101, 116 and 117 East Lullwood were prominent in the *Light*'s real estate section in December 1926. Earl Jacobs bought 117 East in 1929.[41] The McGarraugh home at 106 East, dating from 1927, was the home of the Carl C. Krueger family for more than fifty years.[42]

Among the homes featured in the McGarraugh booklet, 126 East (originally 122) is of solid rock construction with 18-inch-thick walls on a steel beam foundation. Dr. and Mrs. Robert P. Thomas became the first owners in 1928, and afterward the Lucchese family owned it for more than forty years.[43] Newcomers to San Antonio Mr. and Mrs. Henry Deutz, from San Luis Potosí, purchased the McGarraugh-built 131 East Lullwood in 1927. Of modified Spanish design, it featured a tile roof.[44] The Verlin V. Carson residence at 144 East was constructed in 1930. A. Y. Hayes served as contractor for this brick veneer structure.[45]

The "appealing" home at 150 East Lullwood completed by McGarraugh in early 1929 is "an

English type rock house with English tile roof . . . The Payne unit system of warm air heating is used. It brings into the home instantly a flow of fresh air."[46] San Antonio Drilling Equipment Company President John J. Stevens Jr. purchased the 104-foot lot bound by Lullwood, McCullough and Hildebrand from McGarraugh. This 1928 construction at 151 East was more imposing than others along Lullwood:

A beautiful Spanish type home has been completed at the corner of McCullough Avenue and Greenwood Village [Lullwood] for J. J. Stevens, Jr. The building has two stories and is of hollow tile, concrete and stucco construction. One of the features of this new home is a Spanish type tin tile roof, installed by Joe Dean . . . sheet metal contractor. Arnold and Arnold built the building.[47]

East of McCullough on the 200 block of Lullwood, a number of duplexes made their appearance in 1929–30. That at 208 East Lullwood was built for Mrs. J. W. Alonzo of 330 West Summit. M. L. Case contracted for this 1930 structure of rock veneer, concrete and sheet rock.[48] Of similar construction in 1929, the $10,000 eight-room duplex at 214 East was built by T. S. Craighead.[49] J. Frank King had two ten-room duplexes under way at 235 and 261 East in 1930. Both were of brick veneer construction.[50]

Two houses in this block would remain in their respective families for fifty years. The multistory brick at 243 East Lullwood, constructed in 1925, descended to the son of its first owners, Josephine and Cornelius O'Neill. This stately structure with slate roof was designed by Gilberto S. Santa Cruz and built by the Karen Tobias Lumber Company.[51] Lillian and Fred T. Goetting Sr. moved into their bungalow at 250 East in late 1929 for a five-decade residency. Will N. Noonan was their architect.[52]

Only a few homes existed on the 300 East block prior to the close of the 1920s. House number changes make those difficult to identify, but the two-story Spanish rock built by Mrs. Amye Bozarth at 332 East in 1928 is readily validated. Milton Bergel purchased it.[53] The five large rooms with servants' quarters built in 1928 by the South Flores Lumber Company on "Lullwood near Shook" can only be 319 East.[54]

One of the most intriguing and talked about cottages in Monte Vista is the plaster and brick at 327 East Lullwood. Reportedly, it was designed and built in 1927 for his mother by Clemens Fridell, who subsequently moved to California.[55]

While many of McGarraugh's thirty-five homes on Lullwood by 1928 were $15,000 or less, the two-story eight-room Spanish style at 102 West (originally East)

The brick duplex at 243 East Lullwood Avenue (1925, Gilberto S. Santa Cruz, architect) maintains the feeling of a single-family home.

Heavily vertical panels accentuate the linearity of the circa 1930 Deco apartment building at East Lullwood and Shook avenues.

sold for $22,000 to Sterling Burke. "The sale was appropriately reported during San Jacinto Fiesta week, as Burke in 1927 was King Antonio."[56] Later residents included the Louis Kocureks.

Display advertisements of West Lullwood homes, including photographs, could be found regularly in the real estate sections of local newspapers.[57] One of the first McGarraugh completions in 1926, 115 West, opened for public inspection early in 1927.[58] The "typical beauty embodying all those features that tend to make McGarraugh stone and stucco homes distinctive" at 119 West opened in the spring of 1928.[59]

Mr. and Mrs. Robert P. Thompson first owned 123 West Lullwood, a seven-room rock bungalow of English design constructed in 1927. Thomas H. Jarrell purchased this home in June 1930 for $13,500.[60] A nearby completion in 1926, the stucco cottage at 124 West, became the home of Ward H. Miller. Across the street at 135 West, Mrs. Etta M. Little occupied the Spanish stucco featured in the McGarraugh booklet.[61]

Mrs. Bettie C. Ward bought four lots on West Lullwood in July 1928 from Mary M. and Robert McGarraugh for $19,300. Apparently McGarraugh built her spacious English-style rock at 130 West, as he included it in his booklet. Color historian Dan Withers noted that "all exposed wood on this house is stained with opaque stain similar to Franciscan brown. The stain has a gloss and was therefore varnished over after application. The metal frame windows of the house are painted with a gloss enamel to match the stain."

When Mrs. Ward purchased the property, restrictions, to expire on January 1, 1950, required that only residential structures costing "not less than $6,000" might be built. Racial restrictions prohibited the property being "leased, sold, etc. to any person of other than the Caucasian race, or to any Mexican."[62]

The two-story English stone rock home at 200 West Lullwood attracted considerable press upon its completion in 1927. Owned originally by Mr. and Mrs. Louis R. Roth, this spacious seven-room home became the property of Harry Leonard in 1929. San Antonio taste in living room furnishings in the 1920s can be readily detected in the McGarraugh booklet's photographs of this home.[63]

McGarraugh kept his office at 201 West Lullwood until 1929, when he placed that now razed structure on the market for $9,250.[64] One of the most expansive Spanish bungalows in Monte Vista, the ten-room house at 205 West Lullwood, was constructed by McGarraugh for Guy C. Jackson, president of the JHK Ranch in Chambers County, who took up residence in San Antonio so that his daughters might continue their schooling in the city.[65] The Spanish stucco at 209 West went on sale in early March 1929, and the Joseph W. Edwards family purchased it that December. They may have lived there only a short time as H. A. Robard had become the occupant by 1931.[66]

McGarraugh's photo of 210 West Lullwood carries the caption, "Residence of Mrs. T. O. Riley." She could not have resided there long as Nermal L. Huffaker, president of Maverick-Clark Litho, had moved in with his family by 1929.[67] Well-known attorney Patrick W. Swearingen purchased the 1928 stucco bungalow at 214 West Lullwood and lived there several years.[68]

Low ceiling beams added an Old English feeling to the living room of the 1927 random rock Tudor-style home at 200 West Lullwood Avenue, as pictured in developer Robert McGarraugh's promotional brochure.

Completed in December 1929, the "beautiful Spanish type" structure at 215 West Lullwood was sold by McGarraugh to Morris Schen the following April. The three-bedroom, two-bath stucco, sold to the owner of the Juvenile Manufacturing Company, was open for inspection on January 26, 1930, by which time McGarraugh had "designed, built and sold 43 homes on Lullwood Avenue, between San Pedro and McCullough."[69] Fifty-six homes, of which nine were vacant, are listed in the 1929–30 City Directory on those blocks.

Mr. and Mrs. Edwin E. Weise became the first owners of 218 West Lullwood, a stucco with interesting iron design that a recent owner thought to have been constructed as early as 1926.[70] A verifiable date, 1928, would be that of 227 West, inasmuch as Alex G. Krueger purchased this stucco and tile home that year. This was the Krueger home for more than fifty years.[71]

"A Departure from the Commonplace" was the photo caption for 221 West Lullwood in December 1927. A photo of the house "being built" the previous January indicates that these homes did not sell immediately. Time and again photos of these new homes appeared in For Sale advertisements as much as a year apart. Newcomers Mr. and Mrs. L. West Avery purchased 221 West in December 1927, the "sold upon completion" statement being a bit misleading.[72]

More accurate is the description of 228 West: "Originality and Charm of the Exterior Are Fully Carried Out in the Interior Design and Appointments." This steep-roofed five-room stucco bungalow was on the market only a month prior to its purchase by Charles W. Ryan.[73] San Antonio newcomers accounted for a number of Lullwood's earliest homeowners, but as with 232 West, information can be confusing. Presumably recent arrival and contractor Martin L. Case, who "knew of no city in the country that has such a host of admirers and boosters as San Antonio," purchased the 1929 seven-room English stone and stucco bungalow, but apparently Dr. and Mrs. Irving T. Cutter, formerly of 320 West, were the first residents.[74]

Another 1929 structure, the "beautiful new Spanish home" at 233 West, was acquired that year by hydraulic engineer Captain E. J. Carson and his wife.[75]

A central heating plan and millwork by Prassel Sash & Door Company aided "beauty and comforts of a real home" at 239 West Lullwood at Belknap. Mrs. George T. (Elisca) Marshall first lived in the 1927 two-story stucco.[76] While outside the scope of this volume, one of the few non-McGarraugh dwellings on Lullwood should be mentioned. Architect Bartlett Cocke drew the plans in 1932 for Mrs. Edward D. (Louise) Allen's spacious brick colonial bungalow at 240 West. Mrs. Allen was among the half-dozen widows who lived along West Lullwood. Additions were made by Colonel and Mrs. (Tance) Gene M. Patton.[77]

A family home for more than a half-century is the spacious 1927 stucco cottage with steep roof at 301 West Lullwood. Mr. and Mrs. Charles Wiggins were the first owners. In 1964 their daughter, Edith, and her husband, Adolph Grier, became the occupants.[78] M. L. Case built the five-room frame and stucco home at 302 West in 1929, but again contractor Case did not live here. Mr. and Mrs. Chester T. Hager apparently were the first occupants of 302 West.[79] Construction began on 306 West Lullwood in 1928. Mr. and Mrs. Maxie Klemcke were its first owners.[80]

A photo of 308 West Rosewood appeared in a May 1927 advertisement. It was still for sale nine months later. The McGarraugh "stucco structure in the Norman style of architecture" was a departure from nearby homes. M. Leo Dubinski was its first resident.[81] Dr. and Mrs. Herbert Hill became owners of 311 West, advertised first in May 1927:

This home is of Colonial design, delightfully arranged with three bed chambers, commanding the southeast breeze. The balance of the house is most spacious; living room and dining room are of Textone finish and all woodwork throughout stippled. This home is of stucco, and every detail of comfort and correct planning is found here, making your inspection both a pleasure and a source of information in individual design and construction.[82]

Jack H. Bradley purchased the three-bedroom 1928 home at 315 West.[83] Mrs. Annie Krueger bought 319 West, a 1927 stucco with three bedrooms.[84] Dr. and Mrs. Irving T. Cutter bought the stucco at 320 West Rosewood in 1928, the home of the Dave J. Honigblums within a year or so.[85] By late 1929, McGarraugh's "I-Beam Steel Patented Foundation" at 326 West and elsewhere would eliminate "all foundation troubles."[86] Mr. and Mrs. Frank S. Haines got the "well-designed, attractive seven room" at 327 West in 1929.[87]

Unusually thick walls in the stone and stucco at 329 West Lullwood were one attractive feature of this three-bedroom home. Completed in 1928, it was vacant until purchased by Mr. and Mrs. W. M. Harris in January 1930.[88] Another 1928 home, 333 West, also was vacant for some time.[89] So was the English stucco cottage at 334 West, opened for inspection in the spring of 1928.[90]

Concurrent with development of Lullwood came the decision to open Hildebrand, earlier regarded as an alley. During the spring of 1929, work progressed "on opening Hildebrand Avenue, the most important east-west opening that has been made in San Antonio recently."[91]

"A Quiet Exclusion of All that is Ordinary"

12. Bushnell, Oakmont and Rosewood

Twelve acres north of the city rock quarry, bounded by Bushnell, Shook, and Hildebrand, were purchased by Thomas R. Masterson in 1923 and divided into twenty-one building sites known as Oakmont. "A quiet exclusion of all that is ordinary establishes a background for that individuality and personality which the smart world demands of its leaders," ran a promotional piece. "Thus, well bred people seek an environment removed from all that is garish and distracting. . . . If you are in that exclusive group which will consider nothing less than the best, may we direct your attention to the manifold advantages of Oakmont?"[1]

Attorney Masterson turned development of Oakmont over to the W. L. Coleman Company, which offered sites that sold from $6,500 to $7,500 each. Building restrictions of $15,000 guaranteed "dignified and well ordered homes" to attract the city's "best families" to a "lovely woodland [separated] from the drumming arteries of trade. Pervaded by an atmosphere of unmarred serenity, Oakmont lies high above the city, cooly aloof like a fine old English park, its gentle knolls graciously inviting."[2] Formal opening for Oakmont, where "years ago nature did her part," occurred in January 1924.[3]

Masterson himself built and moved into the first completed Oakmont residence at 307 Bushnell Place in 1924. The eleven-room house plus basement, designed by Thomson & Swain of Dallas, cost an estimated $40,000. Artificial stones made for permanent construction and a tile roof added to the stately appearance of this structure overlooking the city.[4] The next home (347) on this block, completed in 1926 and later home

of Myrna von Nimitz and Dr. Peter V. Weston, was described thus:

One of the outstanding homes, marking modern development in San Antonio, is that of Mr. and Mrs. H. M. Harrison on (347) Bushnell Place near Shook Avenue, which is rapidly nearing completion. The site being 220 by 120 foot, high up, and commanding a beautiful view of the city, makes the setting ideal.

Original details along English design of architecture are used throughout. The walls are of rough tapestry brick, with artificial cast stone trim, with tile roof. The main entrance door in the center opens into a large reception hall and stair hall, and the openings to the right are those of the sitting porch and a large living room. The library and large dining room, breakfast room, kitchen and pantry, and service porches, comprise the first floor. On the second floor are four bedrooms, a large sleeping porch, two baths, storage space and maids' quarters. Walsh and Burney are the contractors and Adams and Adams are the architects.[5]

More than one passerby exclaimed that 323 Bushnell "is my favorite house in San Antonio." It remained for a Chicago professional couple to fulfill their dream of returning to their native San Antonio only if they could live at this address. Dr. and Mrs. (Joe Grace) Gary Johnson had admired this house years before as they walked past it in their Mark Twain School days. So a dream came true when they acquired this Atlee B. Ayres-designed structure, for so many years the home of the B. B. McGimseys and, before that, of oilman Joe Owen and businessman Percy L. Mannen. Mannen, local manager of National Cash Register Company, called upon Ayres for the plans. J. M. Oldham was awarded the general contract for $22,334. He completed the two stories of hollow tile and stucco in the summer of 1927.

"Sunny Spain is reflected in the home of P. L. Mannen," ran a photo caption in a newspaper fea-

Typical of the Spanish Colonial Revival houses of Atlee B. and Robert M. Ayres is their use of two massed forms meeting at an obtuse angle, as in their design for the 1926 Percy Mannen home at 323 Bushnell Avenue. Notable features include the arcaded veranda and second-floor balcony.

ture of outstanding new homes in San Antonio. A clay tiled roof with concealed metal gutters underneath, rough timber trellis on the terrace, decorative wrought-iron grills and turned wooden spindles and five interior arches were within sight.[6]

Most of the earliest homes on Oakmont Court have been acquired by Trinity University as residences for senior administrators. Among the most imposing in the city is 106, finished in 1926. Kelwood Company was both architect and contractor:

The residence of Julius Seligmann now under construction on the corner of Shook and Oakmont will be, when completed, one of the finest homes of its type in the city. The design is pure Italian villa style of architecture, every detail having been carefully studied from the standpoint of proportion and precedent. The plan was especially studied with the idea of meeting all requirements and every room is located so as to obtain the maximum amount of ventilation and breeze during summer months. The fact that the house faces north with a corridor running full length along the outside wall gave the architects an opportunity to obtain their effects of large wall surfaces with few windows. The only windows required in the north wall are for purposes of securing cross ventilation for the rooms.

On entering the reception room through the front entrance door, the principal feature of the room is presented on the opposite wall, that of a very large studio window completely covered with an unusually fine wrought iron spiral grille. In the window itself are French doors which open into the garden beyond. A fireplace on one side, vaulted ceiling and a marble floor [are] also features. . . . The tower with its

spiral marble staircase with large Tiffany art glass window and a porte cochere entrance corridor, with its beamed ceiling and marble floor are accessible through a large arch from the reception room. The dining room and breakfast room in this wing are treated in a very simple manner with rough textured walls and wrought iron electrical fixtures. The breakfast room floor will be [of] Italian mosaics.

To the left of the reception room, stepping down two marble steps, is the living room which is entered through a very large archway. This archway is relieved by an interesting wrought iron lunette supported upon twisted iron posts, all polychromed. The living room itself is very spacious and interesting with its large Italian stone mantel and covered ceiling. Cut into the ceiling at intervals are a series of arches, the lunettes of which will contain mural decorations.

One of the most interesting rooms of the residence will be the sun parlor which, though Italian in character will contain the merest suggestion of Chinese influence in order to harmonize with the rugs, furnishings and a number of Italian vases which will be used there. The principal feature of this room will be a large studio window of amber tinted glass set in lead bars. At the base of the window and inset directly into the glass, will be a small stone fountain with a sculptured dragon on its face. The floor of the room will be of Chinese red and black tiles.[7]

Across the way, architect Harvey P. Smith designed 115 Oakmont Court for Mr. and Mrs. Dan Sullivan III late in 1928. This Italian-style brick over hollow tile was completed the following year. At $29,583, the 4,662 square feet cost $6.345 per square foot. Colors chosen included a variegated gray-brown brick exterior, bottle green window casements and shutters, and red roof tiles graded slightly from dark to light. Nine rooms, three baths, a basement, servants' quarters and a two-car garage made for a spacious home.[8] A more traditional residence appeared across the street at 130 Oakmont, built for Roy Campbell in 1928:

Another beautiful section north of the city is nearing completion. A two-story Colonial home is being built on Oakmont Court in Oakmont addition for Roy Campbell, of the Campbell Lumber Company. Allen and Allen, well known local contractors, have the contract for the beautiful structure and are rushing it to completion. The building was designed by H. B. Thompson and F. Gaubatz . . . Its graceful plain lines, broken only by a neat cornice around the top and an entrance of a hundred and fifty years ago, makes this home stand out. . . Some of the features of the home include a beautiful walnut stairway leading from the entrance hall to the second story. . . Panel work on the wall also adds to its beauty. The walls of the bedrooms are finished in pastel shades.[9]

Next door at 138 Oakmont, A. J. McKenzie chose an Italian design of native stone for his own home. Head of McKenzie Construction Company, "among [the] South's largest general contractors," he selected Atlee and Robert Ayres to plan this distinctive structure, completed in the summer of 1930.[10] On the adjacent lot simultaneous construction for Jack Locke Sr. began in the latter part of 1929. Ralph H. Cameron drew the plans for 146 Oakmont, a $40,000 two-story nine-room stucco of modified Spanish design.[11]

While Bushnell, in the popular mind, was to the "oil rich" what Kings Highway was to the "cattle barons," oilman Arch F. Gilliam chose to build at 151 Oakmont in 1926. Glen H. Alvey, vice-president and general manager of the Uvalde Rock Asphalt Company, purchased the home two years later.

Classical arches frame the porte-cochere entrances of the 106 Oakmont Court home built for Julius Seligmann (1926, Kelwood Company, architect). Since 1982 the home has been the Holt Continuing Education Center of nearby Trinity University.

One of the show places of the city to be built during the coming weeks is the residence of A. F. Gilliam in the Oakmont Addition. This pretentious home will be of the English cottage type of permanent construction. It will sit on a large lot, 135 x 200 feet, well back from the street with the front lawn laid out with terraces and winding drives, giving it the atmosphere of a real English country home. Plans for the new home have just been completed by Beverly Spillman.[12]

One other outstanding home on Oakmont, completed at the end of the 1920s, was that of Horace A. Thomson, another leader in the local oil industry. The grand scale of this Spanish design at 150 Oakmont is diminished by the heavily wooded front lawn. Only from the spacious courtyard to the rear does one sense the striking qualities of this residence, home of the president of Trinity University since the early 1970s. Called "Minter House," it recalls the three-decade residency of Dr. and Mrs. Merton Minter.[13]

Rosewood Avenue within Oakmont Addition includes only the 400 East block, and dates from 1928. When the American Building Company first held an open house in July 1928 for its "Everlasting Home" at 401 East Rosewood, ad-

The atmosphere of an English country home was the goal for the Tudor style 151 Oakmont Court (1926, Beverly Spillman, architect). The peak of the stairway turret is partly obscured by oaks.

mission came by invitation only. Upon completion it was "considered one of the finest homes in San Antonio," a somewhat hackneyed comment. The firm of E. F. Albaugh and Henry Steinbomer designed this very English home "with rugged simplicity"—appropriately so, for this rock structure nestled in a thick growth of oak trees.

Albaugh and Steinbomer sought a residence that was spacious, comfortable and livable, and thus practiced restraint in interior decoration. They further enhanced the English motif with large Eternit color-blended fireproof roof shingles made in Rhodesia.[14] Nathan Kaufman was the first owner. His purchase price was $38,000.[15] Subsequent residents have included Pedro Navarro-Sanchez, Dan E. Martin and the Richard Moores. Moore, an architect, made extensive alterations in recent years, though on the street side the original architectural integrity is retained.

Another of Harvey Smith's "architectural beauties," built in 1928, is at 410 East Rosewood.

One of the most charming of the finer homes of San Antonio is that of Mr. and Mrs. Robert S. Yantis on the corner of Shook and Rosewood in Oakmont. It is done in the simple rambling Spanish-Colonial style, so well adapted to climatic conditions, historical background and blending so naturally into our native landscape. This house is built in an "L" shape, with the patio in the angle, catching the southeast breeze throughout all of the rooms. The walls are of solid stone, 18 inches thick. This stone was bought up by Yantis from a number of old buildings recently torn down. In the new house the stone was laid up in a random ashlar method. The texture bending and blending of the different colors of the stone is one of the most beautiful aspects of this home. The walls are furred on the inside so that the sweating of the stone walls does not penetrate to the inner plastered surfaces.

The ground floor contains the large living room, which runs off at an angle itself with a spacious porch on the east end of it. The circular stair hall is in the corner of the building and acts as the main entrance and reception hall. From this stair hall with its winding stairs of solid oak hewn logs and wrought-iron railing, a curved passage with a vaulted ceiling leads to the dining room. . . . The dining room with its coved ceiling, has a plank flooring with wooden pegs in the ends of the boards. All of the other main rooms downstairs . . . have Spanish tile floors and steps leading to and from them of varied colors and designs, so typical of the period. The living room has a wonderful beamed ceiling of adzed timbers and a fireplace. . . . There are numerous wrought-iron gates, railings, balconies and electric light fixtures throughout the principal rooms of the lower floor. The dining room, however, contains a very beautiful crystal chandelier of the period, with crystal wall brackets to match.[16]

One of the most photographed local residences at the time of its completion in 1930 was that at 411 East Rosewood. Mr. and Mrs. Max Roseman chose Beverly W. Spillman and his son, Beverly Jr., to design this singular stone structure, "a type of architecture found in the Spanish cities of Segovia and Toledo. . . The walls are of stone and the roof of the tower, balconies and courts, as well as the house, are covered with variegated Spanish tile. The interior has been carried out in keeping with the style of the exterior, with beautiful stairways, tile floors, wrought iron grills for arched openings and latticed windows."[17]

Modified Italian was the choice of the Robert B. Michaels at 438 East Rosewood in 1928:

Walls are of hollow tile faced with brick in a soft blend of colors. The roof is of Spanish clay tile. Entrance of ornamental cast stone, arched loggia with its stone columns and a patio in the rear enclosed by stone walls, are features of the exterior. On one side of the reception hall is a spacious living room with a sun parlor at one end, with its tile floor and vaulted ceiling. The breakfast-room is also entered through the main hall through richly executed iron gates. This room also has a tile floor of unusual design, and a vaulted ceiling. . . . The home cost approximately $33,000. Robert B. Kelly was architect and Allen and Allen, general contractors.[18]

Mrs. Amye Bozarth, better known for extensive residential building in Olmos Park than in Monte Vista, had architect Glenn C. Wilson plan a twelve-room, $40,000 Spanish-style rock home at 447 East Rosewood, finished on a spacious 100-by-230-foot lot in 1928. Other than the thirty-six-foot living room, the downstairs and two porches had tile floors. Insurance executive Bernard A. Wiedermann bought it a month before completion.[19]

The Spanish stucco Bozarth-built 1928 Oakmont home at 414 East Hildebrand was designed for Ford dealer Robert S. Yantis but purchased from him by Edgar Sweeney in October 1928:

Morning sunlight rakes across the rough brick of the 1928 Tudor-style home at 430 East Hildebrand Avenue, at the northern edge of the Oakmont subdivision.

Seven large rooms consisting of a living room, dining room, breakfast room, kitchen, and entrance hall on first floor; three bedrooms and two tile baths on second floor; large clothes closets, handsome electrical fixtures and beautiful draperies throughout; garage for two cars and servant's room with bath; large lot, 100 x 175, with rock wall around three sides, a wide tarvia drive and flagstone front walk.[20]

Four other homes were built on the south side of the 400 block of East Hildebrand by 1930. Judge George B. Taliaterro, president of Commercial Loan and Trust Company, purchased the spacious rock cottage at 405 Hildebrand in November 1928.[21] Other early residents included Abe Eidleberg (422), George D. Bihl (426) and Benjamin C. Carr (430).

One distinctive residence in Oakmont constructed later than the province of this volume, 139 Oakmont Court, deserves mention. O'Neil Ford designed this modern structure for Mayor Sam Bell Steves in 1950. Two years later it became the residence of the new president of Trinity University, Dr. James Woodin Laurie.[22]

"Millionaires' Row"

13. Bushnell, Shook and Laurel Heights Place

Shook Avenue, Laurel Heights Place and Bushnell Place are essentially products of the 1920s. Most homes were individually designed for a specific owner, not built by speculative developers. Those on Bushnell, "popularly known as Millionaire's Row," are the most imposing.

Some twelve acres, from the southside of Bushnell to Kings Highway, were purchased by architect Alfred Giles in 1884 for $1,350. Giles sold this property, "twelve acres to the north of the theological seminary and adjoining the Francis Smith property (northside of Bushnell) on Laurel Heights," to W. A. Cocke in 1909 for $13,500.[1] More than a decade passed, however, before the prosperity of the 1920s enticed very many home builders to this site.

Some original structures on Bushnell have been moved or razed, but of the extant residences, that at 104 is perhaps the oldest. Built for A. M. Walker in 1914 for approximately $25,000, "the house is distinctively California in design, with brick and mahogany interior finish." Subsequent owner Mrs. Minnie J. Kelley sold the house to attorney Guy S. McFarland in 1922 for $31,500.[2] Immediately to the east (116), W. C. Johnson's new two-story stucco cost $30,000 in 1927. Contractor Clay Dishman built this Spanish-style residence with materials from the Hillyer-Deutsch-Jarratt Company. A multiplicity of built-ins and an electric Kelvinator refrigerator encouraged a local newspaper to run a photograph of this "example of a model kitchen" in 1927.[3]

Facing page: Entrance to the home built for Harry Landa at 233 Bushnell Avenue (1928, Robert B. Kelly, architect), now a branch of the San Antonio Public Library.

The first of the great mansions on Bushnell to be occupied in the summer of 1921, Mrs. Lottie O'Brien's at 126, became the property of Mr. and Mrs. Charles Schreiner, Jr. in less than a year. For nearly three decades it was the William L. Moody III home. Mr. and Mrs. (Beverly) John Copeland did extensive renovation when they acquired this property in 1982. San Antonians watched the original construction with great interest in 1920–21.

The site on which this home is located is in keeping with the structure's massiveness. The grounds have a frontage of 400 feet on Bushnell Avenue, or an equivalent of eight 50-foot lots, and runs back 300 feet opposite Laurel Heights place. Construction on the O'Brien residence began in the summer of 1920. . . . The house was built by Walsh and Burney, San Antonio contractors, from plans furnished by Emmett Jackson, local architect. The house is reinforced concrete construction, finished in tapestry brick and white ornamental stone. The roof is constructed of green tile.

The first floor of the O'Brien residence consists of reception hall, living room, dining room, breakfast room, sun parlor, den, kitchen, servant rooms, porches and terraces. . . . The second floor contains four bedrooms, sewing room, trunk room, three baths and a roof garden. . . . There are four large fireplaces in the home in the construction of which much Rookwood tile has been used. The residence has much equipment that will make for comfort. There is a refrigerating plant, hot-air heating system and vacuum cleaning plant as well as other late mechanical equipment. In the rear of the home is the garage and servant quarters. This building corresponds in style and material to the main residence. On the ground floor is space for three automobiles and a workshop, while on the second floor there are three servant rooms. A pergola is being built to connect the large veranda with a summer garden pavilion.[4]

Wholly different in architectural design, the great house of Thomas E. Hogg at 202 Bushnell Place was completed in 1924. Oilman philan-

Green tiles highlight the Mediterranean-style home at 126 Bushnell Avenue (1921, Emmett T. Jackson, architect).

thropist Marrs McLean acquired this estate in the mid-1930s, and it has been the residence of his daughter, Mrs. William O. Bowers, in more recent years. Atlee B. and Robert M. Ayres were the architects.

The site on which this home will be constructed adjoins that of Charles Schreiner. The grounds front 240 feet on Bushnell Place and are 350 feet deep. A portion of the residence will be parallel to Bushnell Place and the remainder will be constructed at an angle of 45 degrees with that street. It will be of Italian style with a variegated tile roof and stucco walls. It will have two stories and a basement. Woodwork will be stained and interior and exterior walls will be finished in primitive plaster. The first floor will contain a large living room, a library, a reception hall, a spacious dining room, a breakfast room, pantry, kitchen and a den. The second floor will contain the owners' bedrooms with bath, sleeping porch and drawing room. Also on the second floor will be three guest rooms and three baths. These rooms will radiate from a large sitting room. . . .

Being able to stand in the reception hall and look through a pair of wrought iron gates upon a beautiful

informal Italian garden with a fountain is one of the attractive features of the house plan. Another is a circular stair with its wrought iron railing in the stair tower. The entire interior is in early Italian style. The home will have tile floors, solid oak paneled doors and wrought iron gates inside as well as

Spanish Colonial Revival was carried out inside and outside the home built for Thomas Hogg, son of Texas governor James Hogg, at 202 Bushnell Avenue (1924, Ayres & Ayres, architects), which was the first of the Ayres firm's noted Spanish Colonial Revival projects.

High-rise apartments were new to San Antonio, and to Texas, when the elegant seven-story Bushnell Apartments (1926, Kelwood Company, architect), renovated in 1982, were built with "the appearance of a lofty Spanish palace."

outside. There will be a loggia on the east side of the house at the end of the living room which is connected by a broad flagstone terrace which extends from one end of the house to the other along the south side, upon which one can step from the living room, reception hall, dining room or breakfast room.[5]

Adjacent to the Hogg-McLean-Bowers mansion, at 204–208, is an intended deception in the eight-unit apartment building designed in 1930 to appear as a single-family residence. Realtor Gottlieb Sexauer erected this building, based on plans by Carvel and Company:

The building is of Spanish architecture, but very unusual in that it will have the appearance of a beautiful residence instead of an apartment house. It will be one of the most exclusive apartment structures in the city. The character of the architecture and the arrangement of entrances is such that there

will be no suggestion of a commercial building. It is so planned that all apartments will have private entrances and are each in themselves an individual and distinctive home. It is a combination of massive wall surfaces, overhanging wooden balconies, leaded plate glass windows, wrought iron and clay tile, all blended together to create a real atmosphere of Old Spain. Each apartment is arranged so that the living rooms and bedrooms have south and east exposures, opening out into little patios, terraces, or porches.

Spanish atmosphere is carried out throughout the interior. Each living room having massive cypress beams, Spanish fireplaces and mantels, authentic rough texture walls blended in soft pastel shades. All the floors will be clear white oak and the trim a Spanish design. . . . There will be a roll-away bed in the dressing closet, which connects with the living room, allowing for two bedrooms in case of necessity. The entire building . . . will further impress upon each tenant the effect of luxury and comfort in a setting of Old World charm.[6]

The entry hall of the Harry Landa home at Bushnell and Shook avenues, bequeathed to the City of San Antonio in 1946 to be a branch of the public library system, now houses the Landa Library's circulation desk while the former living room, below, houses stacks and a reading area.

1924. Lentz announced plans to spend $10,000 on the property. Newspaper photographs a year later indicated that Atlee and Robert Ayres were the architects. "The residence, of tile and stucco, is a modified Spanish type. Spacious grounds with many trees, as features of the landscape, enhance the beauty of this fine dwelling. The house has 10 rooms in two stories."[7] Antecedents of 223 Bushnell are uncertain, but architect Charles Boelhauwe drew plans for general remodeling of the Louis Sauer home in 1929.[8] Another older home constructed in 1919 for L. R. Mays, 218 Bushnell, was the Curran B. Mendel home for more than fifty years.

Real estate promoter Harvey C. Wood resided in one of the older (c. 1920) structures at 215 Bushnell until he moved into the new Bushnell Apartments and sold his home to Joseph Lentz in

This home (218) is to be two stories with a basement and to be constructed of tile with white stucco on the outside. It will face north on Bushnell on one of the highest locations in San Antonio. There is a terrace across the front with red brick etching and red brick steps. The living room is 15 x 30. The dining room connects with the conservatory and breakfast room. Between the breakfast room and the kitchen is the pantry. On the west is the porte cochere leading to a side entrance. On the second floor are three bedrooms, shower and bath in tile. The woodwork is white with oak floors. The walls are plastered and tinted. The house will be heated by air. Atlee B. Ayres is the architect [9]

San Antonians of some affluence could enjoy a new lifestyle after completion of the Bushnell Apartments in late 1926.

Construction work will begin the middle of December (1925) on the proposed Bushnell Apartments to be built here by the Kelwood Company, according to H. C. Wood of that company. This building, which will be a seven-story structure of fireproof construction, will be erected on Bushnell Place near Shook Avenue at a cost of $300,000 for the building alone. . . . One feature that is an innovation to San Antonio is the use of two high-speed automatic elevators for the service of the tenants. All that one will have to do after entering the conveyance will be to close the door and push the button for the floor where he intends to go and the elevator does the rest. One will not have to worry about whether the elevator boy is asleep or off in some other part of the building talking to his girl, or something like that.

The exterior of the building will present the appearance of a lofty Spanish palace, as that type of architecture features the design of the apartment house. Construction work calls for a frame of reinforced concrete, with hollow tile walls, the exterior to be finished in stucco. There will be 28 apartments in the building—four to each floor—of four, five and six rooms each, none of which will be furnished. All apartments, however, are to be equipped with Frigidaires and will have tiled baths with built-in tubs, showers and hot and cold water. There will be an efficient heating system installed. The Bushnell Apartments are to be built on a large lot, 200 by 300 feet, and in addition to the apartment building there will be provisions for a garage for every apartment.[10]

Facing the Bushnell, Landa Library has become a San Antonio landmark and special gathering place for neighborhood residents, as it is the

A ceramic medallion is the focal point of the short tower designed by architect John M. Marriott in 1926 as the entrance to his own home at 519 Shook Avenue.

only publicly owned gathering place in the Monte Vista Historic District. Several hundred neighbors gather here each July Fourth for a family picnic following the annual Monte Vista parade. Originally the palatial residence of Mr. and Mrs. Harry Landa, this Mediterranean-style structure was designed by architect Robert B. Kelly, who also drew plans for the Bushnell. Mrs. Landa personally supervised the planning and construction throughout 1928 of the "two stories of stucco, stone-tile and other permanent materials." Extensive use of tile, in the trim as well as on the floors, gave a distinctive appearance. A near-page photographic spread appeared in the *Light*:

An art gallery was specially constructed for displaying collections of old paintings, masterpieces from all over Europe. Considerable wrought iron work in the Italian residence comes directly from Italy. A beautiful glass chandelier also comes from Italy. Beautiful marble and tile floors and an unusual handcarved mantel are other features.[11]

New Braunfels textile magnate and philanthropist Harry Landa donated his home to the city of San Antonio "as a memorial to my beloved wife, Hannah Landa," upon these conditions:

Architect Robert M. Ayres won a top award for the design of his own home at 207 Laurel Heights Place in 1927.

The property is to be kept and maintained in a good state of repair and condition with the main building dedicated for use as a non-sectarian free library and with the surrounding grounds dedicated for use as a children's playground, with the right to establish and enforce reasonable rules and regulations for the use and enjoyment thereof. Both the library and playground are to be maintained in a manner keeping with good practices and national standards.[12]

Although less pretentious than those on Bushnell, simultaneous constructions on Shook Avenue, such as the 1922 stucco residence of Dr. and Mrs. James S. Steel at 501, contributed to the "better class of homes being built in San Antonio":

Situated on the crest of Laurel Heights, overlooking the entire city, a charming vista is obtained from the porches and principal rooms. The first floor embraces a spacious living room with fireplace, music room, dining room, breakfast nook, kitchen, serving pantry, store closets, toilet and stair hall, besides a large cement terrace and covered porch. On the second floor are four bedrooms with ample closet space, a serving room, dressing room, tiled bathroom and screened sleeping porch. A hot air heating plant will be installed in the basement and double garage and servant's quarters are to be detached from the house. Phelps and Dewees are the architects and Moeller and Weilbacher are contractors.[13]

Northward, the native fieldstone home at 511 Shook designed for Judge and Mrs. Sam C. Eldridge by Carleton W. Adams in 1932 is just beyond the province of this volume. It is yet another Monte Vista home that has remained within the family for more than a half century.[14]

Architect John M. Marriott designed and built his own home at 519 Shook in 1926; it remained the family home for more than forty years. The spacious stucco over hollow tile bungalow is in the Spanish style. Marriott added such distinctive touches as stencil work on the beams of the cathedral ceiling and stained-glass windows.[15] For one of his early homes in the immediate neighborhood, real estate developer Harvey C. Wood selected Marriott to design 523 Shook. Marriott, in turn, chose contractor James C. Ferguson to build both homes (519 and 523). Construction costs of the Wood home came to $13,500.[16]

A 1930 photograph of 625 Shook Avenue records the home of Dr. and Mrs. Erich J. Arendt much as it appears today. When the Arendts moved to this address in 1926, they set about turning a nondescript backyard into a showplace garden. More than vestigial remains are still apparent. Servants' quarters of ordinary wood construction did not blend with the garden, so the Arendts turned the structure into a log cabin with a roof of thatched palm leaves. Gone are the palm leaves, but remaining is the cabin with a fieldstone chimney that doubled on the exterior as a barbecue pit. Other existing additions to the property abutting the Landa Library grounds include a gold fish pond and walks of flagstone gathered by the couple on trips to the country.[17]

Two other Shook Avenue residences to the north also date from the mid-1920s, with Dr. and Mrs. A. B. McKissack (703) and Dr. and Mrs. W. Huard Hargis (715) being among early residents.

Bounded on the east by Shook and on the west by McCullough, Laurel Heights Place has a few residences as pretentious as some on Bushnell—the parallel street just to the north—and others as modest as those of the 300 block of East Kings Highway, parallel to the south. Few streets in Monte Vista offer as much architectural diversity in residential structures. Overhanging trees, rolling elevation, and individually constructed homes give Laurel Heights Place its appeal.

Insurance executive George C. Eichlitz built the first home on Laurel Heights Place, 101, at the corner of McCullough. Atlee Ayres drew the plans in 1922 for this two-story Spanish-style stucco structure. Eichlitz sold the residence to oilman James A. Chapman, who was already spending considerable time in Tulsa, where he would make his permanent home long before he became the premier benefactor of Trinity University. Chapman sold the property in 1929 to rancher T. G. Hendricks, whose Winkler County oil pool was discovered in 1926. A year after the Chapman-Hendricks deal came the announcement that Hendricks had sold the property at 101 to John B. Smyth, president of the Uvalde Rock Asphalt Company, for $50,000.[18]

Mrs. Minnie J. Kelley sold the southeast corner of Laurel Heights Place and McCullough to Griffith Johnson in 1923 for $6,150. On part he built a one-story frame residence with basement (110), designed by architect Richard Vander Stratten.[19] This has been covered with stucco, while the clapboard (102) which today is actually on the corner is of 1940–41 vintage. Another more recent structure (126) is David C. Baer's design for David Trimble in 1958. Later the home of Dr. and Mrs. R. Gaston Scott, it has parquet flooring (c. 1890) from the demolished Augustus Belknap home on West French Place, a stairway from an old La Villita building, and a mantel from a razed home at 14th and Rio Grande in Austin.[20]

Mrs. Marquis Pope, a New England transplant to San Antonio, desired a home reminiscent of her heritage. Architect Richard Vander Stratten gave her just that at 134 Laurel Heights Place in a Dutch colonial with shingle roof and siding. This two-story and basement frame structure on a concrete foundation, restored in recent years by Laurie and Henry Roberts, cost $9,000 in 1926.[21]

Paul W. Adams Sr. resided at 138 Laurel Heights Place for sixty years before his death. His architect cousin Carleton W. Adams drew plans for this appealing traditional Dutch colonial enclosed by a white fence. Lee Adams, father of the owner, was contractor. Described as "one of the most attractive small houses" built in the spring of 1924, "the strict adherence of the cottage to the Colonial design of architecture, its compactness and all-around attractiveness, have commanded much attention and admiring comment."[22]

"How An Architect Builds for Himself" ran the caption of one newspaper photograph of Beverly W. Spillman's plans for his new home at 142 Laurel Heights Place in 1923. Spillman, a member of the American Institute of Architects, drew plans for additions to the rear of this residence in 1937. Since the 1960s this has been the residence of Mary Lou and Don Everett:

Originality and imported ideas are being adapted to local use by Beverly W. Spillman, architect, in constructing his home on Laurel Heights Place. The interior as well as exterior is carried out in Italian design. The reception hall, entered through a cozy entrance with flagstone floor and stone seats, has an attractive stair with a balcony effect over the entrance. The living room is large and roomy. It has a stone fireplace and a flagstone hearth. The dining room, living room and service pantry open onto a terrace which is floored with red quarry tile. The service pantry floor is also of red tile and fitted with china closets. It has a service entrance from the

Architect Beverly Spillman designed his own home at 142 Laurel Heights Place in 1923.

driveway. The breakfast nook has a flagstone floor and beautifully designed Italian fixtures.

The kitchen is carried out in white and black finish with many devices and cabinets. There are also on the second floor three bedrooms and tile baths. The owner's bedroom opens onto a cool balcony to a tile terrace below. Under this, there is a fern bank formed of honeycombed rock. Mr. Spillman has kept in mind the question of upkeep throughout the entire house, and true to a foreign style, he has spared the use of wood as much as possible. All metal work is of copper, requiring no painting. The roof is of Heinz variegated clay tile. The clay is manufactured by a Mr. Heinz, an Italian, after the fashion of his native country. Ornamental iron is used to a good effect in places where it is needed.[23]

To balance upper-story windows to the left of the entrance of the 1927 Spanish Colonial Revival home at 218 Laurel Heights Place, architects Ayres & Ayres had incised in the stucco an embellishment remarkably similar to a hex sign.

Ayres and Ayres planned the homes at 207 and 218 Laurel Heights Place, both of Spanish design. Though they were photographed extensively in 1927, the paucity of print copy on each is disappointing. Robert Ayres's home at 207 Laurel Heights Place, a "Spanish farmhouse," received the first place award for domestic structures from the West Texas chapter of the American Institute of Architects in January 1927.

Wrote one observer: "Several plain, with only graceful arches, wrought iron grilles and a shell recessed mosaic to relieve its plain lines, this place is representative of the pure Spanish type." Commented another: "Robert M. Ayres, a leading San Antonio architect, believes that San Antonio should erect structures which harmonize with their setting and so in this romantic city which is so famous for her Spanish charm, Mr. Ayres builds his own, featuring the typical Spanish farmhouse type of architecture. . . . Of tile and stucco, it features mass and simplicity."[24] For more than four decades it was the Gilbert Langs' home.

When Edward B. Carruth Jr. began plans with the architects Ayres, he had an $18,000 one-story structure in mind. Something more elaborate was completed at 218 Laurel Heights by August 1927. "One of the most beautiful Spanish types" in San Antonio, this "northside attractive" home was a two-story stucco with a tile roof.[25] For some forty years it was the Richard Gills' home.

Only Paul Adams lived on Laurel Heights Place longer than the late Martin C. Giesecke, who built at 250 in 1927. Shrouded with bamboo canes on the corner of Shook, this is a structure of mystery and intrigue to nearby residents of Trinity University dormitories. Herff and Jones drew the plans, and August Fuessel was contractor:

The home will be of Spanish architecture and will be one of the finest of its type. Materials will include hollow tile, stucco, and reinforced concrete. L-shaped, the structure will have terraces and patio of unusual attractiveness and design. The roof will be of heavy Spanish tile, interior walls will be of rough plaster on metal lath. A steam heating plant and Frigidaire will be installed, the architect states. Work has been started on excavation.[26]

14. Monte Vista Organizes for Preservation

Neighborhood values of the quality associated with nineteenth-century America have been resuscitated throughout the land in the past decades.

Prior to organization of the Monte Vista Historical Association in 1973, however, only residents of the King William area had demonstrated viable concern for their domestic surroundings. Other noteworthy residential districts near downtown—Tobin Hill, Prospect Hill, West End and Dignowity Hill—had suffered irreparable commercial intrusion and deterioration. That Laurel Heights and Monte Vista lay in the path of urban erosion appeared certain.

Younger members of "old families" in Laurel Heights–Monte Vista began to move to the suburbs—"signs of the times," some said—in search of stable home values and better public education for their children. Real estate prices had declined north of Ashby by the 1960s, as unkempt lawns, peeling paint and destruction of fine homes appeared increasingly throughout the area. Witnesses to the razing of their landmark family home on French Place at Main Avenue, the Denman sisters (Molly Branton and Emily Thuss) grew anxious for the future of the neighborhood in which they planned to rear their young children.

Meanwhile, after observing residential decline near the Northwestern University campus in Evanston, Illinois, the writer of this account developed concern for the surroundings of Trinity University, where he served on the faculty. A catalyst appeared in the person of Conrad True, then on the San Antonio Conservation Society staff. He suggested that these three share their mutual anxiety. Whether Molly Branton called the writer, or conversely, has been forgotten.

What followed was an invitation from Emily and Dr. Charles Thuss to some twenty neighbors for an informal gathering at their home, 104 East Elsmere Place, on Thursday night, July 19, 1973. Conrad True joined the group to offer his expertise. Among those present, six couples became the founding Board of Directors of the Monte Vista Historical Association: Molly and Jim Branton, Mary Lou and Don Everett, Elaine and Jack Juen, Frances and John Kuntz, Emily and Charles Thuss, and Virginia and Gus Van Steenberg.

Don Everett, knowing little of which he spoke, contended that only designation as a historic district would preserve the neighborhood. Guests listened intently as the more knowledgeable Conrad True explained legal implications of such a designation and the responsibilities of those who would attempt such an undertaking. He spoke to a group, not without leadership experience in other civic undertakings, but sadly uninformed as to the ways and means of developing esprit de corps in a neighborhood of socioeconomic diversity.

Such an effort would obviously involve the organizational skills of Molly Branton and Emily Thuss; and, little as she could have anticipated that evening, the legal and forensic skills of attorney Virginia Van Steenberg, who would become the first president of this embryonic organization. Few, if any, of this group of burgeoning neighborhood zealots suspected that they would spend hundreds of hours on behalf of a yet unnamed Monte Vista Historical Association.

As originally conceived, Monte Vista Historical Association seemed an appropriate name. Those at the Thuss home that evening lived in Monte Vista proper or eastward across McCul-

The east-west Ashby Place, bottom, marks the southern boundary of the future Monte Vista National Historic District in this aerial view looking north in the late 1950s. North-south streets are, from left, San Pedro Avenue, Belknap Place, Howard Street, Main Avenue and McCullough Avenue. The Trinity University campus is at upper right.

lough. Mulberry Avenue to the south and Hildebrand to the north appeared to be logical north-south boundaries of an identifiable neighborhood which these neophytes would organize. This was not to be. When this writer returned from a three-week vacation, he received the alarming news that the Denman sisters had determined the boundaries should be extended southward to Ashby—"those people need saving more than we do"—and that plans had gone forward for a general neighborhood meeting. Invitees included everyone who lived in the area bounded by San Pedro, Hildebrand, Stadium Drive and McCullough from Huisache south to Ashby. A hand-delivered flyer went out.

You are cordially invited to a neighborhood gathering to discuss the formation of an association for the historic preservation of the Monte Vista area. Wednesday evening, August 29, 1973, 7:30 p.m., Chapman Graduate Center, Trinity University. Please join us!

Neighbors, in addition to the founding board members, who signed the invitation flyer included Mr. and Mrs. Harry Affleck Jr., Henry Amen, Clifton Bolner, John Canty, Kip Espey, Tom Fuller, Jack Hein, James Kazen, Billy Morton, George Newmark, Al Notzon, Joe Owen, James O'Brien, William Priest, Thomas Toudouze, as well as Blanche Barnett, Lillian Berg, Leonard Duce, Mil-

dred English, Gloria Galt, Joanne and Mrs. Charles Holshouser, and Ann Stonecipher.

John J. Kuntz III chaired the organizational meeting at which sponsors for the evening gathered early, uncertain that more than their closest friends might appear. Chapman Graduate Center auditorium filled to capacity. Audience enthusiasm suggested that these individuals would indeed be responsive to the idea of a neighborhood association. Mrs. Gus (Virginia) Van Steenberg presented the charter, which was adopted. Molly Branton, Emily Thuss and Jack Juen presented various plans and proposals from the Board of Directors.

Charter board members selected the first slate of officers, thereafter chosen at general membership meetings. Virginia Van Steenberg became the first president of the Monte Vista Historical Association, the announcement of which came at a general meeting on November 14, 1973. Other officers included Don Everett, vice-president; Molly Branton, secretary; and Emily Thuss, treasurer. Board members filed the association charter as a nonprofit organization with the secretary of state (Texas), who issued a Certificate of Incorporation dated November 8, 1973. The Monte Vista Historical Association charter set forth the organization's purposes:

San Antonio's downtown skyline rises two miles south of Monte Vista, as seen from the roof of the Bushnell Apartments, billed as "The Top of the Town" at their opening in 1926. The spire is that of the 1950s Trinity Baptist Church.

To encourage the preservation of the distinctive heritage of the Monte Vista area; to keep the physical identity of this late nineteenth–early twentieth century district intact; to educate the public, especially the youth, with the knowledge of our inherited neighborhood values which contribute to a wholesome urban environment.

Individuals who joined the organization prior to November 15, 1973, received the designation of charter member. Bylaws provided for annual dues of only $5 per family in an effort to gain widespread support. Although prospects of becoming an historic district had been outlined by Don Everett at the November 14 meeting, board members for more than a year concentrated on developing a viable organizational structure. Membership drive leaders, successful in large part because of support from block captains, eventually enrolled more than eight hundred families in the association. Meanwhile, board members began organizing gatherings and social activities so neighbors could meet one another.

One Monte Vista tradition antedates the association's founding. Janice and Michael Payer had already established a neighborhood Fourth of July parade, the first of its kind in the city. As an addendum, the board began a family picnic on the Landa Library grounds. Early summer block parties attracted as many as five hundred neighbors, and not a few visitors. These were open to the public, but invitations to the annual "I Love Monte Vista" party, generally in one of the "great houses" on the Sunday nearest Valentine's Day, reached members only. To raise funds and bring attention to the uniqueness of the neighborhood, annual Monte Vista House Tours began in 1977.

Local press coverage heightened public awareness of Monte Vista. No publication was more supportive than Lewis Fisher's *North San Antonio Times*. Its advocacy became increasingly important as the board turned toward gaining recognition of Monte Vista as a historic district.

City council passed a revised "Historic Districts and Landmarks" ordinance in May 1974. From this date, board members focused on acquiring that designation for Monte Vista. Welcome encouragement came when the board of the San

Antonio Conservation Society endorsed these efforts in September 1974. Residents were educated about historic zoning through newsletters, newspaper publicity and general meetings where residents could obtain specific information from such city staffers as City Preservation Officer Pat Osborne.

One newsletter explained the proposal, arguing, "only through historic district designation can the irreplaceable Monte Vista–Laurel Heights area be assuredly preserved from a fate such as Tobin Hill and other quality neighborhoods of the past." Composed by Virginia and Gus Van Steenberg and Don Everett, who simultaneously began work on a slide presentation for the cause, the letter presented the arguments in detail:

Jazz musicians led the July Fourth parade, Monte Vista's oldest neighborhood tradition, through its streets in 1971.

Some of the homes in this proposed historic district date earlier than a number in the King William Historic District, although most were built a generation later. Architectural diversity—Georgian, Moorish, antebellum, Victorian, Queen Anne, Spanish, Hollywood bungalow—is more apparent than in King William.

Some of San Antonio's most distinguished residential architects can be found along the streets between Ashby and Hildebrand. Not to be ignored also are several blocks of the already disappearing bungalow types so characteristic of the twenties. Residents can attest to the large number of sightseers attracted to their streets, even before the organization of the Historical Association which has directed widespread attention to the area. Numerous business and civic leaders have lived hereabouts for more than two generations. West Texas cattle barons built their homes on Kings Highway and nearby streets. Residents of the area today are most likely to identify with downtown San Antonio interests, whether they be descendants of these early families, newcomers, or apartment dwellers.

For these reasons members of the Monte Vista Historical Association, Inc., and hundreds of residents who are non-members, believe that this neighborhood is uniquely qualified for historic district designation. Members of the Board of the Association have studied carefully the new "Historic Districts and Landmarks" ordinance passed by the City Council in May 1974, and believe that their aspirations are compatible with the ordinance in both spirit and specifics.

It has never been the intention of the Monte Vista Historical Association to disturb the few business and other non-residential establishments which already exist and have been appropriately zoned within the proposed boundaries of the district. Monte Vista Board of Directors know that this would not be possible and have attempted to inform the general membership that the city ordinance does not "affect the present legal use of property."

As members sought signatures on historic zoning petitions, each carried a copy of the ordinance so residents could understand provisions.

Any zoning decision, including the establishment of historic districts, may reduce the rights of some individuals. Members of the Monte Vista Historical Association believe, however, that larger rewards—tangible and intangible—will accrue to all its residents. The obvious local example is the King William Historic District. Similar meaningful improvements are going on in historic neighborhoods across the nation. Historic zoning for the Laurel Heights–Monte Vista area, moreover, will for generations to come enhance the reputation of San Antonio as one of America's most interesting and historic cities.

City regulations required signatures of property holders within Monte Vista boundaries in support of the board petition for historic zoning. Molly Branton shouldered the tremendous responsibility of organizing volunteers to go door-to-door for signatures. These volunteers, of whom David Yoachum was perhaps the most diligent, spent hundreds of hours explaining the implications of historic zoning. More than 1,600 property owners signed supporting petitions.

Meanwhile, Emily Thuss and her committee spent countless hours compiling the required list of property holders to be called upon by the city to express approval or disapproval. These individuals also received a "Fact Sheet" explaining effects of historic zoning. During the last week of April 1975, San Antonio's Historic Review Board gave the application unanimous approval.

Board members also brought architects, planners and city staffers to an open meeting on May 4, 1975, to answer questions. Ten days later, the initial hearing on historic districting took place before the Planning and Zoning Commission. More than 90 percent of property-holding respondents to notices from the city voted favorably, and the association received another unanimous vote from the Planning and Zoning Commission. Nancy Scott Jones reported the scene in the *North San Antonio Times* of May 22, 1975:

Cheers and a standing ovation from an ecstatic group of Monte Vista residents broke order in the overflowing city hall council room when the commission announced its decision, reached in spite of opposition from a small delegation of property owners who opposed the historic designation on the grounds it would infringe on the rights of property owners and put a "freeze" on the area's cultural diversity, creating "an upper middle class economic ghetto."

The association's rationale for historic district designation was outlined by Monte Vista Association President Mrs. Virginia Van Steenberg of 115 E. Lynwood Ave. and Vice-President Dr. Donald Everett of 142 Laurel Heights Pl. A slide show of homes along the area's spacious, tree-lined streets accompanied the presentation. Mrs. Van Steenberg pointed out that the area is endangered by urban decay, but could be preserved since it qualifies as a historic district by placing changes under the scrutiny of the city's Historic Review Board, which also guards the King William Street and La Villita historic districts.

City staff also endorsed the petition and recommended its approval by city council. Further support came from Ron White in a feature-length article, "Save Monte Vista," in the June issue of *San Antonio Magazine*. Additional backing came in a *San Antonio News* editorial of June 17:

Monte Vista, a part of the city's near North Side, is peopled by residents who want to protect their old neighborhood from decay and demolition. Monte Vista is made up of seven of the city's oldest subdivisions. The homes were built during America's "Gilded Age." There is a marvelous mixture of architecture, from Victorian to Hollywood Bungalow. Its members have petitioned the city to designate the area as an Historic District, giving it the same protection the King William area and La Villita enjoy. Monte Vista's residents

have shown a rare appreciation for their neighborhood. They have worked together to save it, and it deserves saving.

As July 17, 1975, the date set for the city council vote, approached, excitement spread throughout the neighborhood. At the appointed hour, President Van Steenberg and Vice-President Everett made oral presentations to city council similar to those they made before the Planning and Zoning Commission. Virginia Van Steenberg proved to be especially effective in her rebuttals to the four opponents who spoke against historic designation. Once again, Nancy Scott Jones described the scenario for readers in the *North San Antonio Times* (July 24, 1975).

Monte Vista residents—125 strong—hugged their neighbors and cheered San Antonio city councilmen after the council voted in a 7-1 decision at last Thursday's council session to grant historic zoning to the 60-block Monte Vista area despite the threat of a lawsuit by the Trinity Baptist Church.

The council chambers at the outset looked more like the beginnings of an early afternoon garden party. Tanned mothers tucked the skirts of their sundresses under them and sat on the floor to hear the lengthy discussion. Elderly women peered from under their summer straw hats at the eight councilmen. Several men had taken the afternoon off from work to attend the session, and a few children were on hand to see city government in operation.

Cheers and applause greeted Mayor Lila Cockrell, who opened the session and then disqualified herself from voting because she and her husband own property in the area at 254 Rosewood. More applause interrupted the meeting as individual council members praised the association for its two-year-long task in working for the historical zoning as a means of preserving the heritage of one of the city's most distinctive neighborhoods.

So it was that city council passed Ordinance 4550 on July 17, 1975, designating the Monte Vista area as an "H" historic district. Board members and loyal neighbors had achieved their first major objective; the organizational structure was in place.

The time had come to enlarge the number of persons on the board and make it more representative of the entire Monte Vista Historic District. More important, the time had come to attend to those "inherent neighborhood values which contribute to a wholesome urban environment." All the while, numerous social events encouraged hundreds to know their neighborhood.

A Monte Vista button reads: "Older Is Better."

Notes

Introduction

1. Donald E. Everett, "San Antonio Welcomes the 'Sunset,'" *Southwestern Historical Quarterly* (Jul., 1961).
2. *San Antonio Express,* Jun. 14, 1891.
3. Ordinance 45504, City Council, Jul. 17, 1975.
4. "National Register of Historic Places Inventory–Nomination Form," 11.

1. Mrs. Kampmann's Goat Pasture

1. *Express*, Mar. 29, 1916; Apr. 18, 1922.
2. San Antonio *Light*, Nov. 9, 1919.
3. *Express*, Apr. 18, 1922.
4. "City of San Antonio to Estate of D. C. Alexander, Ded'd," Jul. 22, 1870, II, pp. 455–57, Bexar County Clerk.
5. Lee Adams, "Memoir," 73, typescript of Paul W. Adams.
6. Ibid., Adams' Laurel Heights Plat, Feb. 11, 1890, MVHA Files.
7. Cecilia Steinfeldt, *The Onderdonks,* 16.
8. *Express*, Apr. 18, 1922.
9. Adams, "Memoir," 75–76.
10. *Express*, May 23, 1892.
11. Ibid., Jan. 25, 1890.
12. Ibid.
13. Ibid., Mar. 1, 1890.
14. Adams, "Memoir," 7; *Express*, Apr. 18, 1922.
15. *Express*, Dec. 23, 1891.
16. Ibid., Mar. 15, 1890; Apr. 18, 1922.
17. Ibid., Aug. 1, 1906.
18. Ibid., Mar. 7, 1892.
19. Ibid., Mar. 15, 1892.
20. Ibid., Aug. 1, 1892.
21. Adams, "Memoir," 73, 75; *Express*, Jun. 21, 1927.

22. *Express*, Mar. 29, 1916.
23. Ibid., Mar. 19, 1893.
24. Ibid., Oct. 1, 1893.
25. Adams, "Memoir," 73.
26. *Express*, Feb. 6, 1901.
27. Ibid., May 18, 1924.
28. Ibid., Mar. 23, 1901.
29. Ibid., Feb. 14, 1904.
30. *Light*, May 13, 1902; *Express*, Nov. 16, 1904.
31. *Express*, Aug. 26, 1903.
32. Ibid., May 25, 1905.
33. Ibid., Apr. 25, 1929.
34. Ibid., Nov. 25, 1906.
35. *Light*, Dec. 27, 1908.
36. Ibid., Dec. 9, 1906.
37. *Express*, Dec. 2, 1906.
38. *Light*, May 26, 1907. A street such as French Place was actually paved by Uvalde Rock Asphalt Co. in 1917. *Express*, Aug. 17, 1917.
39. *Express*, Oct. 20, 1907.
40. Ibid., Nov. 30, 1907.
41. *Light*, Aug. 27, 1903.
42. Ibid., May 30, 1905; Jul. 8, 1906.
43. *Express*, Aug. 26, 1903.
44. Ibid., Apr. 11, 1905; *Light*, Apr. 20, 1905.
45. *Express*, Jun. 14, 1909.
46. *Light*, Apr. 14, 1907.
47. *Express*, May 24, 1908.
48. Ibid., Aug. 18, 1912.
49. Ibid., Jul. 10, 1893.
50. Ibid., Jan. 15, 1894.
51. Ibid., Jun. 2, 1901.
52. Ibid., Feb. 19, 1893.
53. Ibid., Mar. 1, 1906.
54. Ibid., Nov. 8, 1903.
55. Ibid., Nov. 1, 1910.
56. Ibid., Aug. 5, 1910.
57. Ibid., Apr. 24, 1892; Mar. 5, 1893.
58. Adams, "Memoir," 71, 86.
59. "Session Records, 1895," First Presbyterian Church.
60. *Express*, Mar. 19, 1911.
61. Ibid., Mar. 16, 1913.
62. Ibid., Mar. 2, 1913.

63. Ibid., Feb. 4, 1917.
64. Ibid., Dec. 22, 1901.
65. Ibid., Dec. 25, 1904.
66. Ibid., Apr. 22, 1893.
67. Ibid., Apr. 17, 1907.
68. Ibid., Jun. 27, 1903.
69. Ibid., Dec. 22, 1907.
70. Ibid., Jun. 17, 1908.
71. Ibid., Jan. 20, 1905.
72. Pompeo Coppini, *Dawn to Sunset*, 108–10; *Express*, Apr. 25, 1905.
73. Steinfeldt, *The Onderdonks*, 224; 105n–107n.
74. *Express*, Mar. 17, 1912.
75. Diary of Emily G. Onderdonk, Dec. 25, 1909, Witte Museum.
76. *Express*, Dec. 28, 1902.
77. Ibid., Aug. 7, 1893.
78. Ibid., Jun. 20, 1917.
79. Ibid., Feb. 18, 1917.
80. *Light*, Feb. 18, 1917.
81. *Express*, Jul. 2, 1911.
82. Ibid., Jun. 26, 1921.
83. *Light*, Mar. 23, 25, 1905.
84. *Express*, Jul. 30, 1903.
85. Ibid., Jan. 4, 1903.
86. Ibid., Aug. 7, 1893.
87. Ibid., Jul. 10, 1893.
88. *Light*, Nov. 14, 1902.
89. Ibid., Oct. 26, 1903.
90. *Express*, Aug. 7, 1893.
91. *Light*, Jun. 4, 1903.
92. Ibid., Apr. 14, 1907.
93. Interview, Mrs. E. S. (Ruth West) Emerson, Aug. 18, 1982.

2. Development Expands

1. *City Directory* (1906–1908).
2. *Express*, Apr. 14, 1906.
3. Ibid., May 19, 1907.
4. Ibid., Apr. 28, 1907.
5. Ibid., Mar. 1, 1908.
6. Ibid., Dec. 13, 1908.
7. Ibid., Feb. 21, 1909.
8. Ibid., Mar. 1, 1908.
9. Ibid., Apr. 17, 1910.
10. *Light*, Apr. 10, 1910.

11. *Express*, Mar. 31, 1918.
12. *Light*, Nov. 30, 1919.
13. Ibid., Mar. 30, 1919.
14. Ibid., Nov. 23, 1919.
15. Ibid., Mar. 9, 1919.
16. Ibid., Jan. 19, 1919.
17. *Express*, Mar. 28, 1920.
18. Ibid., Apr. 10, 1920.
19. Ibid., Oct. 3, 1920.
20. U.S. Census, 1900 Bexar County. Also see *City Directory*, 1900–1925.
21. Interview, Mrs. E. S. Emerson, Aug. 16, 1982.
22. Ibid.
23. Interview, Mrs. Frank Churchill, Aug. 17, 1982.
24. Interview, Mrs. Jean Goggan Kuntz, Aug. 17, 1982.
25. Interview, Mrs. Stanley Slavens, Aug. 17, 1982.
26. Interview, Majorie T. Walthall, Aug. 17, 1982.
27. *Express*, Feb. 12, 1928.
28. Ibid., Mar. 15, 1972.

3. Monte Vista Matures

1. *Light*, Oct. 5, Nov. 16, 1919.
2. Ibid., Jan. 19, Nov. 19, 1919; *Express*, Nov. 9, 1919; Jul. 25, 1920.
3. *Light*, May 23, 1920.
4. *Express*, Jul. 25, 1920.
5. Ibid., Feb. 9, 1921.
6. Ibid., Oct. 29, 1922.
7. Ibid., Nov. 26, 1922.
8. Ibid., Dec. 10, 1922.
9. Ibid., Feb. 18, 1923.
10. Ibid., Nov. 7, 21, 1920; Jan. 2, 30, Feb. 20, Mar. 15, 27, Apr. 10, May 15, Jul. 3, 10, 17, 24, 1921; Jan. 28, 1923.
11. Ibid., Jan. 12, Mar. 20, Apr. 3, 24, May 1, Nov. 27, 1921; Feb. 5, Sep. 3, 1922.
12. Ibid., Mar. 5, 1922.
13. Ibid., May 22, 1921.
14. Ibid., Sep. 25, 1921; Jan. 22, Aug. 20, 1922.

15. Ibid., Jan. 9, 23, Jun. 5, Jul. 24, 31; Aug. 14, Sep. 18, Dec. 11, 25, 1921; Jan. 1, 15, 1922.
16. Ibid., Apr. 17, 1921.
17. Ibid., May 11, Jun. 8, Jul. 17, Aug. 3, 10, 17; Sep. 28, 1924.
18. Ibid., Mar. 5, 1922; Feb. 18, Jun. 3, 1923; *Light*, Nov. 18, 1923.
19. *Express*, May 17, 1925.
20. *Light*, Jul. 1, 1923.
21. Ibid., Apr. 1, 18, 1923.
22. *Express*, Sep. 9, 1923.
23. *Light*, Nov. 22, 1925; *Express*, Nov. 22, 1925.
24. "Atlee B. & Robert M. Ayres, Architects," typescript in Ayres Collection, Archives, UT School of Architecture.
25. *Express*, Feb. 11, 1923; Sep. 6, 1925.
26. *Light*, Feb. 18, 1923.
27. "Atlee B. & Robert M. Ayres," typescript.
28. *Light*, Sep. 24, 1924; *Express*, Jan. 27, 1924.
29. *Light*, Mar. 16, 1924; *Express*, Dec. 14, 1924; Mar. 11, 1928.
30. *Express*, Dec. 20, 1925.
31. Ibid., Dec. 13, 1925; Mar. 7, 1926; Oct. 16, 1927.
32. *Light*, Dec. 4, 1927.
33. Ibid., Aug. 12, 1928; *Express*, Mar. 10, May 17, 1929.
34. *Light*, May 15, 1910; Monte Vista Tour Guide (1981).
35. *Express*, Oct. 5, 1927; *Light*, Oct. 14, 1927.
36. *Light*, Oct. 9, 1927.
37. Ibid., Jul. 7, Dec. 22, 29, 1929; *Express*, Jan. 26, 1930.
38. *Light*, Nov. 24, 1929.

4. French and Ashby

1. Steinfeldt, *The Onderdonks*, 15–16.
2. Emily G. Onderdonk Diary, Apr. 18, 1882.
3. Eleanor Onderdonk mss. in Steinfeldt, *The Onderdonks*, 171.
4. *Express*, Dec. 18, 1887.
5. *Beautiful Homes* (San Antonio, 1914), n.p.
6. *Express*, Dec. 18, 1887.
7. *Beautiful Homes*, n.p.
8. *Light*, Mar. 10, 1912.
9. *Beautiful Homes*, n.p.
10. Folder 16, Atlee B. Ayres Collection.
11. J. Fred Buenz Collection.
12. *Beautiful Homes*, n.p.
13. *Light*, Dec. 7, 1913.

14. Ibid., Nov. 17, 1912; *Express*, Dec. 5, 1901.
15. *Express*, Nov. 19, 1901.
16. *Light*, Sep. 20, 1911.
17. Folder 266, Ayres Collection.
18. *Reference Work of Prominent Men of Southwest Texas*, n.p.
19. *Express*, Jun. 25, 194.
20. Ibid., Jun. 25, 1914; Jun. 19, 1921; Dec. 8, 1927.
21. Ibid., Feb. 20, 1921.
22. Ibid., Jun. 8, 1919.
23. Ibid., May 21, 1922; *Light*, Jun. 11, 1922.
24. *North San Antonio Times*, Mar. 7, 1974.
25. "National Register of Historic Places Inventory," Jan. 2, 1980.
26. Dorothy McKinley and Mary Everett mss., ibid.
27. *Express*, Dec. 24, 1916.
28. *Light*, Oct. 18, 1925.
29. Folders 16, 16.1, 16.2, 16.3, Ayres Collection.
30. *Express*, Jul. 16, 1911.
31. Ibid, Dec. 20, 1923.
32. Ibid.
33. Ibid., Apr. 12, 1906; May 31, 1908.
34. Ibid., Oct. 29, 1911.
35. *Light*, Aug. 17, 1919.
36. Appler's *General Directory of . . . Greater San Antonio*, 1924–25.
37. *Express*, Aug. 28, 1910.
38. *Light*, Apr. 15, 1928.
39. Poole-Totten Papers, MVHA file; *Light*, May 24, 1925.
40. *Express*, Nov. 1, 1981.
41. *Light*, Jun. 11, 1905.
42. *Express*, Feb. 20, 1921; Interview, Frank I. Davis, Jr., Jul. 16, 1982.
43. Kinnison Papers, MVHA files.
44. *Light*, Jun. 21, 1903.
45. Ibid., Nov. 4, 1923.
46. Folder 47, Ayres Collection.
47. *Express*, Dec. 1, 1907.
48. Ibid., Oct. 4, 1908.
49. Ibid., Jan. 9, 1910.
50. Ibid., Oct. 24, 1926.
51. Ibid., May 4, 1905.
52. *Beautiful Homes*, n.p.
53. *Light*, May 3, 1925; San Antonio Historical Survey, 1972.
54. *Light*, Nov. 7, 1909.

5. Belknap, Craig, Woodlawn and Mistletoe

1. *Express*, Feb. 7, 1909; *Light*, Nov. 18, 1923.
2. *Express*, Feb. 14, 1925; *Light*, Dec. 6, 1925.

3. Withers, *San Antonio: A History of Color*, 60.
4. *City Directory*, 1947–1981.
5. *Light*, May 18, 1903.
6. Ibid., Aug. 10, 1913.
7. *City Directory*, 1947–1981.
8. J. Fred Buenz, Documentation of Christ Episcopal Church, Sep. 29, 1975, MVHA files.
9. Folder 25, Ayres Collection.
10. *Light*, May 24, 1902.
11. *Express*, Feb. 8, Mar. 15, 1891.
12. Ibid., Jun. 21, 1927.
13. *City Directory*, 1920–1980.
14. *Express*, Apr. 12, Aug. 12, 1906.
15. *Light*, Dec. 16, 1906; *Express*, Dec. 9, 1906.
16. *Reference Work*, n.p.
17. *Light*, Jun. 17, 1928.
18. *Express*, Mar. 5, 1893.
19. Ibid.
20. *City Directory*, 1916–1980.
21. Interview, Mrs. Jack Harris (Virginia) Hein, Aug. 18, 1982.
22. *City Directory*, 1898–1980.
23. *Express*, Jun. 21, 1927.
24. Ibid., Jul. 1, 1906.
25. Interview, Martin Giesecke, Aug. 16, 1982.
26. *Express*, Apr. 11, 1914; *Light*, May 20, 1928.
27. *City Directory*, 1906–1908.
28. *Express*, May 11, 1919.
29. Insurance Maps of San Antonio, 1904.
30. *Greater San Antonio*, n.p.
31. *Express*, May 10, 1918.
32. Ibid., Jun. 26, 1921.
33. *Light*, Nov. 25, 1923.
34. *Express*, Sep. 6, 1927.
35. Ibid., Mar. 3, 1916.
36. *Light*, Feb. 25, 1912.
37. *Express*, Nov. 22, 1908.
38. Interview, Terrell Maverick Webb, Apr. 28, 1975.
39. *Express*, Jun. 17, 1917.
40. Ibid., Jul. 12, 1908.
41. *Light*, Oct. 8, 1902.
42. Ibid., Nov. 14, 1909.
43. *Express*, Oct. 24, 1909.
44. *Light*, Apr. 3, 1910.
45. Ibid., Jan. 29, 1911; *Express*, Mar. 31, 1912.
46. *City Directory*, 1897–1914.
47. Coppini, *Dawn to Sunset*, 118.
48. Mrs. Augusta J. Espy, notes, MVHA files.
49. Harvey P. Smith (copy) Records, ibid.
50. *Express*, Jan. 21, 1906; *Light*, Sep. 13, 1904; Feb. 27, 1910; *Reference Work*, n.p.
51. *Express*, Aug. 20, 1911.
52. Ibid., Oct. 25, 1925.
53. Ibid., Jul. 30, 1922.
54. *Light*, Dec. 7, 1903.

55. Withers, *San Antonio*, 62.
56. *Express*, Jul. 9, 1905; *Light*, Oct. 14, 1906.
57. *Light*, Nov. 23, 1904.
58. Ibid., Sep. 22, 1903; *Express*, Nov. 16, 1924.
59. *Express*, Oct. 27, 1907.
60. Mrs. Frank W. Davis Memo, MVHA files.
61. *North San Antonio Times*, Nov. 23, 1972; Emerson Interview.
62. *Express*, Feb. 11, 1923.
63. *Light*, Mar. 2, 1913; Mrs. S. Finley Ewing Memo, MVHA files.
64. *Express*, Feb. 20, 1893.
65. *Light*, Dec. 29, 1903.
66. Ibid., Sep. 28, 1924.
67. Ibid., Apr. 26, 1908.
68. Ibid., Mrs. W. R. (Fairfax Janin) Nesbit memo, MVHA files.
69. *Reference Work*.
70. *Light*, Apr. 28, 1929.
71. *Express*, Nov. 24, 1972.
72. *Reference Work*, n.p.; *Express*, Nov. 24, 1972; Interview, Mrs. Frank Newton, Aug. 17, 1982.
73. *Light*, Mar. 15, 1924.
74. *Express*, Nov. 24, 1972.
75. *Light*, Aug. 15, 1907.
76. *Express*, Feb. 28, 1910.
77. *Light*, Mar. 20, 1910.
78. Ibid., Nov. 15, 1902.
79. Insurance Maps of San Antonio; *City Directory*, 1906–1946.

6. Magnolia, Huisache and Mulberry

1. *Express*, Mar. 31, 1929.
2. Ibid., Jan. 10, 1909; Interview, Mrs. Lloyd H. Harrington, Jun. 29, 1983.
3. MVHA files.
4. *Express*, Apr. 22, Nov. 8, 1917.
5. Ibid., May 13, 1923.
6. *Light*, Mar. 13, 1927; *City Directory*, 1924–25.
7. *Express*, Jun. 17, 1906; *City Directory*, 1905–06; Interview, Mrs. James C. (Sarah) Talcott, Jun. 28, 1983.
8. *Light*, Apr. 10, 1921; *City Directory*, 1905–06.
9. *Express*, Jul. 13, 1928.
10. Ibid., Mar. 15, Jul. 20, 1913; *Light*, May 5, 1912; Jan. 11, Jun. 14, 1914.
11. *Express*, Oct. 3, 1926; Feb. 20, 1927; *Light*, Feb. 20, 1927.
12. *Light*, Sep. 18, Dec. 4, 1927.
13. *Express*, Feb. 19, 1928.
14. Ibid., Sep. 28, 1930.

15. Ibid , Apr. 6, 1924; *Light*, Jul. 22, 1923.
16. *Express*, May 30, 1909; *Light*, May 12, 1912.
17. *Light*, Jan. 8, 1911; *Beautiful Homes*; *Reference Works*.
18. *Light*, Mar. 8, 1920.
19. Ibid., Nov. 21, 1920; *Express*, Apr. 18, 1926.
20. Ibid., *Light*, Aug. 8, 1920; *Express*, Jan. 30, 1920.
21. *Light*, Jun. 10, 1923.
22. Ibid., Sep. 14, 1924.
23. Harvey P. Smith specs., MVHA files.
24. *Express*, Aug. 7, 1921.
25. Ibid., Sep. 23, 1928; *Light*, Jul. 7, 1929.
26. Folders 4, 4.1, Ayres Collection; *Light*, Nov. 7, 1926; Interview, Mrs. William C. (Agnes) Clegg Sr., Jul. 18, 1976; *North San Antonio Times*, May 10, 1972.
27. *Express*, Mar. 18, 1923.
28. Ibid., Jul. 7, 1918; MVHA files.
29. Ibid., Jul. 11, 1909.
30. *Light*, May 11, 1927.
31. Ibid., Sep. 5, 1915.
32. *Express*, Feb. 13, 1910.
33. Ibid., Oct. 26, 1913; May 29, 1921; *Light*, Apr. 14, 1914.
34. *Express*, Jun. 21, 1925.
35. *Light*, Jan. 7, 1923; *Express*, Jun. 21, 1925.
36. MVHA files.
37. *Light*, Jan. 5, 1913.
38. *Express*, Jul. 17, 1921.
39. Ibid., Oct. 20, 1912.
40. *Light*, Apr. 2, 1922.
41. MVHA files.
42. *Light*, Mar. 22, 1925.
43. *Express*, May 20, 1915.
44. Ibid., Sep. 25, 1927.
45. MVHA files.
46. *Light*, Mar. 13, 1927.
47. *Express*, Feb. 2, 1919.
48. Ibid., May 21, 1922.
49. *Light*, Apr. 16, 1922.

7. Agarita, Summit, McCullough and Main

1. *Light*, Sep. 10, 1911; A. Maria Watson typescript, MVHA files.
2. *Express*, Sep. 5, 1909; Folder 26, Ayres Collection.
3. *Light*, Jan. 16, 30, 1927.
4. Ibid., Jun. 27, 1926.
5. Ibid., Apr. 4, 1920.
6. *Express*, Feb. 13, 1916.
7. Ibid., Jul. 1, 1923; MVHA files.
8. *Light*, Feb. 19, 1909.
9. *Express*, Jan. 3, 1915.
10. *Light*, Mar. 1, 1914.
11. Ibid., May 27, 1917.
12. *Express*, Jan. 3, 1915.

13. *Light*, Apr. 17, 1927.
14. Ibid., Jun. 18, 1922; MVHA files.
15. Ibid., Apr. 10, 1921.
16. Ibid., Apr. 27, 1924.
17. *Beautiful Homes*; *Residential San Antonio*; Interview, Mrs. W. C. (Agnes Terrell) Clegg, Jul. 13, 1983.
18. *Light*, Nov. 29, 1914; Jul. 11, 1915; Feb. 23, Mar. 2, 1919.
19. Ibid., Jan. 28, Feb. 18, 1923; Jun. 11, 1922; *Express*, Jun. 21, 1927.
20. *Light*, Mar. 17, 1929; Interviews, Mrs. Fred Buenz, Apr. 30, 1982; Dr. John L. Matthews, Jul. 14, 1983.
21. Interview, Mrs. Russell W. (Virginia) Fichtner, Jul. 14, 1983.
22. *Light*, Jul. 28,1929.
23. Ibid., Nov. 30, 1924; Mar. 1, Nov. 8, 1925; Apr. 3, 1927; *Express*, Mar. 1, 1925.
24. *Light*, May 15, 1927.
25. City Directory, 1924–25.
26. *Express*, Jan. 25, 1914; Jun. 8, 1919.
27. *Light*, Jan. 14, Mar. 11, 1923.
28. Ibid., Aug. 28, 1922.
29. Ibid., Nov. 23, 1924.
30. Ibid., Mar. 1, 1914; Nov. 23, 1919; *Express*, Jun. 14, 1923; Feb. 9, 1917.
31. *Light*, Jun. 2, 1907; Jan. 12, 26, 1908.
32. *Express*, Feb. 18, 1917; Dec. 22, 1921.
33. *Light*, Sep. 19, 1926.
34. *Express*, May 30, 1920.
35. Ibid., Apr. 6, 1924.
36. Ibid., Jul. 4, 1926.
37. *Light*, Aug. 8, 1920; MVHA files.
38. *Express*, Aug. 27,1922.
39. Harvey P. Smith specs., MVHA files.
40. Interview, Mrs. Frank Churchill, Jul. 14, 1983.
41. *Express*, Nov. 27, 1921; *Light*, Apr. 30, 1922.
42. *Express*, Feb. 8, 1891; Oct. 3, 1920.
43. *Light*, Apr. 26, 1903.
44. Withers, *San Antonio*, 50.
45. *Light*, Aug. 21, 1910.
46. A. Maria Watson, typescript, MVHA files.
47. *Light*, Oct. 19, 1919; *Express*, Feb. 8, 1914.
48. *Express*, Nov. 23, 1919; Feb. 5, 1922.
49. Ibid., Mar. 18, 1923.
50. Ibid., Sep. 19, 1909.
51. *Light*, Aug. 15, 1909; Feb. 23, 1919.
52. MVHA files; *Light*, Apr. 23, 1921.
53. MVHA files.

8. Kings Highway

1. *Light*, Jan. 21, 1917.
2. *Express*, Jan. 20, 1929.
3. *Light*, Jun. 14, 1914; MVHA files.
4. *San Antonio Historic Survey* (1971), n.p.
5. *Express*, Mar. 3, 1912; May 6, 1920; Jun. 21, 1927.
6. Ibid., Apr. 20, 1917.
7. Ibid., Mar. 19, 1911.
8. Ibid., Aug. 16, 1914; Dec. 22, 1916; Mar. 18, 1917.
9. Ibid., Apr. 19, 1925.
10. Interview, Ike S. Kampmann Jr., Jul. 14, 1983; *Express*, Nov. 28, 1922.
11. *Express*, Jun. 17, 1923; Feb. 17, 1924.
12. Ibid., Jun. 21, 1925.
13. Folder 22, Ayres Collection; *Light*, Feb. 9, Nov. 29, 1908; *Express*, Nov. 28, 1908.
14. *Express*, Jan. 3, 1915; *Light*, Oct. 29, 1922.
15. *Light*, Jul. 12, 1914.
16. *Express*, Aug. 24, 1913; Feb. 15, 1914; Jul. 1, 1929; *Light*, Nov. 16, 1913; Oct. 14, 1919.
17. *Light*, Nov. 2, 14, 23, 1924.
18. Ibid., Jul. 12, 1914.
19. *Express*, Oct. 28, 1923; MVHA files.
20. *Light*, Jul. 3, 1921; *Express*, Feb. 11, 1923.
21. *Light*, Feb. 11, 1923; *Express*, Feb. 11, 1923.
22. *Express*, May 13, 1923.
23. *Light*, Sep. 2, 1928; Feb. 2, 1930.
24. Interview, Mrs. Stanley G. (Jane) Slavens, Jul. 14, 1983.
25. MVHA files; *Express*, Sep. 17, Dec. 10, 1922.
26. *Express*, Dec. 20, 1925.
27. Ibid., Dec. 3, 1922; Apr. 8, 1923.
28. *Light*, Jan. 9, 1927.
29. *Express*, Nov. 23, 1927.
30. Ibid., May 10, 1925; *Light*, Apr. 24, 1927.
31. Ibid., Jun. 22, 1924.
32. Vol. 827, p. 582, Office of Bexar County Clerk.
33. *Express*, Nov. 28, 1926.

9. Gramercy, Elsmere and Belknap

1. *Light*, May 25, Jul. 6, 1930.
2. Ibid., Jan. 2, 1927.
3. *Express*, Nov. 13, 1927.
4. Ibid., Sep. 2, 1928.
5. *Light*, Feb. 12, 1928.
6. *Express*, Aug. 26, 1928.
7. Ibid., Sep. 9, 1928.

8. Ann Sheldon Sims in MVHA files.
9. *Light*, May 11, Oct. 12, 1924.
10. MVHA files.
11. *Light*, Nov. 18, 1923.
12. *Express*, Apr. 8, 1923.
13. *Light*, Mar. 2, 1930.
14. Ibid., Feb. 5, 1923; *Express*, May 21, 1922.
15. *Light*, Aug. 26, 1928; *Express*, Apr. 6, 1930.
16. *Express*, Sep. 28, 1928; Dec. 22, 1929.
17. MVHA files. Interview, Mrs. D. B. Ofthson, niece of Russell Brown, Jul. 14, 1983.
18. *Express*, Sep. 7, 1924.
19. Ibid., Dec. 13, 1925.
20. Ibid., Jan. 10, 1926.
21. *Light*, Aug. 15, 1926.
22. Harvey P. Smith specs., MVHA files.
23. *Express*, Jan. 16, 1927.
24. Ibid., Oct. 2, 1927.
25. *Light*, Jan. 13, 1929.
26. Ibid., Aug. 19, 1928; *Express*, Aug. 19, 1928.
27. *Express*, Oct. 9, 1927.
28. *Light*, Jan. 15, 1922.
29. Ibid., Mar. 29, 1925.
30. Ibid., Dec. 30, 1923.
31. Ibid., Sep. 28, 1924.
32. *Express*, May 17, 1925.
33. *Light*, Apr. 6, 1924; MVHA files.
34. *Express*, Aug. 26, 1928; *Light*, Jul. 1, 1928.
35. *Express*, Oct. 19, 1924.
36. Ibid., Jun. 10, 1923.
37. *Light*, Feb. 8, 1925.
38. *Express*, Feb. 11, 1923.
39. Ibid., May 6, 1923.
40. Ibid., Oct. 10, 1926; May 17, 1925; *Light*, Sep. 28, 1924.
41. *Light*, May 10, 1925.
42. Ibid., Dec. 21, 1924.
43. Ibid., Aug. 21, 1921; *Express*, Jun. 1, 1924.
44. *Express*, Feb. 1, 1926.
45. *Light*, Oct. 21, 1928; Feb. 3, 1929.
46. Ibid., Oct. 21, 1928; Aug. 4, 1929.
47. Ibid., Mar. 18, 1923; *Express*, Mar. 18, Sep. 9, 1923.
48. *Express*, Jan. 1, 1928.
49. *Light*, Jul. 8, 1923; *Express*, Feb. 18, 1923.
50. *Light*, Aug. 22, 1920; Oct. 29, 1922; Nov. 16, 1924; *Greater San Antonio*, 93.
51. *Express*, Jun. 21, 1927; *Light*, Jun. 22, 1924; Oct. 3, 1926.

10. Lynwood and Hollywood

1. *Light*, Apr. 18, 1926.

2. *Express*, Jul. 27, 1924.
3. Ibid., Aug. 17, 1924.
4. Bexar County Deed Records, Vol. 583, p. 357.
5. *Light*, Mar. 21, 1926; *Express*, Apr. 18, 1926.
6. *Express*, Nov. 28, 1920.
7. Ibid., May 14, 1922.
8. *Light*, Feb. 5, 19, 1928; *Express*, Aug. 26, 1928.
9. Ibid.
10. *Light*, Mar. 27, Apr. 10, 1927; *Express*, Oct. 30,1927.
11. *Express*, Feb. 8, 1925; Jun. 21, Oct. 10, 1926; MVHA files.
12. Folders 45, 19, Ayres Collection.
13. *Express*, Oct. 11, Dec. 13, 1925; *Light*, May 24, 1925.
14. MVHA files.
15. *Express*, Jan. 23, Feb. 27, 1927.
16. Ibid., Sep. 26, 1920; MVHA files.
17. *Express*, Apr. 22, 1923; Jun. 8, 1924; MVHA files.
18. *Express*, May 4, 1924.
19. Ibid., May 12, 1929.
20. Ibid., Mar. 12, 1922.
21. *Light*, Oct. 12, 1924.
22. MVHA files.
23. *Express*, Aug. 17, 1924.
24. Folder 93, Ayres Collection.
25. *Light*, Mar. 23, Oct. 12, 1924; *Express*, Feb. 27, 1927; MVHA files.
26. *Express*, Sep. 7, 1924; *Light*, Oct. 12, 1924.
27. Ibid.
28. *Light*, Apr. 27, 1924.
29. MVHA files.
30. Folder 46, Ayres Collection; *Light*, Apr. 6, 1924.
31. *Light*, Oct. 12, 1924.
32. Ibid., Oct. 19, Nov. 10, 1924; Nov. 27, 1927; *Express*, Apr. 18, 1926, Mar. 13,1927.
33. *Light*, Sep. 7, 1930.
34. *Express*, Sep. 2, 1928.
35. Ibid., Aug. 27, 1922; *Light*, Feb. 25, Jul. 29, 1923.
36. *Express*, Dec. 18, 1927; *Light*, Jan. 1, 1928.
37. *Light*, Jan. 31, Apr. 4, 1926.
38. Ibid., Feb. 14, Apr. 18, 1926; Oct. 2, 1927.
39. *Express*, Jul. 15, 1928.
40. Ibid., May 30, 1926.
41. Ibid., May 16, 1926.
42. Ibid., Apr. 4, Oct. 3, 1926.
43. Ibid., Feb. 8, 1925.
44. Ibid., Aug. 27, 1922.
45. Ibid., May 14, 1922; *Greater San Antonio*, n.p.
46. MVHA files.
47. *Light*, Dec. 3, 1922; *Express*, Feb. 18, 1923.
48. *Express*, Jul. 2, 1922; Jun.

14, 1924; *Greater San Antonio*, n.p.
49. MVHA files.
50. *Express*, Feb. 13, 1923.
51. Ibid., Jun. 21, 1925.
52. Ibid., May 4, 1924; 1924 clipping and Harvey P. Smith specs., MVHA files.
53. *Express*, Feb. 12, 1922; *Greater San Antonio*, n.p.
54. *Express*, Dec. 25, 1921; *Greater San Antonio*, n.p.
55. *Express*, Sep. 4, Mar. 6, 1927.
56. *Light*, Jul. 12, 1925.
57. *Express*, Jul. 5, 1925; *Light*, Jul. 5, 1925.
58. *Light*, Jul. 12, 1925; *Express*, Feb. 27, 1927.
59. Withers, *San Antonio*, 58; *Light*, Apr. 19, 1925.
60. *Express*, Sep. 7, Oct. 5, 1924; *Light*, Sep. 7, Oct. 12, 1924.
61. *Light*, Jan. 25, May 10, Jul. 12, 1925.
62. Ibid., Aug. 16, 1925; *Express*, Jun. 7, 1925.
63. *Light*, Oct. 26, 1924, Feb. 10, 1925.
64. Harvey P. Smith specs., MVHA files; *Light*, Jul. 12, 1925; Jan. 6, 1926.

11. Rosewood and Lullwood

1. *Light*, Apr. 1, 1923.
2. *Express*, Jun. 2, Mar. 10, May 19, 1929.
3. *Light*, May 12, 19, Jun. 9, 1929.
4. *Express*, Mar. 10, Apr. 14, 1929.
5. *Light*, Mar. 17, 1929, *Express*, Mar. 17, 1929.
6. *Express*, Jul. 24, 1927.
7. MVHA files.
8. *Express*, Nov. 4, 1923.
9. Ibid., Sep. 16, 1923.
10. *Light*, Feb. 7, 1926.
11. Ibid., Nov. 3, 1929; Harvey P. Smith specs., MVHA files.
12. *Express*, May 6, 1928; *Light*, May 13, 1928.
13. *Light*, Apr. 27, 1930.
14. MVHA files.
15. Ibid.
16. *Light*, Jul. 21, 1929; *Express* Mar. 9, 1930.
17. *Express*, Oct. 14, 1928.
18. *Light*, Jun. 28,1930.
19. MVHA files.
20. *Express*, Aug. 7, 1927.
21. Ibid., Nov. 4, 1923.
22. Ibid., Oct. 21, Nov. 18, 1923.
23. Ibid., Oct. 14, 1923; *Light*, Mar. 29, 1925.

24. MVHA files; *Express*, May 19, Jun. 2, 1925.
25. *Light*, Jan. 10, 1926.
26. *Express*, May 19, 1929.
27. MVHA files.
28. *Express*, Jul. 28, 1929.
29. *Light*, Sep. 21, 1930; *Express*, Dec. 21, 1930.
30. MVHA files.
31. Ibid.
32. *Light*, Dec. 8, 1929.
33. *Express*, Feb. 27, Oct. 21, 1927.
34. *Light*, Nov. 30, Dec. 7, 1930.
35. *Express*, Jan. 23, 1927.
36. Ibid., Jan. 17, 1926.
37. Ibid., Oct. 21, 1927.
38. Ibid., Aug. 7, Oct. 16, 1927.
39. McGarraugh booklet, MVHA files.
40. *Light*, Mar. 11, 1928; *Express*, Mar. 4, 18, 1928.
41. *Light*, Dec. 12, 1926; *Express*, May 19, 1929.
42. MVHA files.
43. Ibid.
44. *Light*, Oct. 2, 16, 1927; McGarraugh booklet.
45. *Light*, May 18, 1930.
46. Ibid., Feb. 10, 1929; *Express*, Mar. 17, Apr. 14, 1929.
47. *Light*, Mar. 11, 1928; Apr. 3, 1927.
48. Ibid., May 18, 1930.
49. Ibid., Aug. 25, 1929
50. Ibid., Mar. 23, May 11, 1930.
51. MVHA files.
52. Ibid.; *Light*, Sep. 29, 1929.
53. *Light*, Feb. 5, 1928.
54. *Express*, Sep. 9, 1928.
55. MVHA files.
56. *Express*, May 5, 1929; *Light*, May 5, 1929.
57. *Light*, Dec. 5, 1926; Feb. 13, 20, 1927.
58. Ibid., Feb. 27, 1927.
59. *Express*, Apr. 22, 1928; *Light*, May 6, 1928.
60. McGarraugh booklet; *Light*, Oct. 16, 1927; *Express*, Jun. 22, 1930.
61. McGarraugh booklet; *Light*, Nov. 21, 1926.
62. McGarraugh booklet; Withers, *San Antonio*, 56; Watson deed research, MVHA files.
63. McGarraugh booklet; *Light*, Nov. 27, 1927; Jan. (n.d.), 1928; Sep. 15, 1929.
64. *Light*, Feb. 17, 1929.
65. Ibid., May 25, 1930.
66. Ibid., Mar. 3, Dec. 15, 1929; *Express*, Mar. 10, 1929.
67. McGarraugh booklet.
68. *Light*, Mar. 25, 1928; *Express*, Apr. 1, 15, 1928.

69. *Light*, Dec. 22, 1929; Jan. 26, Apr. 20, 1930.
70. MVHA files.
71. Ibid.
72. *Express*, Jan. 23, 1927; *Light*, Dec. 18, 1927.
73. *Express*, May 22, 1927; *Light*, May 22, Jun. 5, 26, 1927.
74. *Light*, Oct. 6, 1929; *Express*, Nov. 10,1929.
75. *Express*, Dec. 29, 1929.
76. Ibid., Mar. 27, Dec. 11, 1927; *Light*, Apr. 24, Nov. 13, 1927.
77. MVHA files.
78. Ibid., McGarraugh booklet.
79. *Light*, Apr. 14, 1929.
80. MVHA files.
81. *Express*, May 22, Oct. 16, 1927; Jan. 22, 1928; *Light*, Nov. 6, 13, 1927; Jan. 29, Feb. 13, 1928.
82. *Light*, May 1, 8, Sep. 4, Oct. 16, 1927; *Express*, May 1, Aug. 28, 1927.
83. *Express*, Jul. 8, 1928; *Light*, Jul. 15, 1928; McGarraugh booklet.
84. *Express*, Jun. 19, Jul. 3, Aug. 14, 1927; *Light*, Jul. 10, Sep. 18, 1927.
85. *Express*, Mar. 18, 1928.
86. Ibid., Nov. 26, 1929; *Light*, Dec. 15, 1929.
87. *Express*, Aug. 11, 1929.
88. Ibid., Oct. 28, 1928; Apr. 14, 1929; *Light*, Jan. 26, 1930.
89. *Express*, Mar. 11, 1928.
90. *Light*, Apr. 22, May 6, 1928; *Express*, May 6, 1928.
91. *Express*, Apr. 7, 1929.

12. Bushnell, Oakmont and Rosewood

1. *Express*, Oct. 5, 1927; *Light*, Oct. 14, 1927.
2. *Light*, Oct. 5, 1927; Oct. 14, Dec. 9, 1923.
3. *Express*, Jan. 16, 1924.
4. Ibid., Oct. 4, 1927.
5. Ibid., Feb. 6, 1926.
6. *Light*, Sep. 19, Nov. 14, 1926; Jul. 3, Oct. 16, 1927; Plans, Ayres Collection and MVHA files.
7. *Express*, Jan. 10, 1926.
8. Harvey P. Smith specs., MVHA files; *Express*, Dec. 16, 1928; Feb. 8, 1929.
9. *Light*, Feb. 5, 1928.
10. Ibid., Apr. 20, Aug. 10, 1930; *Express*, Sep. 1, 1929
11. *Express*, Jun. 23, Aug. 4, 1929; *Light*, Apr. 20, 1930.
12. *Express*, Dec. 20, 1925;

Aug. 7, 1927; *Light*, Aug. 16, 1925.

13. MVHA files.
14. *Express*, Jul. 22, 1928.
15. Ibid., Jan. 6, 1929.
16. Ibid., Jul. 14, 1929.
17. Ibid., Jun. 29, 1930; Nov. 17, 1929.
18. Ibid., Oct. 18, 1928.
19. Ibid., Mar. 18, 1928; *Light*, Mar. 18, 1928; Nov. 13, 1927.
20. *Light*, Jun. 3, Oct. 28, 1928; *Express*, Oct. 28, 1928.
21. *Light*, Nov. 18, 1928.
22. MVHA files.

13. Bushnell, Shook and Laurel Heights Place

1. *Express*, Sep. 19, 1909; Nov. 16, 1924.
2. Ibid., Oct. 18, 1914; Dec. 10, 1922.
3. *Light*, Oct. 9, 1927; *Express*, Oct. 30, 1927.
4. *Light*, Aug. 28, 1921; *Express*, Feb. 20, 1921; Jun. 11, 1922.
5. *Light*, Aug. 19, 1923; Folder 84, 84a, Ayres Collection; *Express*, Aug. 31, 1924; Aug. 7, 1927.
6. *Express*, Dec. 21, 1930.

7. Ibid., Nov. 16, 1924; *Light*, Sep. 6, 1925.
8. *Light*, May 5, 1929.
9. *Espress*, Jun. 1, 1919
10. Ibid., Oct. 18, 1925; *Light*, Oct. 24, Nov. 7, 1926.
11. *Light*, Feb. 10, Oct. 13, 1929; Mar. 4, 1928.
12. Copy, Landa will, Jul. 17, 1946, MVHA files.
13. *Light*, Jun. 2, 1922; Apr. 10, 1921.
14. MVHA files.
15. Ibid.
16. *Light*, Aug. 30, 1925.
17. *Express*, Aug. 24, 1930.

18. Folder 12, Ayres Collection; *Express*, Jun. 2, 1929; Jun. 15, 1930.
19. *Light*, Nov. 4, 1923; May 11, 1924.
20. MVHA files.
21. *Light*, Jan. 26, 1926.
22. *Express*, Jul. 13, 1924.
23. *Light*, Jun. 24, 1923; *Express*, Jun. 24, 1923.
24. *Express*, Jan. 16, 1927, Jun. 21, 1927; *Light*, Dec. 12, 1926, Mar. 13, 1927.
25. *Light*, Mar. 27, Aug. 28, 1927.
26. Ibid., May 29, 1927.

Selected Bibliography

Adams, Lee. "Memoir." Typescript in files of Paul W. Adams.

Ayres, Atlee B. Papers in Special Collections of the School of Architecture Library, University of Texas at Austin.

Banks, C. Stanley, and Pat Ireland Nixon. *Laurel Heights Methodist Church, 1909–1949.* San Antonio: Laurel Heights Methodist Church, 1949.

Beautiful Homes of San Antonio. San Antonio, 1914.

Carson, Chris, and William McDonald, eds. *A Guide to San Antonio Architecture.* San Antonio: The San Antonio Chapter of the American Institute of Architects, 1986.

Coppini, Pompeo. *From Dawn to Sunset.* San Antonio: The Naylor Company, 1949.

Diehl, Kemper. *Saint Mary's Hall: First Century.* San Antonio: Saint Mary's Hall, 1979.

Everett, Donald E. "San Antonio Welcomes the 'Sunset'–1877." *Southwestern Historical Quarterly* 65, no. 1 (July 1961): 47–60.

Fisher, Lewis F. *Christ Episcopal Church: The First Seventy-Five Years, 1911–1986.* San Antonio: Christ Episcopal Church, 1986.

George, Mary Carolyn Hollers. *Mary Bonner: Impressions of a Printmaker.* San Antonio: Trinity University Press, 1982.

Henry, Jay C. *Architecture in Texas 1845–1945.* Austin: University of Texas Press, 1993.

Insurance Maps of San Antonio, Texas. Sanborn Co., 1904.

Interviews in 1975, 1982 and 1983 with Paul W. Adams, Robert M. Ayres, Mrs. J. Fred Buenz, Mrs. Frank L. Churchill, Agnes Terrell Clegg, Frank C. Davis Jr., Ruth West Emerson, Virginia Crossette Fichtner, Mrs. Jack Harris, Martin Giesecke, Mrs. Lloyd H. Harrington, Ike S. Kampmann Jr., Jean Goggan Kuntz, Dr. John L. Matthews, Mrs. Frank Newton, Mrs. D. B. Ofthson, Ann Sheldon Sims, Jane Slavens, Sarah Talcott, Marjorie T. Walthall, Terrell Maverick Webb.

Kinnison Papers in Monte Vista Historical Association files.

Luck, E.A., comp. *Greater San Antonio.* San Antonio, 1923.

McGarraugh, Robert. *A properly designed Home never becomes obsolete.* San Antonio, 1928.

National Register of Historic Places Inventory, 1980, in Monte Vista Historical Association files.

O'Neill, Perez, Lance, Larcade, comp. "San Antonio Historical Survey," 1972.

Onderdonk, Emily G. Diary in vertical files of Witte Museum.

Poole-Totten Papers in Monte Vista Historical Association files.

Reference Work of Prominent Men of Southwest Texas. n.p., n.d.

San Antonio City Directory. 1897–1981.

San Antonio: City of Beautiful Homes. San Antonio, 1914.

Smith, Harvey P. Architectural specifications in Monte Vista Historical Association files.

Steinfeldt, Cecelia. *The Onderdonks: A Family of Texas Painters.* San Antonio: Trinity University Press for the San Antonio Museum Association, 1976.

The Franklin House. San Antonio: The Friends of the Franklin House, 1985.

Withers, Daniel. *San Antonio: A History of Color and Graphics.* San Antonio, 1977.

Index of Architects

Kinnison, Paul, Jr., 46

Leibsle, Roy W., 96
Lewis, Terry M., 92

Marriott, John M., 34
  510 Belknap Pl. (1928, Christ Episcopal Church parish hall), 50
  138 E. Elsmere Pl. (1928, Henry A. Pagenkopf), 96
  114 E. Gramercy Pl. (1925, D. L. Keiser), 92
  116 W. Hollywood Ave. (1928, Albert Prucha), 103
  330 W. Kings Hwy. (1928, Jesse Y. Womack), 89–90
  519 Shook Ave. (1926, John M. Marriott), 126
  523 Shook Ave. (1926, Harry C. Wood), 126
  334 E. Summit Ave. (1929, Morris Adelman), 77
  101 W. Summit Ave. (1927, V. H. McNutt), 77
McAdoo and Worley
  505 Belknap Pl. (1893, Jay E. Adams), 49, 50
McGarraugh, Robert (designer), 31, 34, 35, 77, 96, 110
  210 W. Elsmere Ave. (1928), 96
  217 W. Elsmere Ave. (1928, Kathryn Johnson), 96
  219 W. Elsmere Ave. (1928), 96
  220 W. Elsmere Ave. (1928), 96
  101 E. Lullwood Ave. (1926, Aubrey Miller), 110
  106 E. Lullwood Ave. (1927, Carl C. Krueger), 110
  112 E. Lullwood Ave. (1928, F. B. Prue), 110
  116 E. Lullwood Ave. (1926, J. R. Murray), 110
  117 E. Lullwood Ave. (1926, Jarell Gose), 110
  126 E. Lullwood Ave. (1928, Robert P. Thomas), 110
  131 E. Lullwood Ave. (1927, Henry Deutz), 110
  144 E. Lullwood Ave. (1930, Verlin V. Carson), 110
  150 E. Lullwood Ave. (1929), 110–11
  102 W. Lullwood Ave. (1927, Sterling C. Burke), 111–12
  115 W. Lullwood Ave. (1926, J. A. Kenagy), 112
  119 W. Lullwood Ave. (1928, Emma Roberts), 112
  123 W. Lullwood Ave. (1927, Robert P. Thompson,) 112
  124 W. Lullwood Ave. (1926, Ward H. Miller), 112
  130 W. Lullwood Ave. (c. 1929, Bettie C. Ward), 112
  135 W. Lullwood Ave. (1926, Etta M. Little), 112
  200 W. Lullwood Ave. (1927, Louis R. Roth), 112
  205 W. Lullwood Ave. (1930, Guy C. Jackson), 112
  209 W. Lullwood Ave. (1929, Joseph W. Edwards), 112
  210 W. Lullwood Ave. (1928, A. H. Staehle), 112
  214 W. Lullwood Ave. (1928, Patrick Swearingen), 113
  215 W. Lullwood Ave. (1929, Morris Scherr), 113
  218 W. Lullwood Ave. (c. 1926, Edwin E. Weise), 113
  221 W. Lullwood Ave. (1927, L. West Avery), 113
  227 W. Lullwood Ave. (1928, Alex G. Krueger), 113
  228 W. Lullwood Ave. (1927, Charles W. Ryan), 114
  232 W. Lullwood Ave. (1929, Irving T. Cutter), 113–14
  233 W. Lullwood Ave. (1929, E. J. Carson), 114
  239 W. Lullwood Ave. (1927, George T. Marshall), 114
  301 W. Lullwood Ave. (1927, Charles Wiggins), 114
  308 W. Rosewood Ave. (1927, M. Leo Dubinski), 114
  311 W. Rosewood Ave. (1927, Herbert Hill), 114
  315 W. Rosewood Ave. (1928, Jack H. Bradley), 114
  319 W. Rosewood Ave. (1927, Annie Krueger), 114
  320 W. Rosewood Ave. (1928, Irving T. Cutter), 114
  326 W. Rosewood Ave. (1929), 114
  327 W. Rosewood Ave. (1929, Frank S. Haines), 114
  329 W. Rosewood Ave. (1928, W. M. Harris), 114
  333 W. Rosewood Ave. (1928), 114
  334 W. Rosewood Ave. (1928), 114
  138 E. Summit Ave. (c. 1928, A. C. Leslie), 77
  333 E. Summit Ave. (1929, Murray F. Crossette), 77
Moore, Richard, 118

Noonan, Will N., 64
  115 E. Gramercy Pl. (1924, Beulah Brice), 92
  135 E. Gramercy Pl. (1930, Logan L. Stephenson), 92
  138 E. Hollywood Ave. (1925, Otto L. Fortman), 102
  250 E. Lullwood Ave. (1929, Fred T. Goetting), 111
O'Neill, Conrad & Oppelt
  510 Belknap Pl. (1990, Christ Episcopal Church education building), 39
Page, Harvey L., 14, 25, 26, 46, 48, 54, 57
  111 E. Craig Pl. (1907, Francis L. Hillyer), 57
  117 E. French Pl. (1925, Taylor Hall), 42
  215 W. Kings Hwy. (1924, William F. Schutz), 87, 88, 90
Phelps, Henry T., 34
  216 W. Craig Pl. (1904, John Taliaferro), 52
  509 W. French Pl. (1907, Franklin C. Davis), 44, 46
  131 E. Kings Hwy. (1921, Ike S. Kampmann), 25, 85–86
Phelps & Dewees
  315 W. Agarita Ave. (1921, Z. E. Bonner), 76
  210 W. Huisache Ave. (1927, W. L. Morrow), 69
  2602 Main Ave. (1923, Laurel Heights Drugs), 60, 82
  501 Shook Ave. (1922, James S. Steel), 126
  100 E. Summit Ave. (1925, Arlington Arms Apts.), 77
  210 W. Woodlawn Ave. (1927, W. L. Morrow), 69
Phelps, Dewees & Simmons, 81
Reuter, H. A.
  228 W. Agarita Ave. (1917, Morris Stern), 75
  102 E. Kings Hwy. (1913, Robert L. Ball), 83
  114 E. Kings Hwy. (1912, H. L. Kokernot), 21, 83–84, 85
Reuter & Harrington
  231 W. Agarita Ave. (1914, Seth S. Searcy), 75
  115 W. Kings Hwy. (1925, Mrs. Hugh Burns), 87
  128 W. Mistletoe Ave. (1914, E. A. Holland), 60
  306 W. Mistletoe Ave. (1913, D. W. Light), 61

Saldaña, Humberto, 109
Santa Cruz, Gilberto S.
  243 E. Lullwood Ave. (1925, Cornelius O'Neill), 111
Schoeppl, C. B. & Co., 31, 34
  122 W. Agarita Ave. (1923, Temple Calhoun), 75
  124 E. Elsmere Pl. (1923, J. L. Felder), 95
  125 E. Elsmere Ave. (1923, J. L. Felder), 95–96
  342 W. Elsmere Ave. (1923, Glen H. Alvey), 97
  130 E. Gramercy Pl. (1923, Randolph Carter), 92
  120 W. Hollywood Ave. (1922, Paul Scholz), 103–04
  202 W. Hollywood Ave. (1922, John Bowen), 105
  310 W. Hollywood Ave. (1922, Fidel Chamberlain), 105
  124 E. Huisache Ave. (1920, C. K. McDowell), 66
  240 E. Huisache Ave. (1924, William M. Fordtran), 68
  111 E. Kings Hwy. (1923, Thomas E. Lyons), 86
  302 W. Kings Hwy. (1922, Mrs. J. D. Houston), 89
  315 W. Kings Hwy. (1922, Edward N. Requa), 89
  321 W. Summit Ave. (1922, Edward N. Requa), 80
Schoeppl & Hardie
  2415 Main Ave. (1920, Winchester Kelso Jr.), 81
Seutter, Carl von
  230 W. Ashby Pl. (1901, Otto S. Koehler), ix, 8, 38–40
Seutter & Simons
  211 Belknap Pl. (1926, Temple Beth-El), 49
Smith, Harvey P., 34, 57, 70, 93
  138 E. Huisache Ave. (1924, Walter McAllister), 66–68
  226 W. Gramercy Pl. (1926, Sylvan Lang), 93
  227 W. Gramercy Pl. (1926, Herman Giesecke), 93
  301 W. Hollywood Ave. (1924, Julius Barclay), 105, 106

General Index

About the Author

For more than three decades Donald E. Everett and his wife, Mary Lou, have lived in a landmark Monte Vista home not far from Trinity University, where Everett chaired the Department of History from 1967 to 1981 and is now professor of history emeritus. A native of Auburn, Alabama, he graduated from the University of Florida in 1941. After completing his M.A. and Ph.D. at Tulane University, Everett joined the Trinity faculty in 1953.

The recipient of several awards for teaching and research, Everett wrote the centennial history of Trinity University and the sesquicentennial history of San Antonio's First Presbyterian Church. His books include *San Antonio Legacy, San Antonio: The Flavor of Its Past* and *Chaplain Davis and Hood's Texas Brigade*, recently reprinted by Louisiana State University Press.

After noting disturbing similarities between residential decline near Northwestern University in Evanston, Illinois, and that near Trinity, in 1973 Everett became a leader in organizing the Monte Vista Historical Association and reversing Monte Vista's decline. He served as the group's president in 1981. With the research incorporated in this book he laid the basis for the effort that culminated in 1998 with the Monte Vista district's listing in the National Register of Historic Places